IRAQ AND BACK

Kimberly D. Olson

An Association of the U.S. Army Book

IRAQ AND BACK

INSIDE THE WAR TO WIN THE PEACE

COLONEL KIM OLSON
U.S. Air Force (Ret.)

NAVAL INSTITUTE PRESS
Annapolis, Maryland

Naval Institute Press
291 Wood Road
Annapolis, MD 21402

ISBN -13: 978-1-59114-527-1

Library of Congress Cataloging-in-Publication Data

Olson, Kimberly.
  Iraq and back : inside the war to win the peace / Kimberly Olson.
    p. cm.
  Includes index.
  ISBN 1-59114-527-9 (alk. paper)
  1. Olson, Kimberly. 2. Iraq War, 2003—Personal narratives,
American. I. Title.
  DS79.76.O47 2006
  956.7044'3092—dc22
  [B]

                                                              2006017238

Excerpts in chapter 22 from Secretary Donald Rumsfeld's question-
and-answer session are reprinted courtesy of the Federal News Service,
Washington, D.C.

All photos are from the author's personal collection.

Printed in the United States of America on acid-free paper ♾

12 11 10 09 08 07   8 7 6 5 4 3

This book is for
those who battle and those who rebuild,
they make it better for having been there
and
for my children,
who will inherit the world we build.

Courage is the price that life exacts for granting peace.

—Amelia Earhart

Contents

Acknowledgments

This is truly the best part about writing a book, thanking all those who took the journey with you. One does not arrive here alone. There are a number of people who made it possible to put this book into your hands.

Special thanks to my exceptional editor Esther Ferington, whose patience and skills made *Iraq and Back* go from good to great. To the two men who read the manuscript and believed in me—Lieutenant Colonel Roger Cirillo, U.S. Army (Retired), of the Association of the United States Army, and Eric Mills of the Naval Institute Press. And to the other outstanding people at the Naval Institute Press who made this book a reality: Linda O'Doughda, Chris Onrubia, Inger Forland, and, especially, Pat Pascale, the press director.

Thank you to Dr. Gorden Rudd, U.S. Army (Retired) and Master Gunnery Sergeant Glenn Kramer, U.S. Marine Corps for sharing their expertise and photos. I am indebted to Colonel John R. Martin, U.S. Army (Retired). A fellow aviator, he helped me in Iraq to navigate the world of the Army. Thanks for being there, JR.

I am grateful for the friendship and wisdom of five extraordinary women: Lieutenant Colonel Nancy Combs, United States Air Force (Retired), whom you meet in this book; Colonel Kathy Conley, United States Air Force (Retired); Renee Martin-Nagle; Colonel Jane Hess, United States Air Force; and Elizabeth Blake. Their gentle persuasion convinced me to write the stories I've been telling for years.

I am honored to have served my country in uniform and I thank all those veterans and active military members who work every day to defend America. You indeed make the world a better place.

I am blessed to live in the small town of Weatherford, Texas, and in a community of friends who wrap me in encouragement, grace, and understanding.

Special thanks to my family: to my parents, Karen and Chuck McNeil, for their love and advice, and to my sisters, Kris and Kellie, and brother, Kevin, for their humor and support. My children, Keegan and Katie, remind me every day of how important it is to be a mom. My deepest love, admiration, and affection go to my husband, Kent, who remains by my side as a copilot, a friend, and the foundation for our family.

Finally, life takes a belief and a faith in something greater than you and I am grateful to have been given that opportunity to serve a greater good.

Thanks for reading *Iraq and Back* and taking this journey.

Foreword

I looked at Kim for a long time; then I wrapped my arms around her and hugged her tightly. I choked up a little, but was finally able to say, "Good-bye, Kimmer; I'll miss you." I turned and walked toward the airplane to begin my international journey home. It was hard to leave! Kim Olson and I had spent every waking hour together for more than one hundred days. I sat down and reflected on our time together.

We had shared good times and hardship; adventure and doldrums; happiness and heartbreak; security and danger. We had been participants in the greatest endeavor of this new century. I realized how blessed and fortunate I was to have had Kim as my right arm. She was a strong, articulate, intellectual pioneer with boundless energy. She was an exemplary officer and a marvelous human being who has served and still serves as a role model and mentor to younger women. For me, she had been instrumental in forming a staff, developing plans, securing funds, producing a budget, arranging travel, coordinating meetings with diplomats, clerics, politicians, military commanders, and Iraqi leaders—Sunni, Shia, and Kurd.

No matter how tough the start, she always ended up winning the race. She was intensely loyal and impeccably honest. She was also tough: she could go without meals, forgo large amounts of sleep, work around the clock enduring intense heat and monumental sandstorms. Throughout all of this, she never lost her talents of negotiation, sound advice, political compromise, and a compassion that embraced the religious, ethnic, and tribal diversities of the hundreds of people she and I encountered daily.

As you read her book, you'll understand, as I do, how we all fed off her energy and drive and what an inspiration she was to the entire team. As you finish the book, you'll be angered and incensed, as I am, over her treatment from the service to which she had dedicated her adult life. Treatment based upon fallacious allegations, undocumented evidence, amateur investigation, and poor senior leadership.

She was a thoroughbred, and I ran her legs off. But the Air Force broke her heart. She is still a thoroughbred, nevertheless, and if I had it all to do again, she would be the first person I would pick for my team. Why? Because they don't come any better than Kim. I know that I would be a little stronger, a little more patient, and a little better prepared, and that each day would be a little easier, because I would have Colonel Kim Olson at my side.

Lieutenant General Jay M. Garner
U.S. Army (Retired)
May 2006

IRAQ AND BACK

CHAPTER 1

Welcome to Baghdad

R aindrops slid down the side windows of the dirty tan Suburban. A gray, solemn sky hung over the city. The procession of SUVs, Humvees, and Bradley fighting vehicles threaded its way through streets littered with garbage, chunks of concrete, and shells of burnt-out cars. My foot tapped nervously against the floorboard. I glanced at my watch. *Come on, come on, we're already late.* I fingered the gold cross around my neck. It was a gift my mother had given me years earlier, the first time I deployed as an Air Force captain to a combat zone. "It will keep you safe," she had promised.

I would need all the protection I could get. Today I was a colonel, riding in the command SUV of a twenty-vehicle convoy en route to a teaching hospital in the center of Baghdad. The view from the car window was one of destruction and desolation. It was a dreary day—April 21, 2003, ten days after the Operation Iraqi Freedom air war ended. The ground war still raged north of Baghdad.

With twenty-three years of military flying experience under my belt, I now had this rare opportunity to inspect the precision of U.S. air strikes. Targeted buildings were reduced to mangled piles of concrete and metal, while neighboring buildings remained untouched by the bombing.

The pilot in me was impressed, but the human being was appalled at all that war produces.

Entire blocks of houses and stores were chewed up and spit out or burned to the ground. What remained was stripped of windows, doors, and roofs. Power lines swayed like suspended snakes where the poles had been removed. Young men dashed down the street, jostling sheets of metal or broken chairs. No one in the vehicle spoke as we absorbed the ruin. Although nothing targeted had escaped the wrath of our weapons, it was the ferocity of the looters that I found so disturbing. It didn't look like looting motivated by greed, but fueled by rage.

The training hospital was a run-down, concrete structure that blended into the gray sky. As we approached the compound, the crowd of a hundred hospital workers parted to let the vehicles into the parking area. Tires crunched over debris and the drivers weaved around the garbage piles. A few dozen Iraqi men packed around a twisted iron gate came forward to encircle the convoy as we rolled in. Bolting from the SUVs, our bodyguards and military police escorts cleared a narrow path through the dark-haired masses, weapons held high and heads scanning the crowd for any threat.

"You ready, sir?" I asked my boss.

He nodded. Before opening the door, I raked my fingers through unruly brown hair and caught my reflection in the rearview mirror. The woman staring back at me was pale with dark shadows under hazel eyes—lack of sleep, the demands of the job, and nervous energy had taken their toll. The makeup I had applied at 0300 had long since faded away. The last six weeks in Kuwait had deepened the lines on my face and made me look older than forty-five.

While we had waited in Kuwait to deploy into Iraq, I had pulled together a rapidly expanding team, now numbering in the hundreds, and ensured they had the boss's directions. Now this fledgling organization was asked to rebuild Iraq. In addition to my responsibilities for the staff, I had juggled the egos and demands of five retired generals (counting my boss), overseen the process of managing $6 billion for the rebuilding efforts, and filtered the daily suggestions from the Pentagon. My office was understaffed, lacked basic communications, and operated in a virtual policy void when it came to the rebuilding effort. Today, I would begin a journey through the demands and dangers of trying to do peacetime work in a wartime environment.

I slid out of the car and stretched my five-foot-nine frame. A pinch in my lower back reminded me of the three-hour airplane ride into Baghdad on an Air Force C-130 under the escort of two gray F-15 fighters. An acidic odor in the city air stung my nostrils and slid down the back of my throat. As it would many times in the days ahead, the smell triggered a memory that unsettled me. I wanted to spit, but I swallowed hard, trying to suppress the raw emotion that stuck in my craw.

The humid day covered my skin like a sticky blanket. I was glad I had worn practical black pants, a white shirt, and a photographer's vest. No one on the leadership team wore military uniforms. I stomped my feet and dirt swirled over my shoes, settling on the hem of my slacks. Raindrops peppered my back and, despite the humidity, a shiver traveled up my spine. I reached into one of the vest's many pockets and fingered my new digital camera, then glanced at the small group of ten reporters who had accompanied us from Kuwait. Now was not the time for me to start snapping pictures. Today, that was someone else's job. Instead, I retrieved a pen and pad. As the executive officer to the leader given the task of rebuilding Iraq, I stood ready to delegate orders, capture significant events, and record history.

A soft clicking sound accompanied the short man who rushed toward us. As he approached, I glanced at his worn, patent leather shoes. The sole of one of them flapped as he walked. Glancing at my new L.L. Bean hiking boots, I felt a twinge of pity and shuffled my feet back among the other boots. In flawless English, he introduced himself as the hospital's administrator and extended his hand to my boss and our leader, Lieutenant General Jay M. Garner, U.S. Army (Retired). Handpicked by Secretary of Defense Donald H. Rumsfeld and charged by President George W. Bush with rebuilding Iraq, the general is a short, barrel-chested man with a ready smile and a big plug nose. He reached out his hand. "Hi, Jay Garner," he drawled. "Glad to meet ya," came his typical greeting.

As their hands met, the contrast was striking. Garner's large, pink, freckled hand enveloped one that was thin, olive-colored, and marked with small scars. I held my breath at this historic moment—we had come to help. But as the liberator and liberated stood face to face, the moment passed with a yawn. There was no rejoicing at our presence, no tears of joy, no pats on the back—just weary resignation from the hospital official. "Come," he said, and turned away.

Garner looked at me.

I shrugged. "You'd think he'd be happy to see us."

A disheveled band of men and teenage boys pressed in to watch the initial greeting. With their hands shoved in their pockets, they glared with squinting eyes at our twenty-member team, especially me. As a senior military officer, I had been in this situation many times before—the only woman in a large group of men. I straightened my shoulders, jutted my chin, and returned their stares. *That's right; women ARE a part of leadership teams where I come from.* As I looked at them, the male crowd blended into a sea of dark pants and grimy shirts. It was the women in dingy-gray nurses' uniforms behind them that caught my attention. These were the first women I had seen not wearing the full, black robes called abayas. Their expressions mirrored the overcast sky, revealing little. I dropped my chin and nodded my head toward them. Some smiled; others flipped their wrists in a half wave.

Our large security detail of contracted bodyguards and a detachment of U.S. soldiers was positioned between me and the Iraqis. I was confident and cool, not because of the display of muscle and weaponry, but because I had cut my teeth in the all-male world of military aviation. I had seen it all, and nothing surprised me.

We had picked this hospital to visit because of its strategic location in the center of Baghdad. It was a logical place to make a first visit and a good public-relations move to show the Iraqi people that our team was here to help. The complex had been without electrical power for a month. The military commanders assigned to the area had relayed the administrator's request for auxiliary power. This particular hospital had the only dialysis machine in the city. Today, it was a useless piece of equipment. Patients needed it to survive and the machine needed electricity to function. We were here to provide the electricity to save lives.

I directed my attention back to our team. As the crowd parted, we worked our way across the parking lot toward the hospital entrance, stomping over rubble, garbage, and debris. "What a mess," I whispered to no one in particular. The reporters forced their way forward, clicking their cameras over their heads. The hospital compound had three buildings in a U-shaped layout. Before entering the center building, I looked up and saw a massive black hole punched in the third-floor wall. The explosion must have showered the grounds with the shards of glass and broken bricks that obstructed our path. Our Iraqi host appeared oblivious to the shattered glass. He continued talking as it snapped and crackled under everyone's feet.

I fell in behind Garner as we entered the grimy hospital corridors. The pungent stench of raw sewage and antiseptic made my eyes water. I cupped a hand over my mouth to keep from gagging. Glancing around, I hoped no one had seen my reaction. Hector, the closest bodyguard, grinned at the smell and mouthed, "Oops, excuse me." I rolled my eyes in response to his adolescent humor.

The dismal hospital wards housed patients sprawled on bare mattresses, curled across thin, frayed blankets, or crouched on the bare floor. The rooms were so dark and damp that it was difficult to see any of the patients. But all of them had family members squatting around them. They muttered in low voices or stared with shadowed faces—resigned to the fate of their loved ones.

The administrator spun around, saying to Garner, "We require a generator." We stumbled into each other in the narrow, darkened hallway, stopped, and tried to regain our composure.

"Carl," the general barked, "let's get these people a generator!"

The hospital workers who trailed our group buzzed in agreement.

"Yes, sir!" snapped Carl Strock, an Army two-star general. A very tall, stoic man from the Army Corps of Engineers, Major General Carl Strock was assigned to Garner's team and tasked to rebuild the infrastructure of Iraq. At this moment, his only responsibility involved a single generator. He made a note in his small binder. Several doctors nodded to one another and the nurses who shadowed us from a distance murmured. Little did they know a generator was already inbound from Baghdad International Airport.

We would learn later that the auxiliary power unit had indeed made it to the hospital and begun providing electricity to the vital machines. Our celebration was short-lived, however. Someone stole critical components from the unit and eventually took apart the wiring and metal pieces. Like the dialysis machine that was supposed to sustain life, the generator became a useless piece of machinery in a hospital that needed help.

Next to me was a storage closet without a door. The administrator explained that looters had stolen most of the supplies and doors. I leaned forward to have a look as the group shuffled down the corridor. A weathered hand reached out from the closet and grabbed my forearm. I jumped. A stocky, heavy-set nurse with gray hair and a wrinkled face emerged from the shadows.

"The children die," she hissed at me. Her rigid posture and hard eyes made me glance toward the bodyguards disappearing around the corner. I resisted the urge to pry her fingers off my arm, and leveled my eyes at hers. This was my first physical contact with an Iraqi citizen.

"Tell me," I said.

"We need water—clean water—running water—any water!"

I followed her gaze as she looked up and down the narrow, dim hallway.

"No kidding." I wrinkled my nose. A slight smile lifted her lined face. I patted her hand. "I'll see what I can do." I turned. She tightened her grip and dug in a nail.

Her tattered smock hung low over her knees and a brown stain ran down the front like a huge teardrop. "Get us medicines—" she pressed on, fearfully looking around.

I nodded. Then I heard the thumping of feet as Hector jogged back around the corner.

"You all right, colonel?" he questioned. His dark eyes glared at the nurse. She dropped my arm.

"I'm fine," I answered, then turned to whisper to the nurse, "Sorry, I have to go."

"You're a woman. You understand these things," she responded, as she faded back into the doorway.

I rubbed my forearm as I jogged to catch up to the group. I knew many things, but how could I understand what she had been through? What had those hard eyes seen or those weathered hands endured? I wanted to know, but there was no time. The time would come soon enough.

As we left the final building of the tour and stepped back into the hazy outdoors, the fresh air filled my lungs. The city odor no longer churned bad memories. Now it brought relief from the stagnant hospital air. I grabbed Garner's shoulder and motioned with my head to the hole left behind by the artillery round, then swept my hand toward the glass and bricks. The general turned to our Iraqi host. "Say, partner," he asked, "why don't you all clean this up?"

The Iraqi administrator looked over his shoulder at the crowd, then answered in a slow, measured tone. "Well . . ." He paused, as if sharing a great secret. "Because no one has told us to do so."

Those words hung in the air for a full minute. Garner and I stared at him. It was going to be a long recovery for the Iraqi people.

We marched toward our convoy as the guards attempted to contain the men and boys jostling to see us. An angry man elbowed his way forward. He cradled a wounded boy and shoved him between Garner and me. I winced at the sight of the injured, lethargic child and the putrid smell of urine and rotting flesh. The man was yelling in Arabic and I turned to our translator. "What's he saying?"

"He claims an American Army truck struck the child, leaving him for dead," the translator answered.

As I reached out to cradle the boy's limp neck and stroke his ashen face, blood dripped from the stained gauze around his thigh and splashed on to one of my new boots. Before the father could place the boy in my arms, the translator stepped between us and spoke. "He wants one hundred American dollars for this atrocity."

I froze in disbelief. My maternal instinct told me something wasn't right. "A hundred bucks for a child? That's disgusting." I balled my fist, drew it to my chest, and glared at the flush-faced father. "Shame on you."

The translator yelled at the father as the Iraqi men pressed forward, joining in the argument. I stumbled back and signaled to our bodyguards, who pushed the arguing men aside. The Iraqis began fighting among themselves and shouting at us. In an instant, the mood of the crowd had gone from docile to dangerous. The guards sensed it and propelled us to our SUVs. It was the first, but not the last, time we escaped unpleasant or dangerous situations behind the human shield of these men.

Once confined to the safety of the vehicle, Garner whispered hoarsely, "We should do something about that young boy." I opened my notebook, but before I could put pen to paper, our jaded translator dismissed this idea outright and explained the reason for what we had seen.

From what others in the crowd had told him, an Iraqi car had actually hit the boy, but the driver had no money. A neighbor heard about the injured child and urged the father to take him to the hospital. The father refused; the sicker the boy, the more money he could get. Extortion was a way of life. The translator cautioned that we must steel our hearts to the human suffering that was Iraq.

The immensity of our task was beginning to sink in. *What have I gotten myself into?* My ego answered, *You can handle it.* I rubbed my temples—*To sacrifice a son for a hundred dollars?* Maybe I could understand what the nurse meant. I looked down at my notebook; the pages were still blank. Was this significant? Our first hour in Baghdad and we had already experienced complacency, extortion, anger, and despair. So much for Iraqis throwing flowers in the streets, as some had predicted.

I leaned back against the rough cloth headrest. Swallowing the acid in my throat, I closed my eyes and shut out the conversations in the car. My mind swirled, trying to remember how an Air Force colonel, trained as a pilot, had ended up sitting next to General Garner as we traveled through the most dangerous city in the world. Although we were surrounded by men with an arsenal of weapons to protect us, there were many more men who were armed and determined to kill us. For now, though, how I got there was not as important as why we were there. Could we make a difference?

I opened my eyes and flipped through the printed schedule. Next stop, the sewage treatment plant. *Oh great, this should be fun.* The convoy crawled down the street. I stared beyond the ruined buildings. *Is there anything out there worth saving?*

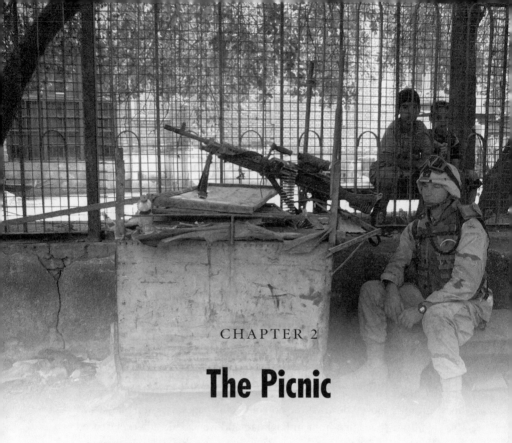

CHAPTER 2

The Picnic

To reach the sewage treatment plant, we crossed the sad city to its
western outskirts. Our convoy choked the intersections and dominated the constricted streets before we pulled through the chain-link
fence surrounding the plant. Except for a dozen filthy squatters at the
entrance, the place was completely deserted. I looked at my watch. We were
two hours late. Perhaps the managers or workers had run away when they
saw our large military convoy approaching. As I glanced round, I could see
that the facility was a sprawling complex of holding tanks, stuccoed buildings, and abandoned equipment. Beige sewer pipes leaned along the side
buildings and lay scattered under bridges and piled in ditches. The two-foot
by thirty-foot pipes looked like huge paper-towel rolls tossed about.

We had been briefed that the Baghdad sewer system dumped five hundred metric tons of raw sewage into the Tigris River, and other cities pol-
luted the Euphrates River every day. These rivers provided the primary water
supply for the entire nation, just as they did in biblical times. Our plan
had been to upgrade this facility, but the dilapidated condition of the
plant would require a complete rebuild. I made a note in my book, *Sewer*

plant-delegate to engineers. For now, however, rebuilding the sewage plant would have to wait. I had more immediate concerns.

The team of nearly fifty people, including our Army escorts, was hungry, and our favorite fast-food places were six thousand miles away. Taking advantage of the complex's deserted condition, I suggested we picnic right there.

"You want to eat here?" Garner replied, raising an eyebrow.

"Sure, it's secure, we got an hour to kill, and everyone is hungry. Besides, we need a bathroom break." He shook his head at my logic.

"There's a plan—picnic and pee at the plant," the general chortled.

We broke open the case of Meals Ready to Eat (MREs) stored in the back of the Suburbans. These brown pouches offered a fine selection of chicken enchiladas, chicken chow mein, beef stew, beefsteak, and tuna casserole. Each one contained enough calories to feed a family of four—twenty-five hundred, to be exact. There was also enough salt to preserve a body for all eternity.

Each MRE included a main meal, a side dish of fruit, crackers, dessert, and condiments. They had come a long way since my deployment days as a young officer, when we would spoon thick food substances from cold pouches. These modern MREs had water-activated heat packs to warm up the pouches. Rumor had it the green gum provided was a laxative.

Some troops swore by them, but I was not an MRE fan—probably because Air Force aviators prefer box lunches. Instead, I scrounged through the pouches, confiscating the rare bag of M&Ms and the shoestring potato chips, peanut butter, and crackers. I hoarded such items in my vest pockets, because the general was terrible about missing meals. I pumped him with peanut butter, crackers, and candy to keep him going when there was no opportunity for a picnic.

Despite the company's claims, by the way, M&Ms do melt in your hands—at least when temperatures climb to 115 degrees. When that happened, I resorted to eating M&Ms with a spoon. Chocolate was chocolate, in any form. I was prepared to go without many luxuries and necessities in Iraq, but chocolate was not one of them.

In the weeks to come, the bodyguards would venture into town and bring me treasures of Mars bars and Kit-Kat bars. I had introduced them to Thin Mint Girl Scout cookies back in Kuwait. After that, my wish was their command. Men can be easy.

Chomping on my crackers, I sat on the tailgate, swinging my legs and surveying the men and women eating around me. The ten-member press pool accompanying us was assigned to capture history in the making. The United

States was going to rebuild a nation. It had been sixty years since we had attempted a feat this complicated. But the Army had worked their rebuilding plan for Europe several years before World War II ended. Today, there was no such plan, and the realities of the last hour collided with our earlier assumptions.

I watched the press pool. Expensive digital cameras hung around the neck of a long-haired male photographer. A young female newspaper reporter scribbled in a small spiral notebook. The TV cameraman struggled to open his MRE. It seemed as though he was always tangling with something. I was used to seeing him juggle his tripods, cameras, and mikes. A National Public Radio reporter put on lipstick and checked her mascara in the mirror of the car. The press had a job to do, but they were ruthless in obtaining just the right picture. Even though I arranged for each reporter to accompany the general in the car to get one-on-one interviews, it was never enough. The longer we were in Iraq, the more intrusive they became, crowding Garner and the Iraqis he greeted or talked with. I watched them step on kids, clobber people in the head with their cameras, and elbow their way around the leadership team. Several times, I thought the bodyguards would shoot them.

The general had been under a gag order from the White House for the entire six weeks we were in Kuwait. Rumor had it the administration didn't want him upstaging the president. Even after the order was lifted, we never really embraced the press, and we sometimes made it difficult for them to get their story. As his executive officer, I guarded Garner's private moments like a watchdog.

One day in northern Iraq, while we were meeting with the Kurdish leaders, the general whispered to me that he needed to use the rest room. I found a toilet and led him to the door. Before I could close it, members of the press pool had raced down the hall, cameras rolling. Stepping in their path, I yelled, "For crying out loud, let the man pee in peace." Lowering their cameras and notepads, they sulkily walked away.

I turned back from the press to look at our leadership team, a study in itself. One key member was an advisor from the secretary of defense's office, Special Assistant Larry DiRita, who was talking on the phone between bites of his meal. Garner said Larry was sent by Secretary Rumsfeld to keep an eye on him and reported back through unfiltered channels. "What, doesn't he trust you?" I had asked, shocked. The general just smiled. Larry quickly became a Garner fan and tried hard to help him navigate through the bureaucratic maze of the Pentagon. But I never saw Larry execute anything. He just watched and reported.

The woman sitting next to me, Ambassador Margaret Tutwiler, was quite a contrast. This beautiful, high-powered, brilliant woman had been summoned by the Bush administration from her position as the U.S. Ambassador to Morocco to help Garner with the press and public diplomacy. She was smart, direct, and knew the political landscape. *How had she done it?* I wondered, as I watched her eat her lunch.

In my experience, there are two types of women who maneuver successfully in a male-dominated world, whether it was my own world of the Air Force or the larger domain of foreign policy and national security. One type keeps her head down, draws no attention, and causes no waves; although she gets promoted, she does little to improve the institution. The second type of woman works within the system, finding the right men as mentors, and changes the system from within. Margaret had been Secretary of State James Baker's spokeswoman during the administration of President George H. W. Bush, the current president's father. She must have been the second kind of woman.

"What did the nurse say?" she asked in her southern drawl.

"She asked for running water and medicine, but there was something else. She was hesitant to talk to me," I replied, chewing on a potato chip.

"Women aren't exactly free to speak their minds around here," she said, sipping her bottled water.

"We need to fix that," I told her.

Margaret stared at the long lines of Humvees, and I studied her pale face, framed by shoulder-length straight blonde hair. Today, she looked older than her fifty-ish years. We all looked older. Margaret was a Washington insider. When she had arrived in Kuwait the previous month, her no-nonsense approach to dealing with the general officers and the staff had been enlightening. She was also a contrast to Ambassador Barbara Bodine, a sharp-tongued woman with little patience who was the most senior female member of the leadership team. Barb was a lightning rod and isolated herself from the very people who could have helped her succeed. *But women* can *make a difference,* I thought, studying Margaret's distant expression.

After eating our lunch, we loaded up the team and headed for Baghdad's power plant, the final stop for the day. Four smokestacks dominated the horizon and could be seen from miles away as we approached the plant. The number of stacks spewing out black smoke would indicate the status of electricity in Baghdad. The entire time we were in Iraq, I saw only one stack emitting smoke.

The protection of the plant was under complete U.S. military control. We rolled into the industrial complex, and the guards relaxed. We entered the building, a concrete structure that smelled damp and acidic. Men in oil-stained jumpsuits carrying large toolboxes wandered on gangplanks around the cavernous building. Pipes groaned and steam hissed as the plant reverberated with the sound of generators spinning.

As we climbed two flights of steel stairs to the control room, Garner gripped the rail and paused. "Knees," he said, under his breath. I understood the need to cover human frailty and moved in to help his ascent. Our footsteps clanked in rhythm as we climbed the stairs. In the control room, a schematic of the electric grid and hundreds of round dials covered the entire wall. It looked more like a museum piece than the controls of an operating power plant.

An Iraqi foreman described how saboteurs had stolen vital pieces of the plant's equipment. During their morning staff meetings, an Iraqi gunman often shot from about two hundred yards away, across the river, into the side of the building. Occasionally a stray bullet would explode through the window, sending everyone to the floor. It was more disruptive than dangerous, he added, tapping his finger to his cheek, but "someone is determined to keep Baghdad in the dark."

General Strock jumped in. "We'll handle that," he said, repeating what he had said at the hospital. He made another note in his book.

Within a week, the U.S. Army took care of the gunman. Equipped with a night-vision scope and an infrared laser mounted on a bolt-action 7.62-mm rifle, an Army sniper and his spotter lay prone on the roof, waiting. In the early dawn hours, two middle-aged Iraqi men approached an area of tall grass on the other side of the river, opposite the plant. One man sighted an AK-47 at the building, while the other stood watch from behind. Before the Iraqi shooter could pull off a round, the Army sniper squeezed his trigger, sending a bullet into the Iraqi's head and throwing him back into the reeds. His accomplice turned to run, but he met the same fate. When the U.S. military police went to retrieve the dead bodies, they were gone. But the morning gunfire into the power plant stopped.

Our conversation with the foreman continued. "Why can't you generate more power to supply all of Baghdad?" Garner asked him. A U.S. Army colonel stepped forward to answer.

I took notes. The lack of electricity in Baghdad was the result of two things: one, saboteurs damaged critical components of the electrical grid, and two, engineers had stopped the rolling blackouts experienced by other cities, a practice previously used to supply power to Baghdad. Currently, the plant was operating at only 25-percent capacity, inadequate to sustain the city.

The inability to burn more fuel oil at a higher consumption rate caused another problem. The colonel went on to explain that refining oil was a complicated and far-reaching process that affected every aspect of life in Iraq. Oil refining occurs when there is a demand for refined oil. Crude oil must move to some destination—either to storage tanks or through pipelines across the border to the ports. The UN sanctions on Iraqi oil since the first Gulf War had tightly controlled the movement of oil, and at the beginning of this war brought it to a standstill.

Iraq's huge oil storage tanks were filled to capacity. Supertankers were restricted from carrying Iraq's oil out of the ports or from the storage tanks. Since no one could purchase or move the oil, the pipeline system was dormant. Now the refineries sat idle, waiting for the distribution system to unclog. The bottom line was that no storage capability meant no refining, and no refining meant no by-products such as gasoline for automobiles or liquefied petroleum gas (LPG) for cooking.

In addition to having Baghdad residents sit in the dark, night after night, in a city with no police or security in place, there was a very real possibility that gas stations would run out of fuel within a week. Cars were already waiting in mile-long lines for gas, and tanker trucks were being driven up from kuwait to avert a fuel crisis. I drew a schematic in my log with a note. *Without relief we will run out of gas & propane, which will drive a humanitarian crisis—exactly what the UN predicted.*

"We got our work cut out," Garner commented.

Exhausted, we walked back toward the cars. Garner and I crawled into the back seat of our SUV. I turned to him. "Well, how do we like Baghdad so far?" He didn't laugh. My attempt at humor fell flat as he stared straight ahead.

CHAPTER 3

Meeting Garner

Early one February morning two months before that day in Baghdad, I walked into my tiny gray cubicle on the third floor of the Pentagon. I was assigned to the comptroller's office within the Office of the Secretary of Defense (OSD). This office was staffed with ten civil-service workers and three colonels—one each from the Army, the Navy, and the Air Force. I was the Air Force colonel. Our mission was to liaise (because you could not say lobby) with the appropriators on the Senate and House Armed Services committees.

These committees were the most powerful on Capitol Hill. Controlling the $480 billion budget of the Department of Defense (DoD) allowed for a lot of pork. The comptroller's job was to prioritize DoD's budget and control the services' gargantuan appetite for expensive technology and weapons. My portfolio included the Air Force budget, military construction projects, and health care issues—a total of $220 billion. Although the job might sound impressive, it was boring—nothing compared to commanding troops, flying jets, or deploying around the world. I missed operations, but so did every other officer in the building. A Pentagon assignment was the price of getting promoted to colonel, but I disliked it.

That morning in February 2003, I was the first and only one in the office until the deputy to the DoD comptroller walked in.

"Colonel Olson, you want a high-vis job?" It came out more as a challenge than a question.

This short ball of a man with a round face and a nasal voice had watched me work the Hill and the halls of the Pentagon for nearly two years. I had proved very effective. But I had told him on many occasions I was ready to go back to any Air Force operational job. "You have to pay your dues here first," he would remind me.

Not only did most officers dislike the Pentagon, but they also disliked the political appointees who dominated the leadership positions in OSD. "Uninformed arrogance" were the words most used to characterize them. An officer was wise to remember that the appointee's loyalty was to the political party in power. It was a sharp contrast to military leaders and their allegiance to the U.S. Constitution. I understood the need for civilian control of the military. For one thing, if it were up to most military leaders, women would never have had a chance to serve in uniform.

But the deputy was a decent guy and I was half-listening as he rattled off an explanation about some retired generals and personnel from various federal agencies forming a team to rebuild Iraq after the war. *War?* I drew back my head. Now he had my full attention. *We are really going to war. . . . Why?*

". . . and they need help. Are you up for it?" he asked.

"Heck, yeah," I responded, glancing at my watch. The time was 7:14, and my life was about to change forever. At first, my mission was to represent the comptroller and get this emerging leadership team the help it needed. Nothing happened in the Pentagon without a funding source and someone to authorize the expenditure. Having worked in the comptroller's office, I knew the system and how to make both happen. OSD had designated $6 million to help with the start-up efforts in drafting this reconstruction phase. With that amount of money, I could provide lots of assistance.

I met General Jay M. Garner the next day at the morning staff meeting. There was an instant connection between us. Although he looked like a typical general officer, his demeanor was anything but. Garner never met a stranger. A three-star general who had been retired for more than ten years, this sixty-four-year-old southern gentleman from Florida had left his position as the president of SYColeman, a Virginia-based technical services and consulting firm, to serve his nation again.

After I had worked for him for a while, I asked him how he accounted for his friendly manner. He was quick to point out that he was raised by a dominant mother. Then he married Connie, who ruled the house, and they had a strong-willed daughter, who eventually had two independent grand-daughters. He boasted that he was surrounded by women. I laughed at this remark, given his forty-two years in the U.S. Army—surrounded by men. But Garner enjoyed the companionship of women. "They're just naturally friendlier and bring a different perspective to life," he declared.

The general had a knack for pulling the best and brightest into his team, and he didn't care about gender. He went after talent. His leadership style instilled loyalty and trust from his followers, an ability few in power possess these days. Garner made you believe all things were possible. He did this by building one relationship at a time. He was a man of the people. It was a natural gift, and he used it well.

In preparing for his new assignment, the first thing he did was to recruit four retired generals he had known since Vietnam as his senior staff. Each was a successful businessman and had a life of his own, but when Garner called, they all flew to Washington within twenty-four hours. When I asked the youngest of the four, retired Major General Bruce Moore, why he came, he answered, "It's simple. Because Jay asked me to." An easy-going Texan, General Moore leaned in, whispering, "Besides, I wanted one last adventure." Slapping his thigh, he threw his head back and laughed from the bottom of his stomach. It always made me grin when he did that.

Within the first two weeks, the original team of half a dozen members had grown to thirty, then eighty, then more than a hundred. It included professionals from the departments of Defense, Treasury, Energy, State, Justice, Transportation, the U.S. Agency for International Development (USAID), CIA, and even the White House. Two active-duty generals joined the team, General Strock from the Army Corps of Engineers and a British major general from the logistics field. An entire military support staff was established to help organize and support the team's mission.

It made sense to recruit folks from the same agencies that made our own country function, but why wasn't the State Department in charge? Rumor had it that DoD was still stinging from the Afghanistan experience and was not about to allow State to lead one of the nation's most critical missions. Instead, the plan was to place the various members of the team as advisors to the Iraqi ministries, and then we would have the country up and running in no time. Sounded good at the time.

This nascent organization was eventually named the Office of Reconstruction and Humanitarian Assistance, or ORHA. ORHA had a three-fold mission. As its name suggested, first, it was to reconstruct, where necessary, the physical infrastructure. Second, it was to handle any humanitarian crisis after the war; at the time, many feared such a crisis would include refugee problems, widespread disease outbreaks, and even the risk of famine. Finally, the team was supposed to begin the process for the governance of Iraq and set up an environment that would encourage democracy to flourish. And, ORHA was to stand all this up in about thirty days. *Hey, right,* I thought, every time a staff member gave that briefing.

It seemed that every day, new faces joined the morning staff meetings. As an advisor, not a member of the ORHA team, I spent most of my time listening and making pointed suggestions when appropriate. Ten days into the process, on a Monday morning, the staff was excited and energized by a rumor that they might deploy within a week. When it was confirmed that Secretary Rumsfeld wanted the ORHA team in Kuwait City before the war began, I sought out Garner.

"Sir, I would be honored to work as your reach-back point of contact in the Pentagon," I told him. Anything would be better than the boring job I had.

He thought about it for a minute, pursed his lips, and shook his head no. I was shocked. Then he added, "Come with us?"

"As what?" I stammered.

"My executive officer." He grinned.

As he awaited my reply, I studied his pale face. Although I had seen my share of deployments, this could be the adventure that comes only once in a lifetime. I had spent two decades flying military aircraft all over the world, but I had never deployed into a combat area on the ground. Air Force pilots see combat from miles above the earth. Add in a chance to get out of the Pentagon for a while. I nearly drooled.

The previous year, my once-promising career had come to a grinding halt, adding to my distaste for this five-sided office building. I pondered the possibilities. Jobs as executive officer to generals are "ball busters," but executive officers to powerful generals can also influence the military and make it better. General Garner could have had any colonel in the military, but he wanted me. *A female assigned to the inner circle of men tasked with rebuilding Iraq. Oh, the difference I could make. . . .*

I stared out the window, then back at him. We had known each other less than two weeks. I wondered if he could handle a female exec, much less a female pilot exec. I swallowed and tried to make this next point clear.

"Sir, if you need someone just to kiss your ass, I am not for you," I said. "But, sir, I'll work my butt off and you won't find a more loyal officer." I paused. *Please say yes.*

He laughed and took my hand. "That's what I like about you, Kimmer, straight and to the point. I don't need a suck-up. I need someone smart, sharp, and aggressive. I like what I see in you. Well, what do you say?"

Relieved, I sighed. "I'd be honored, General Garner."

"Call me Jay."

"Yes, sir."

We shook hands. *Kimmer? Where did that come from?*

My excitement waned as I sat in the typical beltway traffic on my way home that night. The difficult part would be in explaining my decision to my husband and children, who thought they had seen the last of my deploying days.

The next day, ORHA received orders to deploy to Kuwait City. Our mission was to plan and execute the rebuilding of Iraq—after a war that might or might not come to pass.

CHAPTER 4

Departure to Kuwait

O ur team assembled on the cool spring morning of March 16, 2003. Within clear sight of the impact point at the Pentagon from the September 11, 2001, terrorist attack, six buses stood idling, waiting to take 153 Americans into history. Garner gathered the excited and anxious crowd together in the Pentagon's south parking lot. He spoke of the importance of their mission, the sacrifice their families were making, and the appreciation of a grateful nation. Secretary Rumsfeld arrived fifteen minutes later and gave the same speech. Both men waited patiently while the families took pictures and shook their hands. Finally, the secretary and the general patted each other on the back. The two would meet again, but under very different circumstances. I stood next to Kent, watching.

In our seventeen years of marriage, Kent had watched me deploy a dozen times. Over the years, military conflicts had taken me to Asia, Europe, and the Middle East. In all cases, I had been the military pilot flying an aircraft bound for some foreign land. With my responsibilities in the cockpit, I rarely had time to mourn over leaving the family. Today, sitting idly as a passenger in the long, silent hours of this flight, I knew I would miss my children, worry for their safety, and fret over them. Our good-byes earlier that

19

morning had been especially difficult. Katie, the younger, the daughter of my soul, had shoulder-length blonde hair, pouty pink lips, and almond-shaped green eyes. She would turn twelve in my absence. Past deployments had forced me to miss five of her last eleven birthdays. This affectionate girl clung to me as I loaded the car in our driveway. Several neighbors peered out from behind their mini-blinds. Military officers living in the suburbs of northern Virginia seldom deployed.

Katie's beautiful face, usually alabaster, was tear-stained and red. "Mamma, Mamma!" she cried, in a voice too young for her age.

"It will be all right, sweetie," I cooed, stroking her face. "I'll be back before you know it." Her small hands left an imprint on my back. My mother, who had driven up to see me off, watched in silence. I leaned over, hugged her bony shoulders, and reassured her with the same words. "It'll be all right, Mom."

"Be careful, Kim," came her stoic response. I smiled at her demeanor. This is where I inherited my strength and courage. In her late sixties, she, too, had seen me deploy a number of times, but it still did not ease her motherly concerns.

My tall, slender son, Keegan, almost fifteen, jammed his hands in his pants pockets and rocked on his heels. "Come give me a hug," I coaxed. Dragging his feet as teenagers do, he held me tight and trembled. A lump caught in my throat. I drew away and escaped into the station wagon. Glancing back, I saw both kids lunge into their grandmother's arms. She hugged them tightly and I could see her gray face etched in apprehension. Kent and I drove away in silence.

Reliving the dull ache those memories stirred, I began the long-practiced survival technique of compartmentalizing my world. I shut down those maternal instincts and concentrated on the task at hand. I was now the executive officer to Lieutenant General Jay M. Garner, director of the Office of Reconstruction and Humanitarian Assistance. Kent recognized that look on my face and whispered, "It's time to go." He held me tight as I choked down a moan and buried my head in his shoulder. Then we pushed each other away, and he drove off without looking back. I straightened my shoulders, locked my jaw, and climbed on board the waiting bus.

US Airways Flight 1960, destined for Kuwait International Airport, was a grueling eighteen hours long. It would become famous as the last commercial aircraft to arrive in Kuwait before Operation Iraqi Freedom began. The modern A330 passenger aircraft was the pride of the Airbus fleet and contracted with DoD to ferry troops and cargo during the prewar buildup. Most of the senior officers sat in the first-class section of the aircraft, reading or sleeping. Determined to avoid the nagging pain of leaving my family, I ventured into the cockpit and chatted happily with the flight crew. The relaxed atmosphere, the common bond of aviators comparing stories, and the familiar smell of an airplane eased my troubled heart.

While our ORHA team traversed the Atlantic, diplomats from Spain, the United Kingdom, and the United States attended a summit meeting in the Azores in a last-ditch effort to avoid war with Iraq. These negotiations proved fruitless. Hostilities would come in less than one week.

As we touched down and taxied into the deserted ramp area of the Kuwait airport, the view from the cockpit was surreal. Row upon row of tan tents lined the airfield. Trucks, military equipment, and wire perimeter fences with concrete barriers dominated the landscape. Everything had a sepia appearance. Even the afternoon sun hung like a colorless white ball in the brown haze that covered this part of the globe.

Before we deplaned and entered the dusty surroundings, Garner turned to the team and announced, "It's show time!" We were then whisked away through Kuwait City, accompanied by the screaming sirens of police escorts and traveling at speeds of ninety to a hundred miles an hour.

So much for a quiet entrance, I thought, as my fingers dug into the car-door handle.

"It sure would suck to get killed in the first hour of arriving in Kuwait," I joked with the general.

He grimaced. I could see he disliked the black armored Mercedes we rode in, but the recent killing of an American contractor had forced him into this armored chariot. I would soon learn just how much he hated the impression created by Americans when they overdid security. However, the Central Command (CENTCOM) commander, General Tommy Ray Franks, set military policy in this Area of Responsibility (AOR). Policy dictated we travel in a minimum of two vehicles, with at least two passengers and a weapon in each car. I laughed at the irony. No one on the team had been issued their 9-mm weapons yet, and our ammunition was still back in the United States, awaiting transportation.

We arrived at the Hilton Resort compound an hour later and were immediately briefed on the security situation around the hotel. Kuwaiti army units were providing perimeter protection until we could bring in our own forces. The advance team had done an excellent job of bedding down the ORHA contingent. I shared a villa with the three senior generals. The second floor had four bedrooms and the first floor was converted into offices.

Five hours after we landed in Kuwait City, we watched the president of the United States announce to the world his ultimatum to Saddam Hussein. The dictator had forty-eight hours to leave Iraq.

Yep, we are actually going to war, I thought that first night.

Adjusting to the time-zone difference of eight hours made sleep impossible. My first night, I unpacked a suitcase. My wardrobe consisted of two sets of desert camouflage uniforms (DCUs for short), four pairs of khaki pants, one dark navy suit, and several long-sleeve T-shirts. I wasn't going to make a fashion statement with this attire. Opening my duffel bag, I smiled at the ten boxes of Girl Scout cookies that had made the journey safely. They were compliments of my thoughtful neighbors, who hustled around gathering the cookies before I departed.

Rummaging through makeup, shampoo, lotion, and toiletries, I set up the bathroom. As I reached for my family pictures, I discovered my kids' two Gund dogs, Penny and Woffins. Penny, Katie's stuffed animal, still had shiny soft fur and both eyes. Woffins, Keegan's dog, had matted fur, an eye missing, and stuffing hanging from its paw. For those who have read the children's classic *Velveteen Rabbit,* you will instantly recognize such a too-much-loved friend. I breathed in the scent of my children from these stuffed treasures. Katie had hidden them in my bag with a note written in crayon, "Hug them when you miss us." I knew I would get teased, but I displayed the dogs on my bed next to the pillow.

In addition, I stacked some black and white composition books on my dresser. Since this was my first time serving as an executive officer to such a senior official and my first attempt at rebuilding a nation, I had sought the advice of Dr. Gordon W. Rudd— a retired Army lieutenant colonel, who was the ORHA historian— on recording this mission. He recommended buying composition books in which to record the daily events. He suggested that I dedicate two pages for each day. On the left side of the page, I could record the day's schedule by time, events, and people. On the right side, I could provide a narrative of my observations and impressions. "It will become a living document of this journey, Kim." Gordon's prediction was uncannily accurate.

I pulled out my son's old fifth-grade composition book from the stack. Its edges were frayed, but only two pages were scribbled on. The marbled outer cover had drawings of cars, airplanes, and happy faces. It didn't look that professional, but I didn't care. It would stay under my bed, and I wrote in it only late at night. Little did I know that the words I would write in this recycled elementary school notebook would become the basis for a memoir.

Our first full day in Kuwait began with the fifty-minute drive to Camp Doha, headquarters to the coalition fighting staff. We traveled in a four-car convoy, once again at speeds in excess of one hundred miles an hour. White-knuckled, I thought, *Well, if we can just avoid getting killed in an auto accident, we'll be all right here.*

Camp Doha was an austere base surrounded by gray Jersey barriers, concertina wire, and heavily armored young soldiers. Hours of boredom on sentry duty were written on their faces, but their dedication to their mission made me proud. Rows of huge, tan warehouses stood in formation against the desert skyline. A small city existed under their silver metal roofs. As I entered these aluminum structures, the rush of air was so cold it stung my sweating body. I was impressed by the activity inside. During my deployment to the Middle East five years earlier, we had operated out of small tents or within the confines of crowded trailers. Today, uniformed troops rushed about, radios broadcast announcements, and the hum of generators echoed in the cavernous structures.

We were at Camp Doha to receive the latest briefing on the transition and reconstruction phases of the war. It was disturbing to learn there was little to no planning about the integration of the ORHA team with the military postwar phase. Irritation spread over Garner like a blanket and he rocked his chair as the briefer droned on and on.

Immediately after the brief, the general went on the offensive, criticizing the lack of depth and detail in their planning. I suppressed a smile as the remaining military briefers shifted uncomfortably. But the U.S. lack of preparation was nothing to laugh at. It had far-reaching implications, and Garner knew it. "We win the war and you rebuild," was not a plan, yet that was the military's solution. It was obvious our job was to create the transition and reconstruction phases of this war. I copied a graph from the board into my notebook: *Fight-Transition-Reconstruct. Each phase will overlap the other.* But by how much was the troubling question.

I was relieved to crawl back into the black Mercedes. The time-zone difference and lack of sleep was catching up with me. Kuwait's scenery flew by in a blur, and my eyes grew heavy.

"Nice bears," was the only thing Garner said in the car.

"They're dogs," I answered without turning.

Lost in a daze, I glanced at the small green canvas bag that hung from the belt strapped around my waist. It contained a gas mask intended to keep me alive in the event of a chemical attack. *Would I need it, and would it work?*

Forty-eight hours later, Tomahawk missiles and smart bombs from F-117 stealth fighters slammed into command bunkers in central Iraq. In the illumination of a beautiful full moon, the war had begun. This was obviously the Army's war. No aviator wants to fly into combat under a full moon. Oil wells were set ablaze by retreating Iraqi soldiers in southern Iraq. Wavering warning sirens screamed throughout the first night in Kuwait City. Just north of our resort, the desert fell victim to several Iraqi Scud missile attacks. Patriot missiles protected Kuwait City from inbound Scuds with an 80 percent success rate. As the ground war progressed, Marine units quickly advanced and secured southern Iraq. Media sources reported that the initial phase of the war was going well.

I tossed and turned most of the night as sonic booms shook the room and rattled the windows. During the early morning hours, sirens wailed as a Silkworm missile launched from Iraq ripped through a popular shopping mall five miles from our location. Rumors spread that the missile was destined for our compound. Throughout the next few days, the air war continued with a yawn. It was the ground war and the embedded reporters traveling with the Army forces that captivated American audiences. The rush to Baghdad had begun in real time and real life.

CHAPTER 5

The South Africans

W ith the war under way at last, the Kuwaiti Army withdrew from guarding the Hilton Resort compound to protect the border, leaving our team exposed. Requests to the U.S. Army for a security detail were denied. The Army was busy fighting a war. Instead, those in the Pentagon contracted with a London-based company at the staggering cost of $3.6 million. The company, in turn, hired eight experienced South African guards on a subcontract. Protection was essential, given the death threats and other hazards of operating in Kuwait and, later, in postwar Iraq.

The eight-man team joined us in Kuwait in the latter part of March 2003. By then, the growing number of coalition workers at the Hilton required additional security. Fifty Gurkhas—Nepalese retired members of the British Indian, and Pakistani armies—were providing perimeter protection. Later, the Gurkhas complemented the standing U.S. troops in Iraq, guarding the palaces and the occupied hotels. But it was our white South African bodyguards that caused controversy in the early days.

With forty-eight hours' notice, these men had left their families to work for the Americans in Kuwait. They each signed a two-month contract at a salary of $6,000 a month—a substantial amount of money for men in their position. The team was sharply divided between those with police backgrounds and those who had served in the South African Army. Five of the guards had been trained in Special Forces tactics, known as "selection." Selection was an eight-month program designed to grind men into the ground; only the toughest, most callous, and most resilient survived. A typical class began with eight hundred candidates and graduated only eight. These were physically powerful men.

It wasn't our guards' selection training that gave the ORHA staff pause; it was their combat experience. It was rumored that several had been assassins for the old apartheid government, while others had worked as mercenaries in distant jungles and deserts. Several were said to have been embroiled in bloody battles protecting diamond mines. Some on our team argued they would switch sides to the highest bidder.

Then there was the visual impression they created. At six foot two, these battle-hardened men towered over their charges and were an imposing sight. Garner's initial reaction was to say we should cut the team to four. He loathed the idea of being surrounded by grisly brutes toting AK-47s. It gave the wrong impression of ORHA's role. Garner's mission was to lead the rebuilding of Iraq, not battle it.

I was glad the South Africans were on our side, but it was such a contrast to working with U.S. men and women motivated by patriotism and the desire to serve a greater good. Our U.S. team believed in the ORHA mission. Did the guards? I worried about entrusting the general's life and, by extension, my life to them. The reality was that we didn't have a choice. We needed a robust protection team, and they were who the Pentagon sent.

The debate about the South Africans continued for a week after they arrived. Our senior lawyer on the ORHA staff expressed concern about entrusting the lives of the general and those around him to hired guns. He argued that the South Africans did not care about the success or failure of the U.S. mission in Iraq; their loyalty was to a monthly paycheck. There was a serious question as to whose lives they would really save in the heat of a firefight, theirs or ours. The senior staff repeated atrocity stories about the brutality of the former apartheid regime or deeds committed by South African mercenaries, although preliminary background checks uncovered no evidence that these eight men were involved in such activities. The staff also argued that these warriors didn't have much respect for women and were not worthy to work with Americans. I raised an eyebrow.

After much discussion, I brought in Garner to hear the staff's concern about the cost and the character of these South African men and the chances we were taking by relying on them. The general listened and then chose to keep the entire team. He had a knack for seeing the possibilities in people. He dubbed them "the boys." This decision to keep all eight men probably saved his life. "The boys" not only risked their lives for us, at one point they worked for no pay. They continued to support the U.S. mission in Iraq long after Garner left.

Once the decision was made, I moved to establish my authority. Derick, the team's leader, was summoned to brief me and a senior force protection specialist from the Marines on their tactics and operations. It was then I began to learn more about these eight men, who found themselves without jobs in the wake of apartheid. Because of their past employment in the South African Army and special police forces, their military expertise and law enforcement skills were now shunned and despised by the South African government.

Seven of the eight were married. All but one descended from Boers, with their characteristically thick accents and thick bodies. (The eighth was of British ancestry.) Each spoke Afrikaans and English, and four of the men were multilingual, fluent in French, German, and Russian. Six had college degrees. To protect their identities, I'll call them by other South African names—Derick, Hector, Louis, Johan, Paul, David, Neil, and Cecil—instead of using their real names. Each one was a book in himself.

Derick, in his late thirties, who emerged as the leader of the team, stood six foot six and weighed 240 pounds. He looked like a linebacker for the Chicago Bears, with legs as thick as tree trunks, broad, powerful hands, and a large, square head. His dark, distant eyes bore an unsettling look. He struggled with internal demons that would reveal themselves later. Although he cared for his men, he was a harsh dictator. You must lead with an iron fist, he reasoned.

In contrast, there was his best friend, Hector. Hector, who was just as big, was handsome and cheerful, with a simple outlook on life and an innocent, flirtatious way about him. The women flocked to him. Derick and Hector were inseparable, with Derick acting as the father figure. Both were veterans of selection training and had worked at a game capture business after they quit the South African special police force.

As Derick laid out the plan, he and Hector would be the primary guards for Garner. Hector was the driver of our vehicle with Derick as #1, meaning the number one protector for the general. Derick stood the closest and was there to take a bullet for Garner, if necessary. Fortunately, that theory was never tested. Hector was #2, the secondary protector, but he was actually assigned to protect me. He was supposed to take a bullet for me. This theory would get tested.

Louis, with his tousled blonde hair and piercing blue eyes, was the only guard of English descent. He was the intellectual of the group, with a teaching degree in theology and a spiritual view of life. Years earlier, he had escaped death in a brutal ambush in Angola in which the casualty rate was 95 percent. The brutality of that experience left him permanently scarred; he said he lived now on borrowed time. There were days that Louis drifted away in a daze and Derick worked hard to keep him on the sane side of life.

Louis's partner, Johan, was tall and had a broad chest. He had dark, curly hair and a striking face. His smile lit up the room and his mature nature and caring ways drew me to him. We became fast friends as he accompanied me on my evening walks. We were the same age and shared a common outlook on life. He was a worrier like me, but it was nice to have someone watch over me. Having been an art major in college, he had an eye for beauty. Even in war-torn Iraq, Johan could find it in the bloom of a flower, the smile of a young child, or the taste of Iraqi ice cream. A very religious man, he reminded me daily that there was always something to celebrate. The other men on the team did not appreciate his sensitive side, which caused friction.

Louis and Johan were #3 and #4. They commanded the front vehicle of our usual three-car convoy. Their mission was to read the traffic, ensure a safe path, and clear the way. When on foot, they took a lead position out front to protect us.

The next two men on the team were Paul and David. Paul was twenty-three, with a young wife and two children. He had a bounce in his stride and had left his father's cattle farm to join the team. As part of the post-apartheid generation, he suffered none of the emotional trauma shared by the older men. Paul thought this was all just a big adventure. His partner, David, was the informal leader of the group. A dark-haired man with a kind, mature, smart nature, David was a good balance for Derick's rough ways. His specialty was reconnaissance; never once did we get lost or trapped in Iraq's maze of streets and hidden alleyways. Paul and David were #5 and #6, sharing the front and back vehicles. They formed the perimeter behind us when we moved on foot.

Neil was a thin, gangly man with horn-rimmed glasses. He looked more like a professor than a bodyguard. Quiet and soft-spoken, he struggled to understand the English language and hid behind a shy smile. His respectful demeanor made me grin, especially because he always answered "Yes, ma'am" no matter what I asked. He was on medical retirement from the police force and was earning extra money for his family with this assignment. I never learned of his medical condition, but our children were the same age and we shared parental concerns. The final man was Cecil, a polite but distant character who had chartered fishing boats on the African east coast. The sun and time at sea gave him a leathery look and an appetite for alcohol. The longer the tour lasted, the harder he drank. Neil and Cecil were

#7 and #8. They drove the third SUV, protected the rear, and were ready to use their SUV as our escape vehicle if the middle one became disabled. I rarely saw Neil and Cecil when we were on foot, since they spread out to rooftops and around corners. They were the eyes beyond the crowd.

Each of the eight men wore an ear radio and traveled with a short-barrel, collapsible-stock AK-47 or an MP-5 submachine gun, a Beretta pistol, a knife, extra magazines, a flashlight, and other equipment. What they didn't use were flak vests, helmets, or any protective equipment. Derick explained that such equipment would slow them down, and our best chance for survival in urban warfare was the ability to move quickly. This was in complete contrast to the U.S. soldiers, who wore more than fifty pounds of protective gear—battle rattle, as it was called. Garner shared Derick's theory and did not believe leaders should wear flak vests or helmets. He said it presented a more open and approachable image to the Iraqi public. I followed Garner's example.

When the general traveled through the streets and back roads of Iraq, we drove in a convoy of three plain Suburbans. The vehicles were purchased for this deployment and brought up from Kuwait after the war ended. There was nothing special about these standard SUVs. None was bulletproof or armor plated. They were a sharp contrast to the heavily armored military convoys and ostentatious, bulletproof, gold-colored SUV of Garner's successor.

After Derick completed his force protection brief, the Marine sergeant asked a few clarifying questions. Satisfied by Derick's answers, the sergeant turned to me. I still wasn't sure about these South Africans, so I glared at Derick and leaned across the table. "All right, you guys are the experts in your field. But let's get one thing straight. You work for me. I run General Garner's schedule and keep the ORHA team straight. You'll be available whenever and take us wherever we need to go. You got that?"

"Yes, ma'am," he responded, his expression hidden behind hooded eyes.

I didn't give a damn what he thought. I had no time or patience to worry about the egos of these brutes from South Africa or their male chauvinist attitude. I expected them to be professionals and do their jobs. They were working for Americans now, and that meant working for a female colonel.

My concerns were short-lived. A few days later, I found a bag of Toblerones and a card on my desk. It read, "Thanks for watching out for us," and it was signed, "The Boys." Smart men. How had they figured out that chocolate was my weakness?

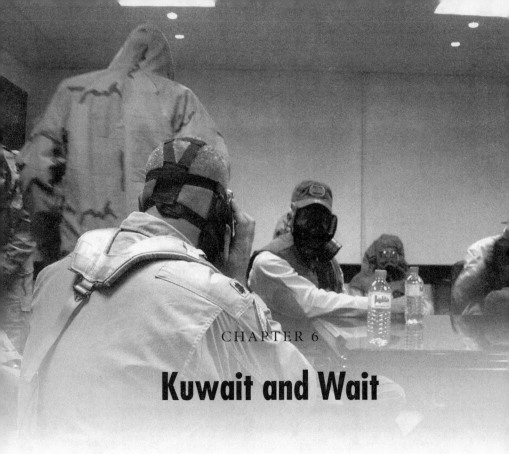

CHAPTER 6

Kuwait and Wait

There was little time to watch televised reports about the war. The next few weeks were demanding, as we settled into a grueling routine. It was the classic "hurry up and wait" situation. Lacking political direction from above, Garner and the ORHA leadership team spent their days flying to CENTCOM-Forward in Qatar and working with the military staff at Camp Doha. I grabbed four to five hours of sleep a night and powered through the day fueled by adrenaline and chocolate. Despite the long hours, sleep sometimes evaded me as my mind raced through that day's and the next day's events. On those nights, I escaped to a seawall just outside the villa.

One evening, I sat with my eyes closed and head tilted toward the inky sky. A light, warm breeze tickled my face, bringing relief from the heat radiating off the concrete. Bouncing my heels against the wall and gazing out into the Persian Gulf, I inhaled slowly. The faint smell of petroleum lingered in the air. I could almost taste the oil in the back of my throat. Hushed waves splashed the darkened, rocky shore as I squinted at the white and amber lights out on the horizon. Soft steps padded across the grass behind me.

"Mind if I join you?" The words rolled off Derick's tongue in a deep voice as he straddled the wall next to me.

I did mind, but I answered, "Sure," without turning. Quiet minutes passed before he spoke.

"Think those are tanker ships out there?" He waved toward the lights.

"Nah, they're buoys."

"Ships."

"Buoys."

In the yellow glow of the porch light, I studied the leader of our protection team. Derick's specialized training was apparent in his cool, assertive demeanor. His violent history was evident on his face—a crooked nose, a scarred lip, and a guarded smile he pulled pencil-thin over his teeth. He didn't walk; he prowled. There was raw power in his athletic physique—wide shoulders, burly arms, and thick knuckles. But it was his dead, dark eyes that unsettled me the most. They looked cold and empty, like a starless night. He seemed comfortable with weapons, invited danger, and dismissed death.

Derick would tell me later, "If I told you what I've done and seen, you wouldn't believe it." Tonight, we sat together in silence, an Air Force colonel and a mercenary from South Africa. I, bound by duty and country—he, bound by a contract and money. We were so different. Back home, he captured wild game: elephants, hippos, and rhinos; I coached basketball, drove kids to sporting events, and taught Sunday school. He had spent a year in the Congo, tracking and killing rebel forces; I had spent a year in the National War College, discussing Clausewitz and Sun Tzu. He was Special Forces; I was a jet pilot. He got his leg shot; I had acid reflux. He had been married fifteen years; I, seventeen. Yet there were similarities: we were both risk-takers, with strong personalities, and both of us were in search of something.

Derick would tell me later he wanted a chance at a better life. It was a dream just out of his reach. Tonight, it didn't matter. There we sat on the wall, an unlikely team with a common mission—to take care of General Jay Garner, the man charged with rebuilding a nation.

"Why did you join the Air Force?" Derick asked in a raspy voice.

"Oh, it's my mother's fault." I chuckled. "You want to hear a story?"

He nodded.

"It was July '79. You were probably still in grade school, and I had just graduated from college with an education degree. I had only two job offers at the time—teach high school biology at a small town in Michigan, or go into the Air Force."

As I began the story, I vividly remembered that decision. At the time, I was spending the summer with my parents in Virginia. My mom and I had gone to a small beach where we had solved many problems over the years. We strolled along the water's edge, the cool surf encircled our ankles, and sand stuck to our bare feet. It was a hot day, and the laughter of children echoed across the seashore. Clear, plate-size jellyfish speckled the beach. Kids just loved to poke at the poor creatures with sticks, and then run away screaming.

I literally wrung my hands as I debated the advantages or disadvantages of each job. My teaching degree from Ohio State was in physical education and science. Teaching was in my blood. My parents, grandmother, aunts, and great-aunts were all teachers. Besides, I really wanted to settle and put down roots somewhere, because my parents were DoD schoolteachers and our family had moved every five years. I had spent my entire childhood overseas, and I never had a hometown. My folks started their careers in Baumholder, a U.S. Army post in Germany. I remember it was cold, damp, and gray. The cold must have gotten to Mom and Dad, because our next move was to Bermuda.

My promised "story" about becoming an Air Force pilot was taking some odd turns, as I began telling Derick about those childhood years in Bermuda. But why not? Bermuda gave me the best years of my life. Our family cruised around the blue waters of the island in our small boat. We camped on deserted, pale pink beaches. Our dog chased crabs and returned, whimpering, with one hanging off her ear or tail. Before I was eight, I could water-ski, snorkel, and swim like a fish in the open ocean. The best part was going fishing with my dad at dawn on Saturdays. He taught me to bait the hook, reel in the fish, and drive the boat. I was the oldest of four kids and it was wonderful to receive his undivided attention. I remember laughter and warmth. We should have stayed there, but it wasn't up to me. After five years of island life, my parents were lured to the exotic Pacific. So, in our next move, we traveled halfway around the world to Clark Air Base in the Philippines—the PI for short.

Those were tough, growing years, but I did okay. I was a cheerleader, class president, sang in the choir, and played three sports. By the time our family returned to the United States, I was sixteen and a senior in high school. Many things had changed. I now had a stepfather and three stepbrothers. My dad, my fishing buddy, had died during our first year in the PI. I was twelve.

As the memories rushed on, I stopped talking and stared at the buoy lights until they began to jump around. It had been thirty-three years. Why did that painful memory follow me to Kuwait, and why tonight, as I sat on this seawall? My head began to spin, and the concrete wall pinched my legs like the base support of a hardwood pew.

I was twelve again, back in that church. Beads of sweat rolled down my back and my clammy hands lay clasped in my lap. The stillness engulfed me. My dad was lying in the open casket. Childish mementos surrounded him—a clown cup, a picture colored with crayons, a brown stuffed bear, and my handmade get-well card. *This isn't happening. This isn't real.*

I caught a glimpse of movement from the corner of my eye. *Here they come. Dad, get up. Please get up. Hurry, before they close the lid.*

I squeezed my eyes shut and jerked as the finality of latching the coffin reverberated off the church walls. *Don't go. Please don't go. You can't leave me, you just can't!*

My memory clouded as a crushing pressure penetrated my chest. *I can't breathe.* I gulped for air as a sob escaped my lips. I was spinning, panting, out of control.

My fingertips ached as I dug them into the cement wall to steady myself. *Jeez, Kim, get a grip.*

"A-hum." Derick cleared his throat and narrowed his eyes on my taut face. I locked my jaw and returned his penetrating look. *No! Don't even ask.*

Forcing my eyes up to the scattered stars, I exhaled and pressed on. "Oh yeah, where was I? Well, my stepfather was an Air Force officer stationed in Ohio and that's how I ended up at Ohio State University. I thought I could settle in the Midwest, and a teaching job sounded fun."

My stepdad, whom I had become very close to, had suggested the Air Force. He loved his career and thought his stubborn, willful stepdaughter would make a fine officer. "Think of the adventure, all those new careers opening up for women. The military offers opportunity, excitement, and travel," he told me.

Honestly, I was a bit unsure—the Air Force was a big institution. Too big, so I decided to follow in my mother's footsteps. That day on the beach I thought she would be pleased when I announced, "I think I'll take the teaching job."

She stopped in mid-stride, turned, and leveled her normally soft brown eyes, now alive with fire, at mine. *Oh no, here it comes,* I thought. She reached out and thumped me on the head with her middle finger. *Ouch.* I rubbed the aching spot. Thrusting her index finger at me, she said in a slow, deliberate tone, "That was my *only* option when I got out of college. Now think again!"

"Okay," I hesitated. "I guess I'm going into the Air Force," answered the parent-pleaser in me. I was such a classic oldest child, always looking for approval and yet rebellious. It is ironic I would choose the military with its authoritative structure.

My mom pressed on. "Look, Kim, stay in for a couple of years and then get out if you don't like it. You can always go back to teaching." So that was my plan—stay in for four years.

I shifted my weight and shook my head. "Well, that was twenty-three years ago." *Where did the time go?*

"So, you come into the Air Force as a pilot?" Derick asked, cocking his square head.

"No, not exactly." I grinned. "You want to hear *another* story?"

"Sure." His large frame leaned toward me. I crossed my legs and rocked back.

"I was recruited into the Air Force as an air weapons controller. Now, having no clue what that entailed, I went to Langley Air Force Base in Virginia—that's where my stepdad was stationed during my final college years. He arranged a visit for me to see the life of a controller."

The controllers worked in a dark, cramped trailer surrounded by large, circular screens with small lights dancing on the glass. Radios crackled from the speakers and cold air rushed around the room. The stale air smelled of cigarette smoke. It was depressing. I asked the young captain about the dotted lights and the sweeping line. He explained this was a radar display and the lights represented airborne jets. His responsibility entailed running intercepts with inbound enemy aircraft. As I listened to the radio chatter of the pilots, something stirred within my soul. I stood spellbound for fifteen minutes and the choice became clear. I didn't belong in a cold, smoky trailer. I belonged in a jet aircraft. Hell, I didn't want to be an air weapons controller—I wanted to be a pilot.

Racing home, I called my trusty Air Force recruiter and announced my intentions. "Great idea, no problem," he said. "Just apply to change your job when you get to OTS in Texas."

The Air Force's Officer Training School (OTS) is the institution where college graduates receive an officer's commission in about ninety days. Elated, I thought it sounded simple enough. I was soon to learn there's nothing simple in the military.

So, with stars in my eyes and dreams of becoming a jet pilot, I entered the Air Force. When I inquired about changing jobs at OTS, I was promptly informed I had to apply and meet a pilot selection board. Not to be deterred, I took all the appropriate aptitude tests, endured the intrusive flight physical, and filled out endless amounts of paperwork. Five men and I applied for undergraduate pilot training (UPT) slots. A couple of weeks later, the board results were released. All five men received UPT slots, but I did not. It seemed my package never made it to the board; in those days, women weren't allowed to apply to UPT while at OTS.

At the raw age of twenty-one years, I was immature. I remember seeking refuge on a set of bleachers to have a good cry. It was early in the evening and a huge yellow Texas moon was rising in the sky. A C-130 cargo plane was flying in the traffic pattern a few miles from where I sat. I could hear the drone of the prop engines in the distance. It was like my own private air show. Every time the silhouette of the plane passed in front of the moon, my resolve to become a pilot grew stronger.

Now that I had gotten over the initial disappointment, I got mad as hell. I wanted to fly jets. My test scores were better than the men's, I had glowing letters of recommendation, and I was a college athlete in perfect health. Why couldn't women apply for those UPT slots? No one had an acceptable answer. It was Air Force policy, they would say. The only way for a female to get a pilot slot was to go through the Air Force Academy or to apply as a commissioned officer. Applying as a commissioned officer, though, would take another two years. I wanted to be a pilot right then, so neither one was an option for me.

For the second time that night I fell silent, as the concrete wall cut into my skin and the bitter taste of discrimination filled my throat. Because I was a woman, I was denied a job. That event ignited a fire in me. *You picked the wrong girl to say no to. You SOBs just watch me.*

Derick again broke the silence. "So, what did you do?"

"What? Well, I kept thinking, this is not fair. Policy or no policy, it was simply not fair. I complained to anyone who would listen. Finally, someone in my class suggested I go down and talk to a Colonel John E. Rush in the headquarters building. Maybe he could help. So I marched down the hill to Colonel Rush's office and presented my case.

He listened politely and asked me why such a nice young girl wanted to fly airplanes. Stunned at his question, I locked my jaw and hissed, "Because I qualified and I know I can." I told him that if he wouldn't help me, I'd find someone else who would. He smiled at my boldness, said he'd check into it, and sent me on my way.

One week later, I was summoned back to his office. With a sheepish grin he asked, "How about a navigator slot?"

"What? Sir, I don't want to be a navigator; I want to be a damn . . . sorry, pilot."

"Okay, okay! Best I could do was a pilot training slot in February."

"All right, thanks, sir!" I jumped up and saluted, anxious to leave his office.

As I marched out the door, I paused and asked, "Will I always have to fight?"

"You . . . I'm afraid so," he predicted.

When I called home to relay the good news to my parents, my stepdad gave me the third degree. "Who did you talk to, Kim?" he inquired.

"Some colonel in the headquarters building. They called him the I-G, I think." My answer was received with dead silence. "What's wrong?" asked the young officer candidate of the seasoned colonel.

He snapped, "For crying out loud, Kim, I've been in the Air Force for twenty-five years and never once have I gone to the inspector general. You've been in training six weeks and are already filing complaints about our service."

It was my turn to be silent, but not for very long.

"Colonel Rush was the inspector general? Oops! But it still wasn't fair, Dad," I protested. Without my realizing it, my visit to Colonel Rush had represented a complaint to the inspector general. This was a clear breach of officer protocol. What on earth could an officer candidate have to complain about after just six weeks? However, after that incident, Air Force policy changed to allow women to enter pilot training while at OTS.

I concluded my story in a triumphant tone.

"You were a groundbreaker," Derick declared.

"Not by choice."

Looking at the dial of his large black watch, he said, "My shift ends at midnight." The green glow from his wrist reflected off his Beretta pistol. "Tell me another."

"No," I interrupted. "You tell me one. I hear you're into game capture. Those pictures I saw of you and Hector with the rhino and the elephant—how do you do it?"

"My English is not so good," he said, dropping his head down.

"It's okay, my Afrikaans is awful." I patted his muscular forearm.

Exhaustion weighed on my shoulders. Chills spread across my body and goose bumps rose on my back. I tucked my legs to my chest and wrapped my arms around my shins. Resting my head on bony knees, I tried to listen.

With his face hidden in the shadows, Derick drew a deep breath. "To capture a rhino, you travel into the thick bush of Africa. This is done by flying in helicopter or traveling in Land Rover. Once the animal is found, you must sedate him. We use a high-powered air rifle, and this is very dangerous for me and the rhino. Too much tranquilizer and the animal goes down, he suffocates—not enough and the rhino can hook you."

"Hook?" I yawned.

"Yes, rhinos are nearly blind, so they use their horn to protect themselves. This animal swings its head in the direction of any movement. . . ." His words faded as my head dropped forward.

"Colonel!"

I was being shaken. "What?"

"You fell asleep, ma'am," Derick said.

"Jeez, I'm sorry. Let's finish this story another time." I stood up, groggy.

"Perhaps another time," he answered.

The cool night air made me shiver. My body ached for sleep and my eyes itched. I stretched out. "Good night, Derick. Thanks for listening."

"Sleep well, colonel."

I felt his eyes follow me as I shuffled across the grass to my room.

He called after me. "Someday, you'll tell me what it's really like to be a female pilot, yes?"

"Maybe," I whispered and climbed the stairs. I glanced back at Derick, who was still sitting on the wall, facing the sea. "Maybe someday, if I can trust you," I said out of earshot. Right now, exhaustion rendered my mind numb.

CHAPTER 7

Southern Iraq

L
ess than a month after arriving in Kuwait, Garner and the ORHA staff were restless. Most days began at 0700 and ended around midnight. Staff meetings, political functions, interviews, phone calls, and feeding the growing appetite for information from the Pentagon and those in Washington dominated my time. I lost fifteen pounds in those weeks and my pants hung from my hips. I gave up exercising and cherished the extra hour of sleep.

Tensions developed between the military officers on the team and the State Department members. The tension was fueled by Ambassador Barbara Bodine, a former U.S. ambassador to Yemen who had been recalled from retirement to join the ORHA team because of her impressive Foreign Service record, which included extensive experience in the Middle East and the ability to speak Arabic. A tall brunette with striking blue eyes, Barb was blunt and direct and showed little respect for the military staff. I recognized that cool aloof leadership style and worked hard to win her trust. She never raised her voice at me, as she did the other colonels, maybe because I knew why she had such a tough exterior.

"We can't work with her," the retired generals complained to Garner one night.

"You want me to get rid of her?" he offered.

The hair on the back of my neck stood up. I had been on the other end of this conversation before. Men couldn't get along with women, so they just got rid of them.

I cleared my throat. "Sir, maybe if you'd just visit with her." The generals looked at me. I pressed on, "She has a lot of experience in this part of the world."

The seven generals (two active-duty, five retired) gathered for a nightly happy hour, a long-held military custom. There they would review the day's events and discuss tactics for the following day. The men did "what if" drills, and after a few rounds of scotch, with their tongues loose, they would tell war stories. Mostly, they reminisced about the rain-filled days of Vietnam, the hot, dry days of Desert Storm, and the long days in the Pentagon. Once in a while I would jump in with a flying story, but these were Army generals, foot soldiers, and unless you fought on the ground, you weren't shit. Most of the time, I just listened and learned; but not that particular night. I pushed them to give the ambassador a chance.

The following morning, I walked to her villa next door. Although it was early, the temperature was already 90 degrees, and sweat beaded on my face.

I tapped twice on her metal door. "Come in," she snapped.

"Hi, ma'am." I eased the door open. "How's it going?"

"Good." Ambassador Bodine eyed me.

"Ma'am, I was wondering if you would consider joining the generals for happy hour tonight. I have to listen to all of their boring war stories, and I heard you held out for months in the U.S. Embassy when Iraq invaded Kuwait back in 1990. It would sure be nice to hear war stories from a woman." I laced my fingers together.

Her cobalt eyes danced. "What time?"

"Say, 1800 hours. By the way, you might want to bring this." I handed her a bottle of scotch. This time, a sly smile crossed her attractive face.

That evening at 1810, Ambassador Bodine walked onto the porch and pulled up a chair like she owned the place. Two of the younger generals shot glances at each other. I suppressed a smile as her cool demeanor hushed the conversation. "I thought you could use this." She slid the bottle across the table. There was a collective intake of breath as Garner picked up the Johnny Walker Blue Label—one of the most expensive Scotch whiskeys produced. Another general reached for the bottle and Garner slapped his hand away.

"Nice choice, Barb."

She nodded and stole a glance my way.

The shot glasses were filled and the seven men toasted Barb. "Tell us about Kuwait, Barb," one of them asked.

"When the Iraqi forces invaded Kuwait City . . ." she began, crossing her legs and settling back into the chair.

I excused myself and went into the office to e-mail a letter I had written more than a week earlier. We had just recently gained the ability to send e-mails, and for now I could send only one message home.

28 Mar 03
Dear Family and Friends,
    Hope this letter finds you all well. As most of
you know, I have deployed to Kuwait City with the
likelihood of going on to Baghdad City. I am part
of the team that is challenged with providing the
humanitarian, reconstruction, and civil administration for Iraq in a post-war environment. We have
been in country 12 days although it seems more like
12 weeks.

(I had started my note several days earlier. Now that I was sending it, it had been more like twenty days in-country. Sure enough, twenty years sounded about right.)

    You might ask, how do you rebuild an entire coun-
try after a war? Good question given that the US has
not attempted this in 60 years. The first thing we
did was gather a team from the different agencies
of the government. We have representatives from the
department of state, energy, treasury, agricultural,
Army Corps of Engineers, civil affairs, all branches
of DoD, USAID, DART (disaster assessment recovery
team), 5 retired generals, American/British Iraqis,
personal protection teams from South Africa, and
international officers. To date there are 230 of us
and our mission is to help rebuild and return Iraq to
its people—24 million of them.
    We are structured in a classic military organi-
zation. The director is Jay Garner, you may have
seen him in the written press and I suspect he will
become more visible when we get in country. There

are three regional and three functional directors
below him. The three regional directors run the
north, mostly controlled by the Kurds, the south,
controlled by the Shiites (majority), and the central, which is Baghdad proper controlled by the
Sunnis (the minority).

The three functional areas consist of directors
responsible for humanitarian aid, reconstruction,
and civil administration. Each of these directors
has resources and various tools at his disposal.
They must rely on other agencies and international
help to succeed.

The first and most important is the humanitarian
aid director. He is a retired Ambassador and a great
American. As you hear on the news there is a humanitarian problem in the south near Basra. If the
security situation was better he could respond to
the crisis. At his disposal are USAID, DART, and
nongovernmental agencies. This director facilitates
the relief efforts identified by the regional teams.
They can do this by providing food, awarding grants,
bringing in medical teams, and preventing human
rights violations. However, nothing can happen if
the environment is still under threat of violence.
This is why a military presence is critical to the
success of any humanitarian operation. Until we can
achieve some stability in these regions, humanitarian aid is problematic.

I deliberately left out everyone's name but Garner's (which was known
to the press) for security reasons. By now, death threats had been made
against several of the team leaders. But time has passed, and I can tell you the
humanitarian aid director I referred to was retired ambassador George
Ward. He, too, had spent a career in the Foreign Service and had been the
U.S. ambassador to Namibia. George had left the U.S. Institute of Peace to
join the ORHA team. He is truly a great American, as I said in this e-mail.

The second tier of our organization is the reconstruction team and they have their work cut out for
them given the results of the air campaign. They can

repair damaged infrastructure: most important is to
restart the water supply and sustain the water sani-
tation process, restore the power grid and repair
dams, roads, and buildings. This team will also extinguish the oil fires by using a contractor and the
Army Corps of Engineers. At present, they and the
Kuwaitis are trying to extinguish the two fields burning in southern Iraq near the border. They are also
trying to get the port of Umn Qasr cleared of mines
and up to operational standards to accept the wheat
that the Australians are offering. The port has lost
power and you can imagine docking a large ship con-
taining 50K metric tons of wheat with nowhere to
store it or mill it. The ship is idling at sea waiting to get clearance into the port.

The third area and the most challenging is the
civil administration (CA) piece. This is the core of
the Iraq governance and where we will work the hardest. There are 23 ministries in Baghdad and we are
planning on repopulating them with a US advisor,
Iraqi-American, DoD reps and pull in native Iraqis.
This team will run everything it takes to make a country function. Education, judicial, health, banking,
investment, culture, and defense are among a few. As
an example, within this pillar are the treasury folks
who are tasked with providing salaries for the Iraq
civil workers. Some might ask, why would the US take
on paying Iraqi workers? Another excellent question—
the answer is that we really need them to come back to
work and we want to prevent a humanitarian crisis.
The Iraq people make about $30 at month. Not a lot of
money, but everything is subsidized: food, housing,
school, and fuel (they use propane to cook and run
generators). You will hear arguments on the proper
amount to pay the workers in the future.

In addition, the long-term goals of the CA are
to write a constitution and to hold elections at the
local, provincial, and national level. The US is
putting together a blue ribbon team to accomplish

this task. We are optimistic the country will run
itself . . . eventually.

Finally, we have a British general who is working
the coalition piece. There are thirty countries who
have stepped forward to offer help with Iraq. Most
of them will bring a particular capability to Iraq.
For example, the Spaniards have a team that can
train a police force; the Japanese want to donate
funds, and the Kuwaitis want to reinvest in the
southern Iraqi businesses.

Now, I must make the point that none of these
functions can happen until the security environment
is settled and for this we rely completely on the
military. Saddam learned from Desert Storm. He has
embedded death squads inside towns to threaten and
keep the locals from uprising or helping the allies.
Until he is gone, it is difficult to win the hearts
and minds.

I just wanted to present the baseline of our
organization and mission. I will try to report once
a week on our progress. The most difficult part
right now is the waiting to go north. We will probably send in the directors north and south before
the main body gets into Baghdad. I look forward to
writing you from Iraq soon.

Kim Olson

My promise to report once a week was overcome by events. I would
actually send only two more letters. There was simply no time to sit and write.

On April 1, a few days after I composed the e-mail, Garner and I got to
accomplish what few Americans had done—travel peacefully in and out of
Iraq. We visited the town of Umn Qasr, just across the border. It was the first
time any of us had been in this part of Iraq. Umn Qasr was a dirty and desolate
place. Poor people, poor neighborhoods, and abandoned facilities marked the
town. Our brand-new Suburban rattled and bounced over the hilly, rutted terrain. The rough ride left me with a backache and a sore neck. I forgot my pains
at the first sight of young children with matted hair, soiled hands, and torn,
frayed clothes. Oversized garments accentuated their skinny arms as they
reached out for money, water, and attention. For all their poverty, they rushed
forward with toothy grins and friendly waves, and pumping thumbs-up.

It seemed that everywhere we traveled, the same type of men and young boys hung along the roadsides and eyed us suspiciously. Some even displayed a hint of fear. A small crowd of young girls waved from behind the men and smiled shyly as we bumped past them. The rare times that I caught sight of a woman, she was normally hidden in a doorway within the traditional black abaya garment. *You shouldn't have to wear that damn thing anymore.* How little I knew about the threats to women in Iraq.

There was 90 percent unemployment in this town. The deepwater port stood idle as Navy SEALs cleared the mines from in front of their small PT boats. They had worked hard to make the water passages safe, but silt runoff had decreased the channel depth, making ship passage impossible without extensive dredging. On the horizon bobbed an Australian cargo ship, waiting to deliver wheat. The wheat would eventually rot. But wheat was not what this town needed. What it needed was a swift injection of imports to stimulate the only port in Iraq and a transportation system to move those goods inland. It would get neither.

Our mission here was to tour the port and visit with the local leaders. The harbor was a massive site with six gigantic cranes, a maze of conveyor belts, and a sprawl of warehouses. The operation must have been impressive, but not today. Its skeletal remains stood rusted and muted. Had Saddam Hussein spent the needed funds to support the Umn Qasr port instead of building palaces, the recovery of Iraq might have been easier.

There was no way for the ORHA team to know just how broken Iraq really was, but we were soon to find out. The port had been the lead-in for the UN Oil-for-Food program. However, it was obvious the local program had scammed their share of money and little of the food or proceeds had made it to those in need. Corruption, greed, and fraud were the hallmarks of this international program. We learned that all the Oil-for-Food managers had fled after the war started and had not returned. Their lives would be at risk if they came back to the town they laid to ruin.

The British military commander assigned to this area was clearly in control. Security was tight and a curfew was in place. We received a detailed briefing from one of my National War College classmates, Captain Mike Tolliston, U.S. Navy. Who could have known when we said good-bye in May 2000 that we would meet again in a spartan building in southern Iraq? He would not be the only classmate I would see again.

Mike's briefing reminded us that southern Iraq is predominantly comprised of Shiites. They took the brunt of Saddam's wrath after the first Gulf War. Unlike the Kurds in the north, these people had no mountains to hide in. Nor could they escape into Kuwait.

Saddam systematically destroyed this region and it was an ecological disaster. When he drained the marshlands and swamps, the wind blew the chalklike silt throughout the south (that's one reason the port had become clogged). The ground was left barren and virtually uninhabitable. He cut off electricity, plunging the towns into medieval times. He also tightly regulated the water supply, stopping it on a whim. The infant mortality rate skyrocketed, and the Shiite population began a slow decline toward extinction.

But human resilience is amazing. Despite all of these obstacles, the people survived. By then, unlikely men rose to lead the townships. We attended a council meeting directed by a retired schoolteacher and a cleric. They took charge and compiled a list of requirements. Their primary concern, much to the surprise of the Americans and British, was to get an ice maker. Summer was coming, and they needed ice to cool their refrigerator boxes which did not rely on electricity. It was impressive to see this forethought and planning occurring. Garner was pleased at our initial meeting with these tough Iraqis.

As the day worn on, I became worried. We were supposed to return to Kuwait before nightfall. Force protection was always on my mind, and the last thing we needed was to be on Iraq's deadly roads after sunset. But I also wanted to see an elementary school; I pushed Garner into looking at Iraq's learning institutions.

The only grade school was on the other side of town. As we drove down the narrow streets, a young girl with long pigtails and a dirty pink dress peeked at me from behind a crumbling brick wall. I waved. Her skinny body froze and she scurried into the house. I instantly thought of Katie. *God, I am glad she does not live here. You are so lucky, Katie. How do mothers stand it? Their children have no food, no water, and no future. Well, we are about to change all that.*

The unscheduled stop at the elementary school seemed like a good idea at the time. The caretaker unlocked a huge padlock put there to prevent looters from ruining the building. As he removed the heavy chain, the door's hinges creaked in protest. We stepped into the musty entryway of the two-story cinderblock structure. The long, dark hall led to empty classrooms. There were desks, but no chairs, no books, no equipment, nothing. A small stick figure drawn on the chalkboard was the only hint that this was a school.

The dull rumble of footsteps and murmur of voices echoed down the empty hallways. I glanced over my shoulder at a steady stream of villagers, running toward the school and shouting, "Americans, Americans." I wished then that we had brought some military escorts.

I looked at Derick. "Can you handle this?"

He nodded without taking his eyes off the crowd. We tried to exit the building, but we were trapped in the doorway. Garner loved the influx of people. He was at his best in a packed crowd. "Hi, Jay Garner. Hi, Jay Garner." He gripped every hand that reached for him. He started to wade into the people when a Japanese TV crew stepped forward, asking questions in broken English.

"What your assessment of Iraq?" the reporter asked.

Garner gave his standard answer. "The coalition forces are here to help the Iraqi people build a new nation."

Considering we had just bombed the hell out of it, it was the least we could do, I thought. As the villagers descended upon us, it became apparent they were happy and just wanted to see us or touch us. Young boys pulled at my vest and reached for my hand. I smiled and passed out chewing gum. Next time, I'd bring candy.

Derick caught my eye and furrowed his brow. He was concerned about the growing crowd. He and I soon created a code of communication with just facial expressions. I would nod and mouth, "Let's go." Then he would stand behind the general and gently push him toward the car. The momentum of these large guards moved us through the crowds without much effort. Or, Derick would raise his eyebrows to indicate something was wrong, and I would whisper to the general that we needed to leave. I knew it was important for the general to maintain an air of confidence and control. The size of the crowds never concerned the protection team; it was the people's attitude. In Iraq, that could change like the wind. We had been lucky this day.

As we worked our way through the welcoming crowd, an irate man approached us yelling about the appalling living conditions and his lack of pension payments. As the elderly man turned his face, his left cheek revealed a repulsive brown scar that pulled down his left eye. I drew back and looked for Hector. Garner tried engaging the man in conversation, but he kept yelling about needing money. Another Iraqi slapped at the scarred man, explaining that he was insane after being tortured and jailed for seven years. His crime—not showing proper respect to Saddam, by looking at him the wrong way. Disfigurements like his served as a visible reminder to all Shiites of the consequences of disobeying Iraqi law. The TV cameras scanned between Garner and the deranged man being shoved around by the crowd. It was time to leave. Nearly a hundred Iraqis stood between us and the cars, demanding payments. "We need money for food!" they yelled.

"Sir, let's go. It's getting late," I urged.

"We will get you all paid," the general told them confidently. The crowd cheered.

"Good to meet ya. Bye," we both waved.

The bodyguards lined up in front of us and created a picket-fence movement, opening a path to the cars. It was their first test as a team. They passed. Later in the car, Garner commented on how well the protection team had handled the crowd without a show of force. "There is no need for violence," he declared.

On the three-hour ride home, I thought about the people we had met and their bleak surroundings. Yet somehow, these Iraqis had gotten married, had families, gone to school, and made lives for themselves. I stared at my boss, lost in his own thoughts, and wondered if one person could make a difference.

When we returned to Umn Qasr ten days later, the attitude had changed completely.

CHAPTER 8

Bismillah

The presidential envoy was five hours late. We were back in southern Iraq, this time at the Tallil aerial port (AP), and we were waiting in sweltering heat and dust-filled wind. Iraqi leaders who could make it to Tallil had been invited to attend the first session that would move toward establishing a new Iraqi government.

The genesis of this meeting took place a few weeks earlier, in an air-conditioned trailer in the Gulf Coast nation of Qatar. Generals John Abizaid and Garner were discussing the continued fighting and Iraq's stubborn military resistance in the north.

"It is a slaughter," General Abizaid stated. This dark-haired, ruggedly handsome, and well-respected man had been my boss on the Joint Staff in the Pentagon a few years earlier. We had worked together when I was the member of the policy division assigned as the Afghanistan desk officer. I helped draft and brief his military options in response to the terrorist attack on the USS *Cole*. I had tremendous respect for General Abizaid and meeting him again brought smiles to both our faces. He allowed me to sit in on his private conversation with Garner.

"As we approach, the Iraqi Army fades away, taking off their uniforms and going home. If any of the young conscripts try to run or surrender, they are shot by their own officers. But it is these young fedayeen [religious fanatics] that we are slaughtering. They come out at night to fight, but there is no night for the U.S. soldier with NVG [night vision goggles]. Every time they make a move, we gun them down. We must give these Saddam loyalists a reason to stop resisting," Abizaid continued.

We were merely ten days into the war, but Abizaid leaned forward and stated, "The pace of the war is too slow." The Army's V Corps had been slowed to regroup and refuel, but Abizaid wanted Baghdad now. Once we occupied the capital, the war was over. So we thought. He complained that the Air Force had the most kills, followed by Army Special Forces; far behind them was V Corps.

"We need to stand up an Iraq-type organizing meeting to show the Iraqi people we intend to listen to them and will give them their country. It needs to be ready when Baghdad falls." (Baghdad would fall within a week.)

General Abizaid, who was of Lebanese heritage and spoke Arabic, would have been a perfect choice as the Iraq reconstruction general, but the Pentagon leadership had other plans. So he sat frustrated in Qatar, waiting to play a more active role in the Iraq war or postwar efforts.

"I'll talk to the deputy tonight and see if we can get buy-in from the Pentagon," Garner suggested, referring to Deputy Secretary of Defense Paul Wolfowitz. "Then we'll have to get Washington to agree."

An expletive escaped someone's mouth. I stared at the wall and the laminated map of Iraq marked with the symbols of military units.

Iraq was divided into three regions: ethnic Kurds in the north, Arabic Sunnis in the central region, and Shiites in the south. It was the conservative Sunni Triangle north of Baghdad that would continue to resist coalition forces. The Sunnis were Saddam's people and had the most to lose with a change of government.

Two weeks after the generals' conversation, the plan was set in motion. While the bloodbath continued in the Mosul area, a meeting was set for April 15 in Tallil, a sprawling military base in southern Iraq occupied by coalition forces. Helicopters were the primary means of transportation, so we flew in from Kuwait the night before. The next morning, in the shadow of ancient ruins, a large, white tent awaited the arrival of U.S. special envoy Zalmay Khalilzad and his team. Khalilzad was the highest-ranking Muslim and native Afghan in the Bush administration's National Security Council.

Khalilzad and his team from the United States and CENTCOM were supposed to arrive around 1000 to begin discussions, break for lunch, and then conclude the talks around 1500. At noon, there was still no special envoy. I finally received word that the plane was delayed and the team would arrive at 1400. "Begin discussion without us," was the CENTCOM direction. Garner was not provided with an agenda, however, because the policy makers and those in the special envoy's party were reluctant to share it. *Typical,* I thought as we waited in the 100-degree heat. Besides, this was not supposed to be a Garner show.

Well, it soon became one. I scraped together an agenda and briefed the general. He gathered the restless crowd of Iraqi expatriates, clerics, local townsfolk, and others inside the tent. His voice echoed through the speakers as the sweltering wind flapped the tent sides. "Bismillah."

"Bismillah," the crowd murmured.

"Let's try that again. Bismillah!" he charged them.

"Bismillah!" they responded.

Sunlight streamed past the open flaps and dust swirled around, dancing through the packed audience. Behind a small lectern, Garner began his first public address to the Iraqi people. It was stiflingly hot. I tapped my foot and watched in anticipation for reactions to the speech. Would the words I had crafted hit the mark? The speech was simultaneously translated into headsets worn by some of the guests.

I scanned the interior of this cloth structure. Reporters with their large digital and television cameras dominated the back of the tent. I was confident this speech would be broadcast worldwide the following day. I never had a chance to watch television—first, because there was no access to a TV, and second, because I was just too busy—so I wasn't sure how the world viewed our efforts. I relied on feedback from family and friends. Once, during a brief call to my parents, my mother told me that General Garner and I should stop chewing gum on TV. It was tacky, she said. When I relayed these instructions to Garner, he laughed and said that is exactly what his mother would have said. We stopped chewing gum.

Iraqi dignitaries sat among the round tables, which were covered in red cloth. Some of the men were dressed in traditional white robes and red- or black-checkered headdresses. At the other tables sat Iraqi expatriates newly returned to Iraq, dressed in business suits. Men dominated the group, but a couple of Iraqi women were there. U.S. Army soldiers, their weapons slung over their shoulders, stood off to the side, looking exhausted, bored, and uncomfortable. I concentrated on Garner's speech as my stomach gurgled and twisted in a knot.

"It is an honor to be here in a free Iraq." Garner glanced up. The crowd waited.

"Before we continue, let us take a moment of silence to give thanks for this day of freedom." He paused a full ten seconds. A few Iraqis bowed their heads. The soldiers folded their hands, and the press continued to film and snap pictures. He went on: "Today we gather in a historic site at a historic moment. This is the cradle of civilization and home to some of Islam's and Christianity's holiest sites. But for nearly thirty-five years, Iraqis have suffered tyranny, war, and oppression. That has all changed. Iraq draws strength not only from its rich history but also its honorable and resilient people. Iraq has been home to some of the Middle East's finest universities, home to some of the most important trading companies. And home to a vibrant culture."

That was referring to the late 1960s, when Baghdad was a cosmopolitan city of the Middle East, but I thought a reminder sounded good.

Today, Iraq has a bright future. A future where the diversity of Arabs, Kurds, and Turkomans, Muslims, and Christians shapes a course to a better life for all Iraqis. Iraqis tell me they hope for a future where their children can attend the best schools and universities; where they can travel freely; where they can speak their mind; where there is a rule of law; where corruption is punished; where citizens can speak freely. We want to help you succeed. As you and I know, there is much work to be done. We must begin rebuilding the country while simultaneously establishing a dialogue with the people of Iraq that will lead to a democratic government. Reconstruction and democracy are parallel processes. We are here to help you rebuild.

Garner looked up from the podium and scanned the audience. They listened respectfully; some tapped their pens, as if to say, "Yeah, we've heard it all before." He forged on.

"This is why I am so honored to welcome you to this meeting. With your cooperation, the Office of Reconstruction and Humanitarian Assistance, the organization I represent, will help you rebuild *your* country. The purpose of our organization is to create an environment in which the citizens of Iraq can build and sustain a peaceful and prosperous life, through a governmental process that represents the freely elected will of the Iraqi people. We are ready to listen to you."

Garner introduced the names of President Bush's special envoy, explaining that Khalilzad was still en route, and of those who would be representing the coalition partners Great Britain, Australia, and Poland.

Finally, the crowd sat up to listen. "This is just the beginning in a series of meetings to hear your voices. We will have conversations and meetings with Iraqis from all over your country. We want to know how you want to build a democracy, and what you want for the future of your country." Garner paused again and addressed the cameras as several of the Iraqis leaned forward. *Would those in the north get the message?* I thought.

Garner took a deep breath, looked straight at the audience, leaned over the podium, and extended his arm for emphasis—careful, though, not to point his finger and thus offend anyone.

"You were invited as prominent members of your communities so that we can hear your ideas and those of your neighborhoods, towns, and cities. The Baath Party tyranny is over. You are free to speak your mind and from your heart. It is your country and it is your future. Today, we gather at the birthplace of civilization. Let us use this day to mark this ancient site as the birthplace of democracy in Iraq." With that, he leaned back and waited.

The audience applauded politely. Then, slowly, they rose in an ovation, increasing the clapping tempo until their applause tumbled out of the tent and down the empty fields, was lifted up into the wind, and swept through Ur, the oldest city in the world.

"Shack, you nailed it, sir." I felt goose bumps jump on my arms and tears well up in my eyes. I was so proud to be there. Who needed a special envoy? Garner had won them over.

He spent the next few hours talking to every single Iraqi in attendance. He listened and I recorded. Finally, in mid-afternoon, the special envoy arrived, but the Iraqis had already expressed their concerns and opinions to the general. The next two hours of speeches seemed moot. At the conclusion of the session, these Iraqi representatives did something that had not been enacted in decades. They voted. They voted to hold a second meeting to discuss the governance of Iraq. Late in the afternoon, the Iraqi representatives left, the special envoy departed, and it was time for us to go back to Kuwait.

It had been a long, scorching day. I had vomited twice and was shaking from food poisoning. Those were the logical explanations for my illness. All I wanted was a cold shower, some toast, and a soft bed. Was that too much to ask?

Our team was scheduled for transportation back to Camp Doha by two Chinook helicopters. They never showed. I teased Garner about the slack Army airlift. Instead, we drove around the air base looking to commandeer a ride back. We found a brigade commander who was willing to fly us back to

Kuwait, but a looming sandstorm threatened the flight. We hustled to load the dozen passengers and get the equipment strapped down in the chopper.

A brown wall of sand obscured the horizon to the east as we tried to beat the storm out of Tallil. Gusts of wind rocked the helicopter and knocked one person down. The crew hurried its pre-flights. I counted the passengers and felt a small tug on my sleeve. It was Sheri, a State Department rep, crying. "What's wrong?" I asked, resting a hand on her back and leaning in to hear her over the howling wind.

"I'm scared. I don't want to do this," she whined.

Women! "Oh, for crying out loud, grow up," I said in disgust and walked away to see about loading the rest of the team. A minute later, Hector grabbed Derick's arm.

"Derick, we have a problem," he said in his thick accent.

The general and I stopped to listen.

"What is it, Hector?" Derick asked, looking over his shoulder.

"Sheri, she is sobbing," Hector answered with a worried face. Derick glanced at Sheri, cowering in the troop seat, then back at Hector.

He rested his large arm on Hector's shoulder. "It is okay, Hector. You won't be able to hear her when the chopper starts up."

Garner and I looked at each other and burst out laughing. Garner doubled over, clinging to my forearm. I braced myself against the fuselage and held on to my side—I almost wet my pants. After I wiped the tears from my eyes, I glanced at Garner, who took off his glasses and rubbed tears from his eyes. *Boy, we needed that,* I thought.

"I'll take care of it," I said, and sat down next to Sheri. I patted her knee, trying to soothe this frightened girl. Not all people take well to flying.

"It'll be all right," I reassured her.

"I'm scared," she cried.

"I know." I hugged her tight.

As the crew prepared to crank the engines, the commander came running out and yelled over the now-roaring wind. "You can't get through to Kuwait. The storm is topping twenty thousand feet. We have to abort."

"Roger that," I yelled back. It proved a wise call.

We hurried back to the bunker to wait out the first gust of the storm. After the initial wall of sand made its pass, we returned to our makeshift campsite on the edge of the airfield. Right before nightfall, the sky opened up and rain pounded the dirt. We stood in a small hut to watch the violent electrical storm. Lightning bolts ripped across the sky like large, jagged spears thrown at the horizon. The cracks of thunder rattled my bones and the concussion hurt my ears. I enjoyed nature's fury, but it was the sand in my teeth and every other crevice I could do without. Besides, I needed a bath. When the thunderstorm let up, the exhausted team crawled into our small pup tents to get some much-needed rest.

As I stared at the cloth ceiling and pondered the significance of the day, there remained many questions. Would the Saddam loyalists in the north hear about this meeting and stop fighting? Was Iraq even capable of governing itself, or had the Baath Party purged or destroyed all of Iraq's intellectual capital? Did the Iraqis have the energy to rebuild? But my real concerns burned deep. I wanted to wake the general and tell him what I really thought. Instead, I lay there looking at the moonless night through the tent screen window.

Although fatigue enveloped my body, I couldn't shut off my brain. Finally, I crawled out of the sleeping bag, lugged a plastic lawn chair into the yard area, and leaned back to admire the brilliant stars. There was such stillness after a powerful storm. Clean, crisp air filled my lungs and the earth's surface radiated a cool breeze. Soft sleeping sounds came from the row of five tents. I sucked on crackers, trying to settle my queasy stomach. Just then, Garner emerged from his sleeping area.

"Hey," he yawned.

"Hey, sir, can't sleep either?" I asked.

He pulled a chair next to me and we sat in silence. I relished this moment because, although I was with him eighteen hours a day, we were never alone. He was always surrounded by people—bodyguards, staff, generals, Iraqis. Everyone vied for his attention. For the first time in two months, it was just the two of us. Tonight was a rare opportunity to speak truth to power. I offered him a cracker. He took it and chewed.

"You did a really good job today, sir. I was very proud for you and of you." I reached over and squeezed his upper arm.

He patted the back of my hand. "You know, Kimmer, we are asking a lot of these people." The silhouette of his face gave him a solemn, sad look as he stared into the darkness.

They're asking a lot of you, I thought.

"They'll answer the call," I replied aloud, unsure if I really meant it. We fell silent. The general never complimented me in person, but I heard through the grapevine he thought I was heaven-sent—an angel. Hardly! The notion made me laugh.

"Sir, may I speak candidly?"

"You always do, and call me Jay."

"Yes, sir." I replied. I swallowed hard. *Here goes.* "We need to involve more Iraqi women. I know it's hard to talk to them in this culture because they are hidden, but they are just as important to rebuilding a nation. Like in our country, they encompass a large portion of the population and they simply view the world in a different way. Remember in Umn Qasr, I saw the town differently from you. While you toured the seaports, I thought of their medical system; when you asked about their school sports equipment, I was thinking about the books and qualified teachers. It's a good thing to have different perspectives. Sir, push to get women represented on the Iraqi government teams and get them involved as we rebuild the ministries."

He turned to face me. "You are so much like my daughter."

"Thanks, given she has an impressive dad."

He looked up at the ink sky sprinkled with stars. "You must have had a rough ride as a pilot."

"Yeah, I was a pistol in my younger days, all MACH and no direction. You know, I think I learned everything I needed to know my first year in the Air Force at flight school," I reflected.

"What's that?" He shifted in his seat.

"Well," I counted with each finger, "boys can be mean, the system discriminates, and if you want something done, it's better to ask forgiveness than permission."

He chuckled.

"Now, I am wiser." I dropped each finger in turn. "Boys can be taught to be nice, systems can change, and it's still better to ask forgiveness than permission."

He looked at me for a long time. "I'm glad you're here with me, Kimmer."

I shrugged and felt my face grow warm. It was his first positive feedback.

After a moment, he asked, "Want to sleep outside under the stars?"

"Sure." We hauled out our cots and placed them next to one another. *This is interesting,* I thought, *sleeping next to my boss under the stars, out in the open, and in the middle of Iraq. Ah, the job of an exec is never done.* I snuggled down into my sleeping bag and heard his breathing slow. Before too long, his snores matched the rest of the camp. *Men like you, Jay, made it possible for me to be successful in my career,* I thought as I watched him sleep.

For the first time that day, I was cold. As my eyelids grew heavy and my mind drifted off, something suddenly jolted me awake. A dark figure sat in the chair next to the cots. I blinked in the dimness, trying to focus on the face.

"Hello?" I whispered. The figure leaned forward.

"Yes, ma'am." The words rolled off the back of his throat.

"What are you doing?" I leaned up on an elbow.

"Watching over you and the general," came Derick's hushed response.

Annoyed by the intrusion of this stranger, I jerked up, and peered into his shadowy face.

"We're all right, go back to bed." I patted his forearm; his skin was cold and damp. I pulled my hand away. "You okay?"

"Yes, ma'am, bad dreams."

"What do you dream of?"

"Death."

I wasn't sure I heard him right, but he stood up and turned away.

I shivered as I watched his massive shoulders hunch over and his dark figure prowl toward his tent. *Whose death?* I didn't want to know.

I huddled further down into my sleeping bag. Tired and dirty, with an aching stomach, I spent a restless night under those stars in Iraq.

CHAPTER 9

Cleared in Hot

L ess than one week after the meeting in Tallil, we got the word to deploy to Baghdad. Garner had been hounding CENTCOM leadership for weeks and he had finally received permission to move north from Kuwait, now that most of the resistance had subsided. At long last, we were "cleared in hot"—a pilot expression for cleared to enter the engagement zone.

The advance team left on April 20. I collapsed at my desk with a thousand tasks left to perform. It was 2200, but I forced myself to finish a letter home that I had started earlier. I needed to tell the story of the week's adventure, our return visit to Umn Qasr.

```
Hello All,
    This is a second letter in the series describing
our adventure in restoring Iraq. As the war transi-
tions, we face the greatest challenge in the peace.
As the boss would say, it is show time. There are a
series of challenges that grip our organization and
the mission of restoration.
```

We have started with the first town, Umn Qasr. It
is a poor port town forgotten by the rest of Iraq.
Yet it is the only deepwater port and was used to
bring in the oil for food by the UN. Today, it is
covered with garbage and rubble and young men just
hang around for lack of work. We visited a school
that had nothing but desks and chalkboards. You
will hear that the residents need water, but they
needed water before the war. The regime used water
to control the population and the system must come
from Basra. We are working this problem, but the
images of water being thrown out the back of relief
trucks to fighting crowds does not help. We need to
show a picture of Iraqis helping themselves (I
don't mean looting). We have Seabees working there
and they have actually graded a soccer field and a
Kuwaiti company donated soccer balls. Nothing is
more telling about our progress then the experience
of being with the people. Two weeks ago we visited
Umn Qasr and the people greeted us with smiles and
waves. Today, the mood had changed considerably.
Instead of waving and cheering, the kids were begging for water and trying to block the cars. As a
mom, I thought, "Why aren't these kids in school?"
Well, school has been out since the war began. Now,
there is no one to pay the salaries of the civilian
and government workers. This presents our major
problem.

We need the workers to come back to work. We
need everything from technicals to labor workers.
However, we need money to pay the workers (they
haven't been paid in 6 weeks.) The money is supposed to come from the Iraqi assets in the US. So,
we have $20 million available in 1- and 5-dollar
bills. Why small bills, you ask? Because we need a
fractional currency, otherwise we will drive inflation. We will use the Saddam dinar for the change
until we can phase out that currency. And even if
we get the money, where is the system to pay the
workers? We need the bank system and pay records

and a mechanism to disburse the money. We can't pay 24 million people in cash. So, we finally found a guy who knows the individuals who run the banks and they are helping us with this issue.

Today, we have folks in the south, at Basar, and folks in the north, at Erbil. Tomorrow we will make the journey to Baghdad. A team of about 20 folks will begin the process of rebuilding a nation. It is interesting that on Easter, the rebirth of Christ, we have a rebirth of democracy. By the time most of you read this note we will have arrived in Baghdad, visited a power plant and a hospital, and introduced our boss to the world.

It is indeed show time. I will write again when we are up and running in Baghdad. I leave you all with a story from Tallil. I was visiting with an Iraqi who had spent time in the Saddam prisons. I expressed my concern that we (US/coalition) really wanted to get this right with rebuilding Iraq and setting the environment for a democratic Iraq. He took my hand in his very weathered hand and said, "Even if you mess it up, it will be better than it was before the war."

Kim

Show time started at 0300 in the morning with the drive to the Doha Camp airfield. As before, however, the Air Force transport plane was late. Garner commented on the Air Force's slack airlift. The flight got us into Baghdad two hours behind schedule and the delay cascaded throughout the day. After our visit to the hospital and the sewage treatment facility, we finished with the power plant at sundown and raced to a U.S. military stronghold before nightfall. Iraqi gangs owned the streets at night.

We spent our first night in a bombed-out palace on the south side of Baghdad. Our precision weapons had destroyed the west wing of this palace; it was rumored the targeted section of the structure was Saddam's sleeping quarters. The windows were blown out, but thick, tattered drapes provided some protection from the elements. Mosquitoes whined around my head. There was no electricity, no water, no toilets, and no food. We ate what we brought. I sent the reporters to a hotel in Baghdad and spent a second night with little sleep trying to work the airlift support for the next day's trip north.

Just before dawn, I was awakened to learn the C-130 cargo plane had arrived three hours early. I couldn't believe the airlift system had screwed this up twice in a row. Garner would never let me live this down. I scrambled to get the team together in the dark palace. When I shook Garner awake, he yawned, "What? Can't the Air Force tell time?"

We flew north to Erbil in Kurdish country—a complete contrast to southern Iraq. After we landed in Erbil, the team split up and rode in two MH-53 Army helicopters to Sulaimaniya. The helicopters flew in formation with the rear hatch open as two youthful Army gunners—snuff protruding from their lower lips—manned the 50-caliber machine gun. They sat on the edge with their legs dangling over the side, in seats fashioned out of lawn chairs. The choppers skimmed the countryside. Hill after hill of golden wheat bent and swayed from the downwash of our rotors. Herds of sheep ran in circles as we approached and shepherds waved from the valley floor. White rock fences were built in perfect squares and divided the landscape into neat blocks.

I leaned over the young gunners, determined not to miss anything, while most of the other passengers gripped the troop seats and concentrated on keeping their scant breakfasts down. Oil dripped from the ceiling lines, the rotor noise was deafening, and with every up-and-down draft we bounced like a basketball. This was flying—two hundred feet above the ground, skimming at 150 knots, and following the contours of the earth's undulating surface.

"I should've been a helicopter pilot!" I shouted at Garner, a huge grin planted on my face.

"You like this?" he hollered over the noise.

"It's better than sex," I joked.

"You need better sex." He shook his head.

"What?" I yelled. He waved me off.

Approaching the base, the lead chopper made a low pass to clear the landing zone. Thousands of Kurds surrounded the airfield, awaiting the return of General Jay Garner, Father of the Safe Haven. Garner had been the U.S. Army's commanding general in northern Iraq during Desert Storm. After the war, he had saved the Kurds from annihilation at the hands of Saddam's regime. Not only did he resolve the conflict between the two warring Kurdish fractions but he also was instrumental in crafting the policy that implemented Operation Northern Watch. The policy established a no-fly zone north of the 36th parallel in order to monitor Iraqi compliance with UN Security Council resolutions. He also crafted Operation Provide Comfort, in which coalition forces delivered more than 12,400 tons of food, supplies, medical aid, and fuel to more than a million Kurdish refugees along the Turkish and Iraqi border.

When the general walked off the back of the helicopter, the crowd of more than a thousand erupted in cheers and swallowed him up. The bodyguards could not get near him, but Garner didn't need them. He was a legend. Young people who were not even born when he commanded in the north rushed forward to offer flowers and packages of sweets. I juggled the numerous boxes as he handed them off to me. Signaling to the bodyguards, I pushed the boxes toward them. Derick gave me a sharp look.

"Get over it," I snapped.

We drove through clean streets lined with children and adults, all cheering and waving. What a contrast to the reception we had received in the south. It was humbling. Even the weather cooperated. The sky was a brilliant blue, the air fresh and breezy. The city streets were lined with flowers. Flowers! Can you imagine? They were actually throwing flowers. Men and women in bright-colored clothing and children in neatly pressed school uniforms greeted us.

Our first stop was a schoolhouse—Garner had listened to my suggestion. Books filled the library and equipment was stacked along the wall. Teachers bragged about what the kids were learning and the exciting projects they were working on. Crayon-colored posters decorated every hallway in the school. First-grade girls and boys ran up to hug my legs. They gave me colorful pictures of their families and I held on tight to each one.

I looked at the general. His face was glowing. "You did this." I patted his shoulders. He had made it possible for the Kurds to prosper and flourish even under a dictatorship. These were proud, productive, and joyous people. This part of Iraq had been basically independent for a decade, and the advantage of this freedom was reflected in their vibrant faces. One person did make a difference, and the Kurds knew it.

I wrote in my log later that night. *He got a hero's welcome. About damn time. We are making impacts in the history of this nation. What a day!* Maybe there was an opportunity for the Iraqis in the south to prosper if men *and* women were given the chance to contribute.

CHAPTER 10

"So, What's It Like?"

Our warm reception in the Kurdish north was a moment to remember. As an Air Force pilot and commander, I had flown and deployed troops to support Operation Northern and Southern Watch, and Operation Provide Comfort. Now I had gotten to walk among the very people we had protected and to witness firsthand the impact of those air-refueling missions flown long ago. What a day, indeed; it was among the best. I thought back to the familiar question Derick had asked me a few weeks ago. What's it like to be a female pilot? Maybe a day like this, experiencing for myself what the U.S. military could achieve, was one more answer to add to my repertoire.

I had been asked the question many times, but I often wondered what those who questioned me were really asking. *What's it like to be in the first generation of female Air Force pilots? What's it like to control those fast jets? Or, what's it like to work with men who don't want you there and to have to prove yourself every step of the way?*

Should I tell them about the early days when military men found a woman in a flight suit a threat, or a potential conquest for bragging rights later on? Should I share with them the toll of being among the first female military pilots at every base where I was stationed? Would they laugh when I explained the games male pilots played in dimly lit bars? Games with names like Carrier Landings, Dead Bug, Sock Check, Bat Hanging, or my personal favorite, Canadian Rodeo.

The Canadian Rodeo game seemed to amuse the Marine pilots, who would select an unsuspecting, attractive woman as a target. The objective was to sneak up, bite her on the butt, and hang on for eight seconds. I guess the men just enjoyed the shocked reaction from women or were so drunk it seemed funny at the time.

During my first year in pilot training I heard rumors about this game. Sure enough, one night in the officers club bar a young Marine pilot swaggered toward me. His baggy, tan flight suit was sweat-stained and he reeked of alcohol. Military bars all smelled the same—beer, sweat, and popcorn. I brought my mug of beer to my lips and eyed him over the rim. In a nonstandard tactic, he rendered a crisp salute, and then slapped five twenty-dollar bills on the bar where my elbow was resting. I looked at the money and back at him. He swayed a little.

"I'll give you ONE hundred bucks if you let me bite you on the ass." He turned to his jeering buddies and pumped a thumbs-up. Leaning into me, he asked, "Well?" I was the first and only female at this pilot training base and my presence in a bar wearing a flight suit had caused a stir. I glanced at the money. A hundred dollars was a lot of money for one bite and a fortune for a young lieutenant.

I put my mug on the bar, pressed my backside to the rail, and held up a hand. "No thanks." I wasn't into pain.

Not to be deterred, the Marine snapped to attention, turned to my classmate Ken beside me, and barked, "Sir, yes, sir, request you hold this lieutenant, and I'll reward you with sixty dollars." My eyes shot open and I stared speechlessly at Ken, a six-foot-three block of an ex-college football player. I thought of making a run for it, but I stood my ground. There was a slight pause as the bar went silent. I inhaled and held my breath.

Then Ken puffed out his chest and bumped the Marine, causing him to stumble back. He glared down and growled, "The lady said no. Now back off, you squid." The Marine snatched his money and retreated to the hoots and catcalls of his buddies. I exhaled and stared at Ken. His reaction surprised me, because I had taken so much grief at being the first female student at this Texas training base. I learned about interservice rivalry that night and the meaning of having someone protect your six. That means the six o'clock position, which is directly behind you. (Hence the expression, "check your six.") That position is the most vulnerable when engaging in aerial combat and when drinking in a bar.

I still chortle at the memory.

So, what's it like to be a military pilot? Well, it's like describing what it's like to be a parent. If you are already a mother or a father, there is no explanation required. If you are not, all the explanation in the world cannot begin to describe what it is like. Each aviator is drawn to this flying world for different reasons, but most stay for the same reason. We love to fly. I entered the aviation world because someone told me women don't fly. *Oh yeah? Watch me!* was my response. But I was seduced by flight the same as any man, drawn to the control, the power, the test of talent, and the sheer fun of it.

Air Force pilot training was boot camp with wings. The flight training program took young people in their early twenties, most of whom had never flown before, and made them the best trained pilots in the world. It was an intensive twelve months, packed with endless hours of military exercises, academic study, rigorous simulator flights, and hundreds of stress-filled hours flying fighter-type jets. Most days started at 0300 and ended some eighteen hours later with an academic book open and a face stuck between the pages, fast asleep. The program was designed to weed out those who didn't have the physical ability, the mental aptitude, or the emotional attitude to handle the pressure of military flying. Needless to say, it was a tough year, but there were moments when it was all worth it.

For me, such a moment came late one afternoon after I soloed for the second time in the T-37 aircraft. I had silenced those around me who doubted whether a woman could make it through this first phase of flight school. Airborne in the western sky of Texas, I watched the orange ball of the sun descend over the distant horizon and the sky turn a milky gray. A patchwork of ranches blanketed the ground as far as the eye could see. It was quiet and peaceful and for the first time that year, the pressure to perform was off. It was just me, the jet, and the pure enjoyment of flying.

The aircraft became an extension of me, slipping gracefully and effortlessly through the atmosphere. I rolled her (airplanes are the female gender) up on a wing and swung her back to the opposite wing. Back and forth I rocked, like we were riding on a gigantic swing. I began humming the tune "Somewhere Over the Rainbow" to the swaying of the jet. Soon I was singing joyfully, "Somewhere over the rainbow/Way up high,/There's a land that I heard of/Once in a lullaby./Somewhere over the rainbow/Skies are blue,/And the dreams that you dare to dream/Really do come true."

I couldn't recall the next verse, but my voice grew louder. "La-la, la, la, la, la, la, la, la, la. La-la, la, la, la, la, la, la, la, la, la, la, la."

Then I belted out the last verse at the top of my lungs. "Somewhere over the rainbow/Bluebirds fly./Birds fly over the rainbow/Why then, oh why can't I?" I leveled the airplane and sighed. *God, I love this job.*

As I turned the jet to head for home, a laughing voice came over the radio frequency. "Hey, Dorothy, you might want to check your mike button the next time you start singing."

Sure enough, my knee had accidentally engaged the radio button and everyone on the frequency had heard my rendition of that song. *Oh shit, I'll never hear the end of this,* I thought as I descended into the field. But I didn't care. I really loved to fly. The next day after the morning briefing, I found a little pair of red shoes in my helmet bag. I had found a home in the Air Force.

Aviation is not a world that is flattering for women. The black flight boots wore calluses on my ankles. The military flight suit was a drab olive-green that washed the color from my face. Constructed of a fire-retardant Nomex fabric, it made me sweat and give off a sharp odor. The suit zipped from crotch to neck with pull tags to cinch the waist. The chest area had more than enough material for a man's body, but left most women looking very flat chested. The cut also had plenty of room in the crotch, which hung down to my knees. There were zippered pockets everywhere—two on the side of the calves, two over the thighs, two directly over the chest, and a small one over the left bicep. With seven pockets available, I never had need for a purse.

Your flight suit was a walking explanation of who you, as a pilot, were: what you flew, where you worked, and why you served. An embroidered name tag, with your silver pilot wings positioned over the left breast, told of your experience level. Slick wings, as they were called, meant you had less than six years of experience. Wings with a star above them indicated a pilot with six to twelve years of experience, and after that, you wore a wreath around the star. Your military rank was worn on the shoulders.

On the right breast of your flight suit was the command you were assigned to; most pilots were in Air Training Command, Tactical Air Command, Military Airlift Command, or Strategic Air Command. Later, the Air Force reorganized and changed the names, but their missions basically stayed the same: one command trained, the second command transported stuff, and the third command did the fighting. On your right upper arm was the aircraft or squadron patch. Finally, the left arm was reserved for the American flag, a daily reminder of why you served.

Some would say there is something sexy about a woman in a flight suit. I could never understand that logic. Combat boots, a stinky suit, and a flight cap were not very appealing. But I certainly turned heads when I walked into any place wearing that uniform. Was it just the novelty of a female pilot or did I look good? I never felt attractive in the flight suit, but when I stepped into it, I zipped up my coat of armor. I could take anything—I felt invincible.

In the early days before sports bras and jockey underwear for women, undergarments were tricky for female pilots. The regulations required us to wear all cotton under the flight suit. The concern was that nylon undergarments would melt to your body in an aircraft fire. Trying to find decent all-cotton panties was a challenge. I always thought, *if it gets hot enough to melt my bra or underwear, that's going to be the least of my worries.* In a rebellious act, I wore the sexiest nylon underwear I could find. I figured it helped me retain some femininity.

The flight suit wasn't the only unflattering thing. For the five years I flew high-performance jet aircraft, I wore an eight-pound, form-fitted helmet that crushed my hair. The thick rubber oxygen mask cut into my face, leaving a circular imprint on my nose and cheeks, and under the chin. After a flight, my curly hair, wet with perspiration, remained plastered to my head, and any attempt to comb it out made me look like I had French-kissed a wall socket. It was tough debriefing a ride as an instructor pilot when your hair looked just like Bozo the Clown's. I didn't bother to wear any makeup because it interfered with the seal of the oxygen mask. Besides, temperatures in the cockpit under the Plexiglas canopy regularly climbed to 120 degrees. Makeup would have run down my face and neck.

In addition to the helmet and oxygen mask, I wore a forty-pound parachute strapped to my back. The webbed straps buckled across the chest and between the legs—tight, really tight. I endured the pinch of the straps because a tight parachute greatly improved survival if I had to eject from the aircraft.

Because I was an instructor in a high-performance jet, my training program included aerobatics, formation flying, and navigation work. For this kind of flying, I also wore an antigravity suit, known as a g-suit. The g-suit looked like green chaps. It zipped up the inside of both legs and, similar to a corset, laced up the outside of each leg. Worn low across the hips, the g-suit connected to the aircraft with a hose. Air was pumped into the small bladders in the g-suit, compressing my legs, thighs, and lower abdomen. This prevented the blood from pooling in the lower extremities, which could otherwise cause a loss of consciousness during flight.

Experiencing g-force made your body feel like its own weight times each G. For a 150-pound person, pulling two Gs equals 300 pounds of pressure. Our high-performance training aircraft routinely pull four to six Gs, exerting up to 900 pounds of pressure on a 150-pound pilot. G-forces strain the heart and slow the circulation to vital organs—most importantly, the brain. Without a g-suit, pilots wouldn't last more than ten seconds at three Gs.

To stay conscious during aerobatics, we not only wore the g-suits but we also performed L-1 breathing maneuvers. We would bear down—like having a bowel movement or like pushing when giving birth—taking short, gulping breaths to draw fresh oxygen into our lungs. This kept blood in the upper extremities, mostly in the heart and brain. Talking was done through grunts and clipped phases. Early physiological studies proved that women were actually better at sustaining Gs than men. The researchers discovered that because most women carry their mass in their hips, below the heart, as opposed to men, whose mass is in the chest area, women could retain blood in the upper extremities longer.

After a typical one-hour sortie in these high-performance aircraft, I'd emerge soaking wet from sweating off five pounds. But I loved the ability to control and teach in a rocket of an airplane. I loved to maneuver it through the sky, performing aileron rolls (twirling the aircraft in quick tight circles); barrel rolls (slow wide spirals); and a lazy eight (tracking the nose through the horizon in a figure eight). To dance with a jet among massive, cotton-ball clouds at speeds of 300 to 550 knots, and at times going supersonic, was such a rush. Practicing landing in the traffic pattern and flying instrument approaches pitted me against the weather, winds, and runway conditions. Every time I flew, it was a test to see how good I was, and whether I could get better. The best part of flying was the company I kept—a man-made machine, Mother Nature, and me.

While most women of my generation were entering the corporate world or breaking into other nontraditional fields, I was a part of the best air force on the planet. Like all pilots, I had war stories. These stories are not necessarily about war, but about flying—the "There I was" story.

So, there I was at 0300 in the morning climbing out over Dallas, Texas. By the early 1990s, I was an instructor pilot in a KC-135—a modified Boeing 707 used for aerial refueling. We had just finished two hours of flying in the traffic pattern, practicing instrument approaches. We were cruising at twenty thousand feet. My young copilot, 1st Lieutenant Roe Jones, had rotated to the jump seat, the chair between the two main pilot seats in the cockpit, to allow another pilot some flying time. Thunderstorms were towering all around us and it was time to return to our home base.

A sliver of the blue light known as St. Elmo's fire began to dance down the windscreen. Lieutenant Jones leaned forward and touched the metal end of his pen on the windscreen glass. The St. Elmo's fire attached to the metal tip, which he dragged across the glass as if he had caught an electric eel. At the same time, a silver-blue cone began to form off the nose of the aircraft, resembling a tornado.

"That's awesome!" he exclaimed, still playing with the pen. The hair stood up on the back of my neck and my skin began to prickle. Experience taught me to lower my eyes. I knew we were about to get nailed by a lightning strike or a significant electrical discharge. But before I could tell the lieutenant to sit down and look away, the negative charge of electricity waiting to connect to its positive mate exploded with a brilliant flash of white. The blue tornado was gone and a burnt metallic smell permeated the air.

I heard Lieutenant Jones scream, "I'm blind, I'm blind," as he fell back into his seat. I wasn't too worried; the effects of flash blindness wear off in a couple of minutes. My immediate concern was another electrical tornado forming on the nose. A second strike might blow a hole in the aircraft, or us to pieces.

Taking command of the flight controls from the pilot who sat across from me, I keyed the intercom and barked to my navigator, "Get us out of here."

One of the navigator's jobs was to interpret the weather radar, so we could thread our way through thunderstorms and adverse atmospheric conditions. My navigator replied in a weak voice, "I lost the radar."

"Damn."

The discharge had disabled all the external antennas, leaving us blind and mute. No radar and no radios. I shoved the throttles forward and made the decision to climb out of the clouds to get above the threatening weather. I said a silent prayer that there was nothing above us. It was a big sky, and I gambled against the chance of hitting another aircraft versus the likelihood of taking any more lightning strikes. Another strike could severely damage the aircraft, blowing off large portions of wings or shattering the vertical stabilizer. If that happened, I would completely lose control of the aircraft and we would tumble to our deaths.

"Can you guys see? I'm blind, I'm really blind," the young lieutenant whined, as he rocked in the jump seat with his face buried in his hands.

Before I could comfort my frightened crew, the young enlisted airman who had been standing in the galley way rushed into the cockpit, yelling about a fireball moving down the inside of the aircraft.

"What?" I snapped my head around.

"Yeah, a damn fireball flew past my head." He hovered over the copilot and looked over his shoulder like it might come back to get him.

"Listen to me carefully," I began in a strong, measured voice. "The discharge just went down the metal air-conditioning duct and probably exited out the tail. You need to check the back of the aircraft to make sure that nothing caught fire."

My firm voice and calm face masked the somersaults in my stomach at the thought of a fire *inside* my aircraft. An internal fire in a plane climbing from twenty thousand feet is a deadly combination.

As if a monster awaited him, the enlisted airman glanced back again. "I'm not going back there by myself."

The KC-135 aircraft had only three small windows, no passenger seats, and dim lighting, which made the fuselage area very dark.

"Well, take Jones with you," I ordered over the roar of the engines.

"But I'm blind!" the lieutenant whimpered.

"Just go."

A scene that will forever stay with me is of my crew members staggering like two scared kids into the darkness—the airman with one arm hooked around a fire extinguisher and the other hooked around Lieutenant Jones, the lieutenant's hands groping along the inside of the aircraft as they made their way down the long, dark fuselage. I shook my head as they disappeared from view. *God, let me live so I can tell this story. Someday, it'll be funny.*

Minutes passed. I could feel their footsteps reverberate in the floor before I could see them. They both came charging up to the flight deck, pushing on each other. "No fire," they announced in breathless voices.

"Good," I answered, as if they had told me we were having chicken for dinner.

"I can see!" cried Lieutenant Jones.

"That is even better," I said. "Now, get back to work. Nav?"

"Yes ma'am, take up a heading of two seven zero. I have the radar back."

We were safely climbing out of the threatening weather and communicating with the Fort Worth center.

Thanks, God! I chuckled under my breath. *I lived to fly another day.*

So, what's it like? Moments of sheer joy, fear, and pride—and everything in between. Most adventures are like this. Iraq was no exception.

CHAPTER 11

Republican Guards

W
e had only been in Baghdad for merely thirty-six hours and already Garner was pacing his office like a caged animal. The trip to northern Iraq had energized him to accelerate the rebuilding efforts. The impatient general knew he couldn't rebuild Iraq if he was holed up in the security of the Green Zone. He wanted to get out and meet the people on the streets of Baghdad.

"Okay, sir, let me get the boys to recon a route first. We'll leave right after lunch." I had tried to keep to a fixed schedule, but the general changed plans to accommodate the demands of the rebuilding effort.

The ORHA team had settled into one of Saddam's old palaces. The Republican Palace, as it was called, was located on the Tigris River and formed the core of the Green Zone. This massive two-story beige structure was in a half-moon shape, divided into three wings with a domed center. There were two huge busts of Saddam on each roof. The heads would be removed later in the year. Behind the palace was a long narrow rose garden with beautiful pink flowers and ornamental orange trees lining the pathways. Inside, the ceilings vaulted up to more than twenty feet, with marble and tile dominating the interior. In the center was a large ballroom with smaller rooms flanking the sides; that's where we set up our offices. A huge mural of Saddam passing a brick to a laborer was the first thing you would see when you entered the palace. Within the first few days that picture got covered by a tarp.

For weeks, we worked with no furniture, electricity, or running water. Eventually, furniture was discovered in a nearby warehouse, carefully stored and labeled. It looked like an early French brothel design with gold leaf, cheap veneer wood, and crushed-velvet-like fabrics. Someone had anticipated the bombing and removed it from the palace for safekeeping. We furnished the palace with the recovered furniture, giving Garner a massive desk with a multicolored design and carved animal heads. He hated it.

Our air strikes had taken out the electrical power station for the two-square-mile complex, so generators were brought in to power the tremendous amount of equipment needed to run it. The rose garden would wither and die, and the trees were cut down to make room for house trailers, Port-a-Potties, and portable showers.

Finding staff in this cavernous place was an adventure in itself. The bodyguards were no exception. They normally lounged around their sleeping quarters, waiting for the next tasking. It was uncomfortable for me to enter a room that housed eight giant men in varying states of dress and surrounded by a small arsenal of weapons and ammunition. It always seemed that one of them was entering or exiting the connecting bathroom partially clothed. Our agreement was that I would knock three times and go in when cleared. They thought it was comical that I kept my eyes downcast to keep from staring at their muscular chests and legs. These boys had no shame, and I was modest enough for everyone.

Theirs was the only room with a door that locked. They had cleaned the surrounding grounds of booby-traps and collected a large assortment of weapons and ammunition. They stored these spoils of war with the staff's laptops and other critical equipment in their locker. Most days when I came down to my desk, my laptop, a hot cup of tea, and a pink rose from the garden in a white plastic cup were waiting for me. I smiled, and learned later that Johan was responsible. I drew the line at his offer to wash my clothes. Some people are just natural caregivers.

"Recon a one-hour route and be ready by noon," I ordered. I retreated from the room, but not before I stole a glance at the naked body with a towel around its waist emerging from the bathroom. *Augh, I've been deployed too long.*

Shortly after lunch, we piled into the Suburban and started on our second adventure through the Baghdad streets. This time the convoy was six deep. In the lead was a U.S. Army Bradley fighting vehicle with a jutting five-foot gun barrel that could unleash two hundred beer-can-size projectiles. It was capable of turning a three-story concrete wall into Swiss cheese in less than sixty seconds. The Bradley also carried seven four-foot missiles created to annihilate enemy armored vehicles within a two-mile radius. This display of tremendous military firepower was sure to crush or deter any attackers. If we were ambushed, smoke-grenade launchers would produce an instant screen to obscure the enemy's view and provide an escape cloak for our convoy.

Behind the Bradley vehicle, the three Suburbans were tucked between two light-armored Humvees equipped with 50-caliber machine guns and manned by baby-faced soldiers. The young troops made me nervous when they swung the barrel of one of their guns toward our cars. *Hope that safety's on.*

We stayed safe and secure under the protection of our bodyguards and an umbrella of military technology. If we would just stay in the cars, we would be okay. After exiting the confines of the Green Zone, we rumbled down the streets at thirty miles an hour. At the checkpoint, Garner stopped to chat with the young Army soldiers who stood guard next to their Abrams M1A tanks. When we had first arrived at the palace, four tanks were positioned right outside the gates. Garner told me to get rid of them. The perimeter was expanded and now they guarded various bridges.

We crossed over the July 14 Bridge, and turned onto a street paralleling the Tigris River. Halfway down the block, Garner spotted a group of men and boys sitting on the front steps of a long three-story apartment building.

"Stop!" he ordered. The tires screeched to a halt, and before I could object, Garner jumped out of the car. I shoved the translator forward to catch up with the general as the guards tripped over themselves trying to form a secure perimeter. I cursed under my breath. The Bradley vehicle ground to a stop and spun its turret around at the apartment building. Garner strolled over to the men with his right hand extended. Climbing the six steps two at a time, the general pumped everyone's hand.

"Hi, Jay Garner. Nice to meet ya." He smiled at their shocked faces. The four men replied politely, stealing questioning glances at each other. Knowing the Iraqi people were generally hospitable, Garner asked about their history. A tall, distinguished gentleman of fifty bowed his head and asked us to join him inside for tea. As we entered the small apartment hallway lined with family photos, the wife shot her husband an aggravated look at our unannounced arrival. I imagined her swearing under *her* breath, "damm . . . company."

"Jay Garner, Jay Garner," the Iraqi called out in his own defense. The four women and three children sitting on the floor of the cramped room scrambled to move out of the way, attempting to straighten the room as they departed.

It was the first time I had been in an Iraqi home. I scanned the drab living room. A white couch and two tan chairs were the only furniture. A worn Koran lay open on the black scratched coffee table. The dirty window overlooking the river was covered by a drapery with a pattern of large red and pink flowers on a gray background. The dated décor looked like the 1970s.

I watched the women while they brought in tea and bustled around us. Their clicking words and quick gestures made me smile as they continued straightening up the room. *Ah, women are the same everywhere, trying to clean up for the guests.* Black and white family portraits decorated the dingy white walls. I noticed an empty nail and the dirty outline where a ten- by twelve-inch picture had hung. I leaned over to Garner and whispered, "I bet that wasn't a picture of Jesus Christ." He chuckled in response. I would also bet the picture of Saddam Hussein was stuffed behind the couch. They knew he was still alive.

As Garner began visiting with the men, I wandered down the hallway to the small kitchen area. The heavy smells of cooking oil and warm bread mingled in the air. I leaned in through the doorway. Two middle-aged women were huddled together over a boiling pan of water. They glanced up, eyes widening and unsure smiles crossing their faces.

"Do you speak English?" I asked.

The elderly woman nodded. Her simple dress and headscarf reminded me of a peasant; her demeanor was so different from the nurse I had encountered a week earlier.

I shoved my hands in my pockets, crossed a foot over my ankle, and leaned on the doorjamb. "Tell me what we can do to help you."

The woman pulled a young girl out from behind her long skirt and patted her on the head. "The children," she answered with a sharp sigh.

"She's beautiful." I gave her my best motherly smile and squatted down.

"Children," the women repeated in an exhausted tone. "Get them back in school. Been out too long."

I nodded and grinned. She was right. The kids in Iraq had been out of school for more than three months. At first, they had been forced inside by the bombing; now it was the presence of military troops and the absence of any police force. *Yep, mothers are the same everywhere.*

"Oh, I hear you. After the summer break in America, we are so ready to get our kids back in school." I heard my name being called from down the hallway. My knees popped as I stood up.

"I'll see what I can do," I promised. The women smiled and the little girl waved. I winked.

I entered the living room just in time to hear the translator state that the family members were refugees from Mosul. In fact, the older gentleman explained he was a retired colonel in the Iraqi Republican Guard and showed the team his military ID card. He had fought in the Iran-Iraq war and was looking forward to enjoying his children in his retirement days. Garner nodded with an air of understanding for this military officer. The colonel went on to say that this apartment complex was for members of the Iraqi Republican Guard or Special Forces and their families. As my eyes flew wide open, the blood drained from my face. *Oh my God, we are going to die. We are going to walk out of this apartment and die.*

In slow motion, I mouthed to Derick, "Get us out of here."

Trying to regain control of my rising panic, I blurted out, "Sir, it's time to go to our next appointment."

"Nice meeting ya." Garner shook the older man's hand. Derick and Hector shoved us out the door and down the steps. Barking hushed orders into their headset radios, the team snapped off the safeties on their weapons. The military vehicles pointed their mounted guns at the apartment building and I heard the clicking sound as they charged the weapons.

The hair on my neck stood up and my shoulders cringed in anticipation of the first round of gunfire. But none came. We hustled to the SUVs without incident.

Once inside the car, I turned on the general and snapped, "You sure know how to pick the places to stop, sir! Jeez, we could've been killed."

"Nah," he responded in his southern drawl. "Look, Kimmer." The male members of the family stood on the steps and waved as we pulled away.

Placing both palms on my clammy cheeks, I muttered, "What were you thinking?"

"Look at the place." He gestured with his thumb. I glanced back. What I saw were the women outlined in the windows waving and the kids running down the sidewalks after us. He saw something different. "It's not looted."

He was right. The apartment complex stood untouched. "Now, we know why. There's probably an AK-47 in every living room," he chortled.

That's why you're the general, I thought.

His voice grew forceful and serious, and his hand gripped my shoulder. "Besides, sometimes you have to walk right into the lion's den and show no fear. Now they know that we know where their families live."

I stared at him in silence. *Gutsy move! Guess that's why you're a three-star general.*

Clearing my throat, "Sir, we need to talk about the Iraqi kids. . . ."

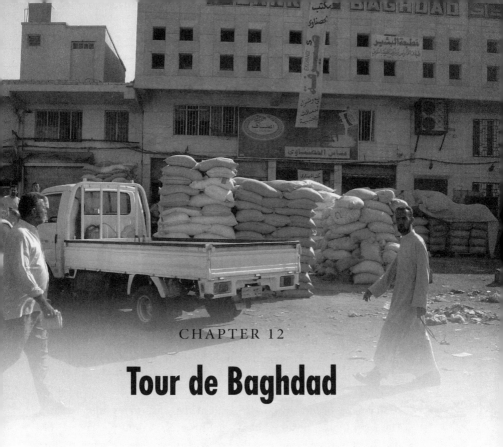

CHAPTER 12

Tour de Baghdad

We made at least three trips a day into the city of Baghdad and the surrounding suburbs. The general was leading Iraq by building one relationship at a time. One day, we drove into the conservative Sunni district to meet with some leading clerics. This meeting was arranged by our Sunni contact Saad. Its objective was to convince the religious men in this sector to help in the rebuilding efforts and to suppress any talk of an insurgency. Garner was also trying to get the Iraqis to disclose, surrender, or destroy the large caches of weapons hidden in the city.

Our convoy parked next to a cinderblock wall that enclosed a gray stucco house. The entrance was crowded with men in white robes. I stepped into the parlor area as the general shook hands with the men. A short, fat Iraqi with bad teeth and bad breath stepped in front of me.

"You must cover." His voice dripped with disgust. I got the impression he had enjoyed living under Saddam's dictatorship and could care less about rebuilding Iraq.

Cover this! My first thought was of Lieutenant Colonel Martha McSally, one of the Air Force's first female fighter pilots. She had sued and won on this issue, changing the requirement that military women wear abayas during deployment to a Middle Eastern country. Then I thought again. *Jay needs these people on his side.* I took the scarf I used for protection during sandstorms from around my neck and draped it over my head. As Garner entered an interior room of the home, I excused myself. I knew that women did not enter the inner sanctum of the meeting area, which was reserved for religious and formal events. My presence today could prove more of a liability than an asset for Garner. Stepping outside and removing the scarf, I leaned against the car door. Louis, the scholarly bodyguard of the group, drew a long drag on his cigarette. His blue eyes darted around the street.

"I'm impressed you actually covered," he said, in his crisp English accent.

I folded my arms across my chest. "Hey, sometimes there's a greater good at stake. I know how to keep my ego in check." He blew a long trail of gray smoke into the air and nodded without comment.

Some time later, the bad-breath Iraqi reappeared at my side, puffing out his fat stomach. "I said you must cover." Everyone stopped talking and turned to watch. I was a good head taller than the man and pivoted to look down on him.

"Can you say occupying power?" I jammed my fists to my hips.

The Iraqi looked unsure and averted his eyes. "Could you cover?" he repeated, but this time he noticed the bodyguards who were glaring at him.

I turned my head to Louis. "Tell this man I am *not* covering out here."

Louis swung his AK-47 around to his waist. "She will not cover," came his terse response. His blue eyes sparkled like ice.

The Iraqi's mouth dropped open and his pudgy face beaded in sweat. "I, I," he said, his lips smacking together like the mouth of a fish out of water.

I stepped in front of Louis and pushed the muzzle of the weapon down. "I mean no disrespect, but I am not in a mosque and I am not a Muslim. Military women do not cover," I stated in a flat, forceful tone. *Thanks to Martha.*

The Iraqi stumbled back and almost collided with Garner as he passed through the wrought-iron gateway. The general strolled over to me. "What's happenin'?" he asked, raising an eyebrow.

"Oh, just working on a little international relations," I commented, opening the car door for him. Garner looked at Louis and back at the retreating Iraqi.

Louis smiled, flipped his cigarette butt, and strolled to the lead SUV.

We made our way to the Baghdad slum called Saddam City, later changed to Sadr City. There was an ecological balance to these filthy streets. Raw sewage pooled on the broken sidewalks and along the curbs. The center median of the street was filled with debris and garbage. Scavengers picked their way through the rubbish, selecting discarded food, metal, and bits of material. A bent old woman retrieved a broken eggshell with her crippled, weathered fingers. I could not imagine what she would use it for, but then again, I wasn't starving. Farther down the road, sheep grazed on what remained of the garbage. A red X was painted on the hindquarters of the sheep, symbolizing the ewe had been bred. It seemed as though all females wore a mark in this country.

An open market lined the broken streets. Young boys rushed forward to sell bottled water, soda, or Chicklets chewing gum. Flies buzzed around the butchered meat that hung in display cabinets. There was a familiar pungent odor that stung my nose as we exited the car.

"Watch your step," I cautioned the general.

We climbed up a flight of rickety steps to a cramped room over a small grocery store. There, several older shopkeepers complained to Garner about the state of their town. They sat in a semicircle with the general facing them. I stood in the corner near the window. It was so hot. The smell of body odor permeated the air.

"Electricity. We need electricity and running water." The older man gestured with his fist, thumb pinching his index finger, a scowl on his tan, wrinkled face.

"Security. No police patrol here. They are afraid," added a plump, middle-aged Iraqi in a sweat-stained shirt. His dirty feet stuck out of torn sandals. They had reason to be afraid. Many of the criminals that Saddam had released from the prisons during the war migrated to this predominantly Shiite area.

"All right," Garner began. "Who among you will volunteer to patrol your neighborhood?"

Silence. A car horn honked in the street below.

I made an entry in my notebook. *Once again no one steps forward. What is it with these people?* I circled it with my pen. *What's it like to be them?* I added.

"Okay, who will ask their sons to work for the police department?"

Dead silence. Flies buzzed around the sweltering room.

"I see." The general took off his glasses and rubbed the bridge of his nose. He looked around the room, withdrew an index card from his shirt pocket, and wrote some notes. The Iraqis squirmed in their seats and looked sideways at each other.

"If you get us more electrical power, then we have lights. We go out into the streets at night," the eldest offered, scratching his chin.

"Deal," said Garner.

We exited the shop and walked across the street to an electrical transformer station. The guards banged on the gate until a young man in a soiled blue jumpsuit peeked out from behind a steel door.

"We want to talk to your boss," Garner barked.

The translator relayed his request and the young kid ran back into the building. It was yet another meeting with an Iraqi who was ineffective and unresponsive. Frustration was planted in the middle of Garner's forehead when we left the station.

"You got any aspirin, Kimmer? I got a hell of a headache." He took off his glasses again and gave the bridge of his nose another rub.

"Yes, sir." I tapped out a pill from the small bottle I carried in my vest and handed him bottled water. He got Tylenol. I knew his stomach was bothering him, too.

The next day we were scheduled to meet with Congressman Dave Hobson at Baghdad International Airport. Four members of Congress had decided to drop in to see how the postwar effort was going and to visit the troops. Congressman Hobson, from Ohio's 7th District, was the powerful chairman of the House Appropriations Military Construction Subcommittee and a senior member of the House Defense Appropriations Subcommittee. I had worked with him several times as an OSD congressional liaison. I guessed that he remembered me because I had graduated from Ohio State University and because there are so few female military pilots on the Hill. When the congressman and his staffer saw me get out of the car at the Baghdad airport they made a beeline for me and each gave me a big hug. I introduced General Garner and they chatted for a while. The meeting didn't last more than fifteen minutes, but the general pushed the congressman hard to call for terminating the UN sanctions, which would alleviate the gas shortage.

Garner laughed as he climbed back into the SUV. "Is there anyone you don't know?" Earlier in the day, he had seen me greet another National War College classmate, a new member of the ORHA staff in Baghdad. She and I talked like old friends over a quick lunch. And now a congressman knew my first name.

"You know, sir, I like people and tend to stay in contact with lots from my past," I began. "You want to hear a funny story from my younger days?" I asked, as we drove out of the airport.

The general looked up at Hector and raised an eyebrow.

"Not that kind of story," I scolded. "When I was a captain T-38 instructor pilot at the Air Training Command headquarters base near San Antonio, it was standard practice for experienced instructor pilots to fly orientation sorties with the local businessmen. The squadron commander told me I was flying with Bill. He called him a local car salesman."

There I stood at the operations desk, waiting for the life-support technician to finish fitting Bill's helmet, oxygen mask, g-suit, and parachute.

I heard the technician announce from beyond the swinging door, "Now, sir, come meet your pilot for today."

When Bill came through the door, his eyes went wide and his mouth gaped open. Dark, silver-streaked hair framed a surprised face.

I read his thoughts and advanced on him in two strides. "So, you don't want to fly with *me!*" It was more of a statement then a question. I had learned over the years to go on the offense. It put doubters off-guard and reminded them I had earned my pilot instructor ratings like any man.

"No, certainly not." His voice carried a slight edge. "That's not it at all." He leaned away from me, clutching his helmet bag and raising it between us. I cocked an eyebrow and narrowed my eyes as I studied him, waiting for him to finish. "Indeed, I am simply impressed," he continued in a measured, precise tone. "Impressed by the fact you are a female instructor and you have a great responsibility for training other pilots in the skill of flight. You are a credit to your profession." He waved his helmet bag for effect.

Yeah, right. Don't patronize me—you car salesman, you. I gritted my teeth and smiled.

"Okay, sir, let's go." I swung my forty-pound parachute over my shoulder and marched onto the windy flight line, hot from the afternoon sun, with Bill hustling to catch up.

The mission was to take him out to the practice areas and fly around for about thirty minutes. Orientation flights didn't go above eighteen thousand feet because the passengers were not trained in the altitude chamber. Most instructors also refrained from performing aerobatics, because those always made inexperienced passengers sick. Nobody throws up and hangs onto their dignity, whether they are a CEO or a car salesman.

As we flew, Bill chatted about his time in the Air Force as a radar instructor during the Korean War. He explained that he had wanted to be a doctor, but ended up going to law school instead.

Why do you sell cars if you went to law school? Something didn't add up. I made a slow turn over central Texas. It was perfect day for flying—white fluffy clouds dotted the blue sky, the visibility was fifty miles, and the air was as smooth as a baby's behind. That's pilot talk for a calm day.

"Is this all we are going to do, fly straight and level?" he asked in the nasal voice caused by the tight-fitting oxygen mask.

"What do you want?" I asked, glancing in the mirror toward his face, hidden behind the dark visor.

"How about some acro?"

"You got it." Even before I finished my response, I slammed the stick to the right, tumbling the jet in an aileron roll. The earth's horizon spun around the front of the aircraft. I snapped back to level flight, jammed the throttles forward, pushed the jet over, felt the afterburners kick in, and accelerated to 450 knots. I pulled the aircraft straight up toward the clouds, then over on her back, filling the windscreen with farm fields. The wind noise screamed over the canopy as I grunted through a four-G loop. Glancing in the small mirror, I saw Bill's head flopped to one side; I had probably blacked him out. I eased the aircraft into a lazy eight, then back to straight and level flight, and waited.

"Whoa," was all he could say. The next thing I heard was the sound of him vomiting. I was impressed he got his oxygen mask off and the airsickness bag open before losing his lunch.

I smiled under my oxygen mask. "Sorry."

"I just wasn't ready for all that." He coughed and spit.

I chuckled. *Works every time.* "Here, it helps if you fly the aircraft. Go ahead, take the stick and I'll teach you a maneuver."

Bill lurched the aircraft through a few simple aerobatic maneuvers and then we headed west toward the airfield.

"I can't believe I got sick."

"I'd have been surprised if you hadn't," I reassured him.

"What will I do with this bag?" he asked.

"One of the rules in flying is: If you get sick, you carry out the barf bag." I was feeling nice that day. "I'll tell you what. Just leave it in the map case and I'll take care of it."

"Okay," he mumbled. "Boy, that was sure fun, though."

When we landed I was surprised and impressed that the commander of the Air Training Command, a four-star general, came out to meet us. Well, not us, but Bill. They shook hands like old friends and Bill's face was bright with joy as he used his hands to mimic the maneuvers we had performed. I watched their exchange from the other side of the aircraft while I filled out the standard post-flight forms. With my elbows propped on the wing, I waited for the photographer to take a picture of the general and Bill. *Who is this guy?* I wondered.

Before the photographer could focus his lens, Bill turned to find me. "General, we can't take a picture without my favorite female pilot." He waved me over.

Hey, you are all right! At least he wasn't mad that I had made him sick. I strutted over, hung an arm around his shoulder, tilted my head, and smiled brightly. Click! *Well, that's that. At least he'll have a nice photo to remember his flight with his favorite, read "only," female pilot.* So I thought as we said our good-byes. But life has a funny way about it.

Several months later, I was talking to my mother on the phone. She knew about my flight with Bill, and she had scolded me for making him puke.

"Have you read the papers? Do you know where Bill is?" she asked.

"No. We didn't stay in touch," I responded.

She chuckled. "Better yet, do you know *who* he is, Kim?"

"No. Why?"

"Well, sis, President Reagan just announced that Bill Sessions is the new director of the FBI."

"WHAT!" I gasped. "Holy sh—!"

"Only you, girl, only you!" she laughed.

It took a week, but I looked up the FBI's number and dialed. I didn't have a clue what I was going to say. My foot began its nervous tap. I wondered if he would remember me.

"Director's office, may I help you?" came the drawl of a woman's heavy southern accent.

"Hi, I would like to speak to the director. Can you please tell him his favorite female pilot is on the line?"

Silence.

One potato, two potato, maybe I should hang up? I held my breath.

"Hold, please." Her curt response stung my ear.

Five seconds later, his distinguished voice filled the line. "Captain Kim Olson! How are you?"

I heaved a sigh. "You know, sir, had I known you were somebody so important, I would never have made you sick in that jet," I joked. *The director of the FBI, for God's sake.*

His laugh crackled across the phone line for a long time. "Good to hear your voice. Where are you, Kim?"

"Sir, I am now stationed here at the Pentagon on a one-year internship."

"Excellent. You come have lunch with me next week and let me show you the bureau," he offered. "I won't lock you up," he finished with a chuckle.

"I'd be honored," I answered William S. Sessions, former Chief Judge for the Western District of Texas. It seems I had made the judge of the largest district in the United States sick as a dog when I flew him that day on his T-38 orientation sortie.

I shook my head at the memory. I sure missed flying.

"So, what happened?" Garner asked.

"Well, sir, we had lunch the next week and have remained friends for nearly twenty years. Judge Sessions now works for a law firm in D.C., and whenever I call, he makes time for lunch. He still calls me his favorite female pilot, and he still reminds me it was the only time he ever got sick in a jet. He's such a gentleman. Heck, he even came to the ceremony when I was pinned as a colonel. You'd like him, sir; you two are a lot alike."

"You're something, Kimmer," the general chuckled.

The smile melted off my face. *Yeah, we all used to be something.* I stared out at the brown haze beyond the window and tapped my foot.

CHAPTER 13

Palace Life

"You live in a palace?"

"Yes, Sweetie," I answered my daughter during one of our weekly long-distance phone calls.

"Cool!"

It was anything but cool. It was hot. Every breath burned. Every step exhausted me. Everything I touched stung my hands. The tips of my fingers were red and swollen from typing on the hot laptop. Even my bedroom offered no relief as temperatures reached a blistering 125 degrees. Located on the second floor, it was an eight-by-eight-foot square with a fifteen-foot ceiling. There was no door for privacy, just a rusty upturned bed frame in the doorway with a tattered drape hung over it. The bare window looked out over a roof where many soldiers slept during the night.

The room was decorated with two cases of bottled water in the corner, a small metal bed with a thin mattress, a plastic-cushioned chair, and a second upturned bed frame leaning against the gray wall from which I could hang my clothes to dry. Most of my wardrobe lay scattered in the corner. I always wore shoes because the tile floor burned my feet. Later, I discovered my room was directly above the kitchen stove.

The dry desert heat was relentless and there was no escaping its energy-draining effect. Even when the sun descended over the horizon, there was no relief. After baking all day in the sun, the concrete structures pulsated with heat throughout the night. As darkness crept in, the outside lamps bathed my room in an orange glow, resembling the fire from a coal furnace.

The metal bed frame was too hot to touch, and the thin mattress provided little comfort to my parched body. I tried to drink a quart of water before bed, just to keep from being dehydrated. My lips cracked and bled, my skin itched and flaked, even my bones felt hot. As I laid down my head, the pillow breathed hot stale air. I stared at the ceiling, forcing my body to lie perfectly still. A ball of sweat formed on my chest and slid off my ribs. Sleep was slow in coming. Within an hour, my T-shirt and sheets were soaked. I changed them in the middle of the night before dragging myself off to go pee.

The night air was so full of dust that it was stifling. Just as I drifted off, gunfire cut the silence in sporadic intervals, jerking me awake. Return fire answered the barrage, and so it went throughout the night. I dreamed of an explosion rocking my room, and I awoke trembling with a foreboding that gnawed at me. But the real nightmares involved my children. *Katie is lost and I can't find her*—I awoke in a panic. *Keegan is drowning and I can't save him*—I struggled awake again, whimpering. On those sleepless nights, I was kept company by the whine of mosquitoes and the murmur of voices down the hall. The marble palace echoed the hum of machinery, the shuffle of people, and the clicking of rats across the floor.

Morning brought an eerie calm, as the sun's first rays brushed away the darkness. In the hours just after dawn, the silence was unsettling. No birds sang, no wind blew. Everything seemed suspended under the steady, dull pressure of the heated air.

I rolled out of bed and surveyed the pile of salt-stained clothes. Weeks in the soaring temperatures and endless dust had left everything I owned filthy. With a box of Tide in one hand and a garbage bag full of laundry in the other, I strolled outside to the overgrown garden. A stiff garden hose connected to a faucet provided a tepid gray liquid—the only running water available. Filling a cracked blue five-gallon bucket, my knees popped as I squatted down beside the milky mixture of laundry soap and gray water.

Washing laundry is a chore few women relish. I was no exception. I remember my grandmother on the Iowa farm scrubbing "delicates" in the same manner. Rubbing the soft fabrics, I shook my head. *Reduced to washing my damn underwear in a bucket. Oh well, at least I'm not living out of an Army tank or taking a weekly bath using a box of baby wipes.*

The temperature was already 100 degrees, and perspiration rolled down my flushed face. The huge fig tree offered some shade from the blazing Iraqi sun. After I finished scrubbing, soapy bundles of clothes lay stacked at my feet. The comforting smell of detergent and water made me long for home. Mesmerized by the foam, my mind wandered back to my children's bathroom.

"Bubbles! Bubbles!" The tile walls echoed with squeals of laughter as two blonde-haired toddlers splashed and kicked in the warm water. The tub was overflowing with Mr. Bubbles. Keegan's and Katie's soft, slick skin wiggled under my touch. My attempts to retrieve them from the tub were met with more squeals. "No! More bubbles, more bubbles!" Giving up, I plopped on the cool floor with my face and hair covered in suds. These beautiful babies were the joy of my life. I loved being a mom. Life at home was the only time I could let down my guard and enjoy uninhibited emotion.

As a military officer, I stayed guarded inside an emotional fortress. I had to, to protect myself from the onslaught of institutional prejudice and the cruelty of some military men. The fortress safeguarded my ego and my self-esteem as a female pilot in a male-dominated environment. I needed its protection to withstand the unwarranted and spiteful comments about my flying ability, my leadership capabilities, and my qualities as an officer.

My very first squadron commander was a short, cigar-chewing plug of a man. He was weathered, hard, and very conservative. Within a week after I reported to my first flying assignment, he called me into his office and shut the door. Chomping on his unlit cigar, his dull eyes burrowed into mine as he kept me standing at attention. It was my first lesson about power and control.

"Let's just get something straight, Lieutenant. I don't think girls belong in the military, much less in the cockpit. So as long as we understand each other, we'll get along fine." He dismissed me with a wave of his hand.

Kiss this, I thought. I had just as much right to serve in the Air Force as he did. I earned my wings just like he did. Yet who was I kidding? It really didn't matter what was right or what I had already earned. I was going to have to prove myself over and over.

I stayed out of his way for most of my tour. And I learned to steel myself whenever someone felt compelled to tell me his personal feelings about how women didn't belong in the Air Force or in airplanes. Heated debates ensued with my contemporaries, and I always believed I had to defend my right to serve as an officer or a pilot. The central theme of those debates in the early 1980s was that women weren't emotionally equipped for the job—they weren't emotionally capable of handling combat, or leading troops, or even being taken seriously. So I learned at the ripe old age of twenty-two to keep my natural, female emotions in check. Caring, compassion, and crying were liabilities, weaknesses, and I was not about to be weak.

Thus began the construction of my emotional fortress. Each building stone represented a cruel comment, a critical look, another rejection by my peers, or simply my loneliness at being the only woman. I compartmentalized my fears, my sexuality, my nurturing instinct, and my ability to care, and stowed them away within the fortress walls.

Breaking into the male club of military aviation required persistence, guts, and a little luck. I was determined to prove myself every step of the way. But the battle I had accepted took its toll. My personality was guarded, abrasive, and tough throughout most of my career. I existed within my fortress, but the self-isolation came at a price. They gave me the call sign Ice Queen. It made me feel bad, but it was a fair representation of the woman I had created—hard, cold, and not very compassionate. If that was the image I needed to succeed, then so be it. There could be no middle ground. For example, if I accepted a date, I was perceived as a woman on the prowl. If I turned down a male's advances, I was a lesbian. Neither were accurate reflections of who I really was.

I acted cocky and confident, and my favorite saying was, "I am so good, I could fly up your ass and out again, and you wouldn't even know it." Yep, I was trying to be just one of the boys. I would drink with them into the late hours of the night, curse like a sailor, and brag about my flying exploits. It was all in a vain attempt to fit in. The harder I tried, the farther away I moved from myself. My lifestyle consisted of flying, eating, and sleeping, and it had little room for romance. Although the exploits of male aviators were well known, women pilots did not share the same adorations. This tough persona masked a real need to be accepted, loved, and appreciated. It would take nearly a decade for me to feel accepted by the Air Force. We had a love-hate relationship—I hated the Air Force's dogmatic management, risk-averse mentality, and discrimination against women. But I loved the discipline, flying those cool jets, and the chance to teach and lead.

After I was promoted to captain, I became a T-38 supersonic jet instructor pilot, earning the distinction of being the number one graduate in the otherwise all-male class. As a new instructor, I worked every day for weeks at a time. I was demanding, relentless, and tougher than tough. My students used to joke that I could teach them to fly a broom. Flying was serious business, and every year half a dozen pilots and students lost their lives in aircraft accidents. With five hundred hours of flying time under my belt, I was considered an experienced pilot and would tell my students, "The only thing between you and death is me. When I tell you I've got the aircraft, you let go of that control stick." Screaming toward the ground at 500 knots is no time to get into a pissing contest as to who has control of a jet. I told my students that if they did not release the controls when ordered, I would pound them into the ground. For effect, I added, "If I can't beat you, I'll find someone who will." The instructor is always the ultimate authority, and establishing that early on with my students was critical to staying alive.

In the early days of my career, the officers club was the place to go. Getting drunk with older pilots and hearing their war stories was expected and encouraged. Some were veterans of the Vietnam era. They were the gods of the flying world because they had flown in combat. I would sit spellbound, listening to them tell of dogfights with MiGs over North Vietnam, lobbing bombs into Laos, and taking midnight runs into Cambodia. Most aviators longed for a chance at those glory days; little did I know my chance was coming. The stories in the "O" club, the hours in the air, and my tough, outwardly unfeeling attitude defined my life. And then. . . .

"Happy Valentine's Day," Kent grinned. It was early 1984 when we met. Besides my flying wings, Kent was the best thing I found in the Air Force. Male pilots were such studs in their olive-green flight suits, and Kent was no exception. His broad chest, trim waist, and tall, slim body made my heart pound. Kent was painfully shy, and he informed me later that he thought I was so mysterious. Although we worked together as instructor pilots for more than two months, it wasn't until some of us went dancing as a group that I knew I had him. He held me tight as we swayed to a slow country song, and when the music sped up, he continued to rock me gently. I knew this man was going to be the father of my children. We were married less than two years later. I might have stayed the Ice Queen had I not met Kent, but becoming a mother sealed it.

When I had my son, emotions I had never known overwhelmed me. To be a mom, to experience such unconditional love, and to nurture my baby was a revelation. Discovering the joy of motherhood left me feeling giddy and alive. Almost overnight, my new call sign became Jetmom. At work, I tried to remain an ice queen, but the protective fortress was beginning to deteriorate.

After Keegan was born, Kent separated from the Air Force and flew for a major airline. Our daughter was born a few years later. I had it all—a husband who supported me, beautiful kids, and a great job flying. But when those extended flying deployments demanded that I leave my babies for weeks and months at a time, the guilt nearly suffocated me. I longed to smell them, to touch them, to hold them against my chest, and to watch them sleep. To survive, I continued to compartmentalize my life and emotions. Expressions of love existed only in the safety of my home. When in uniform, I remained stoic and aloof—it kept me alive. I loved my children, and I loved to fly. The two loves were in direct conflict. Or were they?

Now, in this overgrown garden in Baghdad, the memories caused the familiar tug in my heart and made me ache for my children. They were no longer toddlers, but teenagers. I was no longer a captain, but a colonel. I had done it all—raised a family, commanded troops, and achieved a sterling career. Today, I was trying to rebuild a nation. Sighing, I reached into the bucket and scooped out a handful of suds. Blowing across my palm, the bubbles floated upward and hung suspended. The sunlight reflected a rainbow of colors in each globe. I popped one with my finger, then smiled at the simple pleasure of blowing bubbles in the middle of a war zone.

As I dumped out the water, it sizzled and spread over the hot concrete. More gray liquid trickled out of the worn hose into the cracked bucket. Enjoying the solitude in the garden, I rinsed each soapy ball of clothing. Stretching up, my skinny, bug-bitten arms snapped out a shirt, then pants, then pieces of underwear. Mosquitoes danced around my head and sang their high-pitched songs. I brushed them aside, flinging droplets onto my cheeks. Reaching up, I patted my face. *Tears?*

The familiar questions haunted me. *Should I have given up the career and stayed home with my children? Have I made any difference in the military at the expense of my family? Will I make a difference here?* I searched the garden, but I was the only one with the answers.

With wet laundry in one arm and my box of Tide in the other, I walked back toward the dominating bulk of the Republican Palace, my new fortress—home to thousands of military and civilian personnel, guarded by tanks, security teams, and a battery of weapons. I paused and looked up. "Yeah, Katie, I live in a palace."

CHAPTER 14

Lions

"They know human meat," cautioned John, the wildlife specialist from Kruger Park, South Africa. We stared at the lion as he prowled back and forth near the cage door. His snout drew up in a snarl, revealing long, yellow fangs. He gave a low, menacing growl and hissed at us. Although his ribs protruded at his side and his mane was mange infested, this predator was a formidable sight. Two lionesses paced near the back wall and kept their four cubs away from the large paws of the male. One curious cub did not heed his mother's warning growl and ventured forward. He cried out as he was sent tumbling into the side wall by a swipe of the male's powerful paw. The mother reached in with her teeth and dragged the cub back to the corner of the cell.

Humans brought food, and this lion was starving. John, a large-game veterinarian, explained that in their natural habitat, the male would eat first, followed by rest of the pack. Lionesses in the wild hunted and ate every three or four days. These animals had been without food for a week. U.S. troops had discovered them in Uday Hussein's palace more than three weeks prior. Taking pity on the animals, the soldiers had fed them MREs and bottled water. But the lions were malnourished. They needed protein and medical attention or they would die.

John and his small rescue team had flown up from South Africa on a different mission: to save and relocate the animals that had survived a tank battle at the Baghdad zoo. I had met him when I toured the damaged zoo and asked him if he could help these lions, too. I later found out he knew Hector and Derick from their game capture days. It was strange how often we all ran into old acquaintances in this seemingly remote city.

John had brought some donkey meat for the lion pack and was trying to separate the male lion from the feeding area so he could enter the holding cage.

"How do you know they like human meat?" I asked, studying the stalking lion.

"Come, I show you," he said in a halting accent.

With a prod, he backed off the agitated animals and locked them in a different compartment of the cage. John swept his flashlight around the darkened corners of the den. The temperature had already reached a sweltering 110 degrees. Flies swarmed around my head. The putrid smell of urine, animal dung, and decay stung my nose. I looked back to make sure the lock on the metal gate between us and the lions was holding.

"Here," he said.

I followed him into the shadows, and there a human body lay crumpled in the corner. The beam of his light illuminated a crushed skull. The arm and leg bones were scattered among the lion's feces.

"J-e-e-z," I exhaled.

John bent down to inspect the corpse. I wanted to look away, but I couldn't. "How—"

"Looks like he was dead before he got eaten. See the bullet wound to the front of the head?" He pointed the light toward a black hole in the corpse's forehead. The face had been torn off, but the matted black hair was still intact. I'd seen enough.

"So, they shot the guy and let the lions eat him."

"Yep," John said in a clipped voice.

"Sick bastards!" I whispered.

He laid out half the donkey meat and released the male lion. The tan cat pounced on the raw, red meat and gulped down large chunks of pulp. As I watched, I imagined the animal sinking its fangs into the thigh or stomach of the human body we had found torn apart in the corner. Wiping my wet brow with the back of my wrist, I shook the vision away.

The lion began to purr like a small engine as he filled his stomach with protein. The lionesses waited in the back corner, snarling at one another as the cubs cried in high-pitched mews. The smell of the blood and raw meat permeated the air. When the lion had had his fill, he sauntered away, curled in a ball around his protruding stomach, and closed his eyes. John reentered the cage and placed another batch of donkey meat for the rest of the pride. There was a pecking order even among the lionesses. The older female ate first and then allowed the other lioness, and finally the cubs, to feast. As I watched Mother Nature in action, I thought it amazing that even in captivity, animals followed their instincts and a semblance of order. Too bad human nature was not like this.

White contractor trailers now dominated the grounds of Uday's palace, a sprawling complex of concrete buildings, hidden passages, and courtyards. Coalition military units occupied the compound. The bodyguards relayed to me disturbing rumors about its past from the Iraqi workers. Saddam's sons had appetites for money, booze, exotic animals and cars, and women. Within the basement of the palace, coalition forces discovered entire rooms full of expensive, rare wines and liquor. Other rooms held precious statues, paintings, and furniture. One vault contained millions in cash. Crisp U.S. twenty-dollar bills were stacked on pallets five rows deep and six feet high.

It was evident the economic sanctions had done little to impede the greed of this dictator's family. The sanctions had only served to deprive the Iraqi people of food, water, and medicine. After UN sanctions were levied, Saddam built more than seventy palaces from 1991 to 2002. The Oil-for-Food program had actually funded these construction projects, at a great cost to the Iraqi people.

Uday, Saddam's oldest son, had a sadistic and psychopathic nature. The guards told me stories of how he enjoyed torturing men. He would pull out their fingernails, sear their skin, or shock them with electrical leads. I had heard this all before, but it was his treatment of women that angered me most. Uday would prowl Baghdad college and high school campuses scoping out the women. Women covered their faces with head scarves or hooded abayas to keep from being noticed by Saddam's sons or his cronies. When an unfortunate girl caught Uday's eye, he would take her and a friend back to his palace. Women did not say "no" to men in the Baathist regime. For most of the women, it was the last time anyone saw them alive. I now understood why some women felt secure inside the black garments that covered their bodies. Like my flight suit in my early days of flying, the abaya for Iraqi women served as a coat of armor.

According to what our bodyguards heard, the injuries Uday had sustained from a would-be assassin had made him impotent. But that didn't stop him from deriving pleasure by abusing and beating women savagely. If a woman refused his advances, he would take her and her friend up in a helicopter and push the friend out, laughing as she tumbled to her death. If by some miracle a woman survived the beatings and rape, she could not return home because she was now soiled and, by Muslim standards, brought shame to the family. There were no counseling centers for abused women in Iraq. Most women committed suicide in the wake of an encounter with Uday or his men.

I left the palace and the sleeping lions with a knot in the pit of my stomach and acid burning in my throat. I could understand the lions hunting for food, but what did these men hunger for? What made them hunt humans? The stories and the body in the lion cage not only sickened me, but inspired me to push harder in rebuilding this country. No one should watch her best friend plummet to her death, no one's body should be ripped apart by lions, and no one should torture one human being to entertain another. And as this dictator built yet another palace at the expense of medicine, the children died. We just had to get this right.

Garner and our team were trying to get it right. In the morning meeting, he outlined the priorities for the ORHA staff. The seemingly endless problems and demands of Iraq had the military and civilian personnel reeling. There was little support from the policy makers, and the funds needed to begin reconstruction were caught in the bureaucratic quagmire of the Pentagon and other federal bureaucracies.

Every day, Garner asked for funds to begin paying the Iraqi pensioners, civil servants, and service workers, as he had promised in Umn Qasr.

Every day, the answer was the same: "We are working on it." The frustration and disappointment at being unable to get things started wore lines in the faces of Garner and the ORHA staff.

Garner brought the team together one morning and explained that we needed to work with what was available. A focused approach could channel our limited resources and concentrate our efforts on areas of immediate concern. If the general could score a few quick successes, he would go a long way toward winning not only the confidence of the Iraqi people but also that of the leaders back in Washington. It seemed as though the very people who hired him did little to ensure his success. He knew his window of opportunity to affect change was closing.

I wrote feverishly as he talked through the ten goals: *pay salaries, establish police and judicial system, restore basic services, fix fuel crisis, purchase crops, solve food distribution, install town councils, meet public health needs, bring ministries to a functional level, and establish better security.*

Although it was listed as the tenth task, security was the first priority. Garner traveled to the military command headquarters twice a day trying to get the military to help with his plan. The various military leaders gave Garner a gentleman's agreement, but they did not report to him. They only aided the ORHA mission when and where they could. Most of the Army generals had worked for Garner at some point in their careers, and he pressed the limits of those relationships. He also understood he needed the men and women in uniform if the mission were to be successful—a fact most civilian leaders ignore. Even though Garner knew the Joint Task Force commander, the commander's troops were stretched thin and had other security concerns to tend to in Iraq. Without an integrated plan with the military, OHRA was on its own.

Garner commented to the military staff on a number of occasions, "It would be a damn shame to win the war and lose the peace." The key to maintaining peace was paying salaries. It was the only goal the ORHA staff could impact directly. It took nearly a month, but the salaries and pension payments finally began on May 18. Garner had kept his promise. Without any banking system in place, the staff improvised a method to pay the Iraqis twenty dollars each. Under Saddam's Baathist regime, most of the services had been subsidized. But with the shortage of gas, propane, water, and food, inflation began to climb. No one in Iraq had received pension payments in three months. On the first day that payments resumed, forty thousand pensioners received Iraqi dinars, but the currency had lost its value and they demanded U.S. dollars. We eventually used the cash found in Saddam's and his son Uday's palaces to make payments in U.S. currency.

The logistics and accountability of trying to pay millions of Iraqis with no banking or distribution system presented incredible challenges. Leave it to American ingenuity to solve. The procedure was for two ORHA staff members, accompanied by one heavily armed U.S. soldier, to transport the cash to a payment center, normally a school building or office building. The money was then counted and signed over to an Iraqi supervisor. Tables manned by two Iraqis each were set up inside the building, and the actual payments were made through the window. Although every pensioner had to supply two forms of ID, a roster was used to verify the information. The windows had letters for names starting with A-C, then D-G, and so on. On the first day, the A-C line was nearly a mile long. It seems that almost everyone had al-something as a last name. We learned that lesson the hard way.

As thousands of Iraqi men and women stood in the blistering heat, people began to lose patience and push their way forward. The U.S. troops who were there for crowd control carried long sticks and batons. I cringed when I saw that, but at least it gave the soldiers another way to manage the crowd besides lethal force. The first week of payments went well. I noticed that when the Iraqi supervisors completed paying the pensioners, they turned back the remaining money to the Americans. They reasoned that carrying the cash home would only invite a mugging, robbery, or death.

Next, the ORHA staff addressed the police force. Although thousands of police officers had returned to their stations, the men refused to do foot patrol and would only go on mounted patrol with U.S. military forces in their vehicles. Old scores were being settled, and several policemen lost their lives in the aftermath of war. As a result, no policemen patrolled after sunset. The police station closed every evening at 1800 and reopened around 0800. Besides, there were no holding facilities or jails to use if individuals were detained, nor were there guards to watch them. A U.S. Army military police brigade established a holding center at the Baghdad airport. Rumors of violence and rape among the prisoners filtered their way through the staff and military channels.

Several ORHA staff members with experience in the Middle East cautioned against rehiring the previous prison staff. They strongly recommended destroying the existing facilities, which only served as reminders of the brutality of the Baathist regime. Garner and I went to tour a prison twenty miles west of Baghdad. The prison was one of the most notorious in the country because of its brutal executions, horrific torture, and filthy living conditions. As we stepped into the parking area, we could see that the huge, deserted complex had been stripped of everything. It wasn't just the doors, windows, wiring, and furnishings that were gone. Most of the brick walls had been dismantled and removed.

The first building had a long corridor with cells on either side. The twenty-by-twenty-foot rooms were bleak and lifeless. On the second floor at the end of the hall was a large room. Our Iraqi guide opened the door and stepped back. Cold air rushed out, despite the 100-degree temperature outside. None of the bodyguards moved.

"Evil lives there," Johan whispered to me. I raised my eyebrows at him. "Torture chamber," he warned.

I stepped around him and peered in the doorway. Big russet stains covered the chipped and cracked walls. Black burn marks and long scratches cut the floor. Large iron hooks dangled from the walls and ceiling. It reminded me of a slaughterhouse. With no windows and concrete walls a foot thick, there was no escape.

An invisible force emanated from the empty room and we all drew back. A bitter chill cut through me. I shivered. My imagination took off. A dismembered body dangled beaten and broken, blood pooling on the floor. The screams of pain and pleas for mercy echoed in my head. The smell of burnt flesh, sweat, and blood sent a wave of nausea through me. Black, hollow eyes stared out, and skeleton hands clawed at the walls. Johan reached out to steady me. I was panting.

"Pure evil," he repeated.

"Let's go." I swallowed the bile.

Back in the car, the general asked, "Could you feel that room, Kimmer?" He rubbed the bridge of his nose.

"Sir, demolish the place. Nothing good will come from it. Nothing," I answered.

"What is the name of that prison?" he asked.

I flipped through my notes. "It's called Al bu-something."

Johan made a curious comment as we drove on. "In all of creation, it is only humans that torture one another." No one spoke during the hour-long ride back to the palace.

And we torture ourselves, I thought, as I glanced at the general. We still had seven of the goals to address, but we tackled the leadership of Iraq next.

CHAPTER 15

The Council of Seven

O ur vehicle stopped in front of the worn, six-story cinderblock hotel. Short Kurdish guards stood at the perimeter eyeing the convoy. Garner strutted to the crowded entrance. We were greeted with the glare of bright lights as the cameras recorded our first meeting with the Council of Seven.

"Good day," he drawled, stretching out his hands to Masoud Barzani, one of the two Kurdish leaders. He treaded his way through the crowd, grinning and shaking hands. "Hi, Jay Garner. Hi there, Jay Garner." Everyone wanted a piece of him. He was the visible American general. It didn't matter that he was retired; he was the general who listened to them.

In the absence of any direction from policy makers in the White House, DoD, or State Department—and at the urging of prominent Iraqis— Garner formed the Council of Seven. The theory was to put Iraqi faces in the governance of the country and to create a working body of leaders who represented the majority of the Iraqi population.

Two Sunni Muslims—Masoud Barzani, the leader of the Kurdistan Democratic Party, and Jalal Talabani, the leader of the Patriotic Union of Kurdistan who later became Iraq's president—represented the kurds from the north.

Representing the Shiite majority were four men. Ayatollah Abdul Aziz al-Hakim was a cleric who came out of exile from Iran. Garner was uncomfortable with this Shi'a leader, but the Kurds said it was better to have Hakim inside the tent than outside the tent. Ibrahim al-Jaafari was the soft-spoken doctor who later became Iraq's prime minister. Ahmed Chalabi was the Pentagon-backed expatriate who Garner neither liked nor trusted, believing Chalabi had no power base in Iraq. Dr. Ayad Alawi was a secular Shi'a who was later nominated as the first Interim Prime Minister.

Eighty-year-old Adnan al-Pachachi, the only Sunni Arab, had a secular, liberal outlook but was unable to make the trip from his home in London. Garner had wanted an eighth position to be reserved for a Christian. It was never filled.

The meeting was set on the fourth floor of the hotel. An old spiral marble staircase opened into the lobby and we started the ascent. Bodyguards with their AK-47s, reporters with their microphones and cameras, and assistants with their notepads all crowded around. As we climbed the stairs, the general gripped the rail and I moved up behind him.

"You all right?" I asked. He waved me off. I motioned to Derick, who knew the drill. He gripped the general by the arm and leaned over talking to him as he helped Garner up the stairs. No one was the wiser.

As the group climbed the next two flights, I asked, "Why the stairs?" A Kurdish assistant explained that the electricity was not reliable and no one wanted to risk getting stuck in the elevator. *No kidding.* I couldn't imagine it, given the stifling 110-degree temperature and the massive amounts of cologne that Iraqi men wore. We reached the conference room, dominated by a thirty-foot-long battered table and mismatched wooden chairs. I could see through a screen partition that divided the room in half. The guards were asked to wait in the makeshift area behind it. Some houses in Iraq have a tent or a waiting room, like a formal parlor, for the drivers or security guards who routinely accompany the well-to-do populous in the Middle East. This hotel was no different.

The Council of Seven positioned themselves around the table. Four were accompanied by their translators, with two jockeying to sit at the head of the table. The remaining leaders flanked Garner. They wrinkled their brows and looked around the table with a sense of importance, nodding to one another in respectful greeting. Young boys wearing dark, pajama-like clothes served warm, sweet tea. The rest of the group settled in their chairs, eyeing each other. The room was hot and quiet and the mood tense as the general began.

In his southern drawl, he delivered his standard "rebuilding the country and you are important to the future of Iraq" speech. From the end of the table, I watched their faces and saw nothing encouraging. They had heard it all before from the military leadership and the dictator who had raped this country and brutalized its people. Every man at this table had experienced the terror of the Baathist regime. Each had lost a son, a father, or an uncle, either in the Great War with Iran or at the hands of the Iraqi secret police.

These leaders had also battled one another. The Kurds had fought among themselves, and yet both factions were the enemies of Saddam's Sunnis. The Sunnis had brutalized the Shi'a. The Iraqi Shiites had clashed with the Iranian Shiites. I doubted whether any member of the Council of Seven trusted another, but they needed each other to survive.

The men listened politely as the general continued outlining his vision of a collective body to govern Iraq until a constitution was written and general elections held. Iraq needed Iraqi leaders, and these men had the power and resources to keep most of the Iraqi population in check. Given that each leader had been the enemy of the others at some point, the idea that they could work toward a common goal was probably naive. The "seven" wanted to secure their power bases, and if the Iraqi people benefited, that was secondary. The general knew he had the authority of the coalition. What he needed was cooperation from these men to succeed. The council members would do what Garner requested—for the short term.

The discussion began with the standard complaints about the lack of security in sectors of Baghdad and the surrounding suburbs. I focused on the body language and watched the reactions. They droned on about the lack of electricity, water, and jobs. The two Shiites at the head of the table complained the most, pounding their fists on the table for effect. As the black-robed old man went into a tirade, his fist slammed the table. Simultaneously, the lights failed, plunging everyone into darkness. I could hear the guards' shouts and the sharp clicking of shifting weapons. Heavy footsteps echoed around the room and down the hall.

"Crap," I whispered, bending over to take cover under the table. From the far end of the table, I heard chairs scrape across the floor. I imagined it like the scene from a mobster movie when gunfire explodes in a room for a full minute. Then, dead silence. When the lights come on and the smoke clears, there, sitting among the blood-splattered walls and overturned chairs, is the lone survivor. In this case, he would run a country. I held my breath. But no weapons fired, no smoke filled the room, and no chairs overturned. Instead, beams of light streamed from the flashlights that swept around the room. Within thirty seconds, the fluorescent lights flickered back on. Audible sighs escaped the mouths of those around the room.

I still had my head under the table when the lights returned. I popped up in time to see I wasn't the only one with a wild imagination. I smiled wearily at the young Kurdish aide across from me who emerged at the same time. He winked as if we had just shared a clandestine adventure. I showed him the pen in my hand and he showed me his reading glasses. I grinned. The remainder of the meeting was uneventful, despite two more power failures. This time we chuckled at the darkness, and candles were lit within seconds.

The Council of Seven may have succeeded in keeping the violence at bay or starting the rebuilding process, but it alone could not change the course of a nation that had suffered under a brutal dictatorship. As an institution, the Council of Seven would not survive Garner's successor. But it was only intended as a temporary measure. Rebuilding a society requires its entire people—both men and women. They must be active participants in both changing their leadership and running their institutions. People need to feel they have a voice and can make a difference.

I know this concept all too well. The integration of women into the military has been my own experience, but I believe that experience has been mirrored in other predominantly male professions. Changing long-held habits is a difficult undertaking. People can demand change, legislate for change, or fund change, but most institutions resist it.

Women pioneers, some would say, had to break invisible barriers or shatter glass ceilings. I did not subscribe to the glass-ceiling analogy. Slamming into those ceilings hurts. The toll of shattering barriers can be emotional and personal and can sometimes cost a career. If you break a glass ceiling, chances are the shards of glass will not only rain down on you but also make it more difficult for those who must follow in your wake. The repercussions can last for years. Finally, sometimes those very same ceilings turn out to be the floors of support you need for the next level of your professional journey. I found another route to success in my military career.

Rather than smashing ceilings, women in nontraditional careers should start by unlocking the doors of opportunity. The secret is in finding those enlightened men who hold the keys. General Garner was one of them. Seeking out the best talent regardless of gender takes courage and foresight. A common trait among these men is a relationship with strong women in their family—a daughter serving in the military, an independent wife, or a powerful mother as a role model. These men have a strong sense of self and are not threatened by powerful women. They give women the opportunities needed to succeed or fail. When we succeed, the challenges keep coming. When we fail, they help us learn and try again. As I think back on the enlightened men who unlocked those doors for me, there are several, but two come particularly to mind.

Lieutenant General John Jackson, now retired, was my wing commander. My first memory of him is when I was summoned to his office as a new captain instructor pilot in 1985 at a flight training base in Arizona. He wanted to send me to Squadron Officers School, a six-week program for company-grade officers. My own boss had not recommended me for the school, but General Jackson took a chance. He made it clear I was to return as a distinguished graduate (DG), one of the top 10 percent in the class, or not come back at all.

Well, call me an overachiever. Not only did I accomplish this feat, I also received an additional top graduate award for being in the top 1 percent in a class of eight hundred. This set me on a path for an internship program at the Pentagon, and then an assignment to the first cadre of pilots to train and instruct in the Air Force's newest jet trainer. Although I was still very rough around the edges, General Jackson saw my potential and took a gamble at a time when women were still considered a social experiment in the military. He would be my mentor and role model for a decade, teaching me how to serve God, family, and the Air Force—in that order.

When he retired, I learned another valuable lesson. A good leader passes on those he has groomed and mentored to the next mentor. Colonel Arthur Lichte, now a lieutenant general, entered my life after General Jackson asked him to watch out for me.

It was General Lichte, with his white hair and Irish humor, who called me in 1996 to ask if I was ready to command. I nearly jumped through the phone line. He had just become a wing commander and was building his squadron commander team. He hired me as the first female to command a KC-135 air refueling squadron at Fairchild Air Force Base in Washington. He would eventually select more than ten women to command positions. This general was indeed an enlightened leader.

Talk about unlocking doors. That command tour defined me as a senior officer and afforded me the opportunity to prove that woman leaders were not a novelty but a necessity. During that tour, I had the privilege of running a squadron of 120 exceptional men and women and to teach them how to balance service to their nation and responsibility to their families. I also worked to balance the authoritative leadership style prevalent in the military with a more nurturing approach to commanding troops. I didn't know if it could work in this environment, but it was what my instincts told me to do. In wartime, leaders need to be decisive, confident, and results driven. But in peacetime, there is room for other leadership styles. That's where I worked the hardest during my command tour.

My command philosophy was best portrayed in the movie *Jerry McGuire*. In fact, I played that clip during my first commander's call. The movie scene was set in a locker room, where Jerry, the agent, is arguing with his client, an average football player. Jerry makes a compelling plea. "Help me, help *you*. Help *me*, help you. *Help* me to help you."

Simple lines, but they became the backbone of my command tour. When I mentored troops or required them to take on extra duties, I would refer to this line. "Here is where you are helping me to help *you*." Or if one of my troops got in trouble or began to complain (which pilots do a lot), I would ask, "Are you helping *me*, help you?" My goal as a leader and commander was to inspire greatness in others and to teach them to reach beyond what they thought possible.

My first year of command was so successful I thought nothing could top it. With my squadron in the lead, we earned an "Outstanding" rating from the Air Force Inspection team on our Operational Readiness Inspection, a first in forty-eight years. Our wing received numerous awards and trophies. We continued to excel once we deployed to Saudi Arabia in 1997 to refuel planes patrolling the no-fly zone over southern Iraq.

But there were times when the situation demanded an authoritative leader, too. In 1999, during the final part of my command tour, I deployed to Italy to lead the air-refueling mission for a huge and complicated bombing campaign during Operation Allied Force, the air war in Bosnia.

When the number of sorties flown over Kosovo exploded from ten to nearly a thousand a day, the demand for air-refueling aircraft was staggering. Confined airspace, enemy ground-to-air missiles, and the risk of midair collisions threatened the lives of pilots and the success of the operation. Urgent calls came from the Combined Air Operations Center in Italy, where the war was being controlled, identifying an immediate need for a refueling commander to restructure and execute the air-refueling missions. The request went from the war-fighting general of Air Combat Command (ACC) to the general in charge of Air Mobility Command (AMC) to every air-refueling wing in the Air Force.

One Thursday morning, I was informed that my name had been forwarded to fill the requirement for an experienced commander. My first thought was "Yes." Then doubt set in. Would the war-fighting side of the Air Force accept a woman directing the refueling requirements of sixty-one NATO squadrons and working side by side with the coalition fighter pilots? My doubts proved unfounded; two days later, I was on a plane to Italy. When I arrived, I reported as ordered to the commanding ACC three-star general and saluted. For a moment, my heart sank. He looked a lot like the cigar-chomping commander who had berated me so many years earlier. But that ghost disintegrated with his first words. He looked up from his desk, pointed a finger at me, and barked, "Fix my air-refueling problems and get those bastards from AMC off my back."

"Yes, sir," I replied, and left the room. I had my marching orders. It had taken twenty years, but this general did not care about my gender. He wanted his air-refueling problems fixed, and I was to lead the team to do it. And fix the complex problems we did. The driving factor was inefficient use of aircraft and the air space. Within two weeks, we had realigned the air space, changed the refueling procedures, and built discipline into the flying system. This was the first major modern battle with no loss of coalition military lives in combat, and I am convinced our team made that possible.

After my two years in command, our squadron's successes resulted in my selection for a prestigious military school and promotion to colonel ahead of my peers. Enlightened men, and my professional achievements, had made the opportunity for my command tour to happen. When it came, I balanced leadership skills cultivated as an officer, pilot, teacher, and mother. It worked.

So, I was an empowered woman, trained in a male environment, taught to lead effectively in an authoritative manner, but also able to combine that with a nurturing leadership style that proved itself in action. Can this be applied to women in other jobs?

That is the challenge for our society. Women struggle to break into the executive levels of leadership in America. Even though we are 51 percent of the population, women are underrepresented on a national level in both the U.S. Senate and the House of Representatives. Women make most of the spending decisions in the United States, yet our faces rarely appear as CEOs or members of the board of the Fortune 500 companies. Women make up a huge part of the educational field, yet only a handful of them are superintendents. Military women comprise 15 percent of the armed forces, but fewer than ten are general officers, and there has yet to be a female four-star general. The service academies still cap the number of women who can enter at 15 percent, even though 60 percent of the freshmen entering most state universities are women.

Our country has work to do. Why? Not because it is the right thing to do—although it is—but because, for our nation's survival, it is the only thing to do. I knew what it took to get the military institution to change and for me to be successful in a command tour. But trying to translate those lessons into rebuilding a Muslim nation was different—or was it?

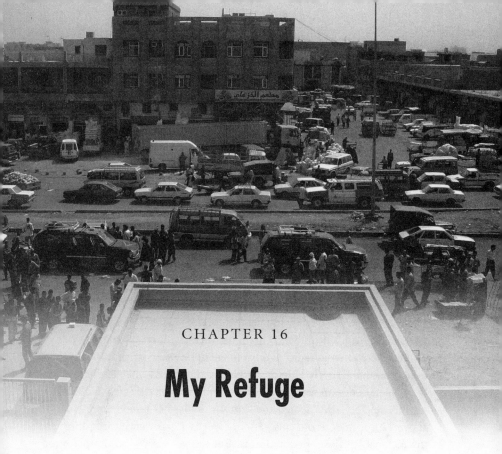

CHAPTER 16

My Refuge

The first month in Iraq included extensive travel throughout the country. We put more than five thousand miles on our vehicles. When the demands of the job and the overwhelming pressure threatened to crush me, I found refuge in a most unlikely place, the second-row bench seat of our 2003 tan GM Suburban. That plain SUV became my sanctuary. There I could escape the foreign smells, the city noises, and the excessive heat. This was my cocoon of safety as long as we were moving—so the bodyguards informed me. It could be a coffin on wheels if we were trapped in traffic.

I always felt safe and sound in this American car. I ignored the fact that a round fired from an AK-47 could pierce the side doors like a sewing needle through fabric. The bullet would tear apart the first person it struck and fatally wound the second. Unaccustomed to the dangers of ground war, I knew little about the commonly used TM-57 land mine, which could have hurled our thirty-five-hundred-pound vehicle twenty feet in the air. The blast would have peeled off the metal skin and ripped apart the axles. If we survived the explosion, the crushing force as we hit the asphalt would have finished the job.

I didn't think at the time about the danger of a well-placed rocket-propelled grenade (RPG). Later on, I learned that a single RPG could enter the vehicle, creating one-foot entry and exit holes and leaving everyone inside burnt and shredded with shrapnel. I had no clue about the improvised explosive devices (IEDs) that later became a serious threat. They could have disintegrated our vehicles in a second, leaving nothing but torn, charred metal and dismembered bodies.

Such weapons were the reason we traveled so fast on the roads. The faster you moved, the more difficult it was for the enemy to time an ambush. The objective was to move the convoy through kill zones as rapidly as possible. Yet the Suburban was the place I felt the safest while traveling in Iraq. It was an illusion I created to deal with the constant threats that existed just beyond this plain, tan SUV.

SUVs wore out quickly in the harsh Middle Eastern climate and rough terrain. The windshield looked like a roadmap, with cracks running everywhere. There were no radio stations to entertain us, so when our conversations ceased, the steady hum of wheels speeding across the pavement filled the air. The common new-car smell was replaced by a stale air-conditioning scent. The cloth seats spared the skin on my legs as temperatures soared above 120 degrees. From this vessel of safety, I experienced Iraq through the rectangular glass window frame. But the vehicle was also a place for comic relief.

Hurtling down the highway on another road trip north to visit the Kurds, I reached from the back seat and touched Hector's shoulder. As usual, he was driving our vehicle.

"I have to go." I whispered.

"She's got to go," announced Hector into the mike.

"Again?" The reply crackled from the radio. Hector shot me a mischievous wink. I rolled my eyes.

For a female, going to the bathroom in Iraq required the detailed planning of a space shuttle launch. Rest stops, so common along America's highways, did not exist in this country. The occasional toilet you might find in a shop consisted of a keyhole-shaped porcelain bowl sunk into a dirty concrete floor.

The familiar stench of an outhouse was not the issue. What was challenging for Westerners was the requirement to squat down, spread knees, and take aim. It was harder than it sounded; losing your balance was the clear and ever-present danger. Iraqi women must have strong thighs and iron knees. It was a better workout than the Thigh Master. I could never figure out which way to face: toward the wall or toward the door? Either way, I always seemed to miss. My trusty bottled water came in handy when a small hose or bucket of water was not available for flushing. Toilet paper was the user's responsibility. I made the mistake of assuming it would be supplied once—*only* once.

It proved just as easy to stop along the side of the road. Never mind that the Iraqi landscape was mostly desert. In the desert, it is tricky to find a small ditch or a private place when you need one. In addition, the eight body-guards grumbled because they had to sweep the area for land mines and establish lookout positions for snipers. The last thing I wanted was to perish with my pants around my ankles.

Today, Hector found picking the right spot amusing. He pulled off the road to an area as flat as a tabletop.

"How about here?" Derick teased in his thick Afrikaans accent.

"You guys are cute. Find me a ditch. Now!"

He broadcasted my order through the radio. "She wants a ditch," he said.

"You say she's a witch?" a voice returned.

Garner suppressed a laugh.

"Don't encourage them," I snapped. By now, my foot was beginning to tap and the pressure was mounting. We sped out, kicking up gravel and leaving a small dust cloud in our wake. "This is not funny, you guys. I've had two kids," I groaned. *I wonder if local women have this much trouble when they need to go to the bathroom.*

"Women!" whispered Derick. "How about here?"

Hector pulled onto the dirt shoulder. By now, I didn't care if it was Grand Central Station—I had to go. Before I could get my seat belt off, ten men from the three cars bolted out, stood in a line with their backs to me, and relieved themselves.

"Just checking for land mines," they joked.

"Super," I breathed through clenched teeth. I loosened the belt on my trousers and tried hard not to dance. After they finished, I stumbled into the small ditch, tugging on my zipper. Through frequent practice, I had perfected the art of pulling down my pants and squatting. It was not very digni-fied, but my goal was to minimize exposure of my white butt. I thought it a brilliant execution of modesty and necessity—poetry in motion, almost.

In midstream, I could hear the boys chuckling from over the hill. Then I recognized a squeaking sound. Was I hearing wagon wheels?

I looked up to see a rickety, donkey-pulled cart top the dirt hill. An old man in a flowing white robe with a dark wrinkled face and gray hair sat on the bench seat. He'd caught me with my pants around my ankles. There was no stopping. I did what any American would do—smiled and waved.

He stared in disbelief, then returned a toothless grin. Shaking his head, he snapped the reins over the sad donkey, and continued on down the dusty road. I think both sets of my cheeks blushed. I stood up, buckled my pants, and glared at the retreating farmer. I could see his shoulders shaking with laughter.

Men!

"That will be the highlight of your day," I thought of shouting after him. Climbing up the hill to the car, the howls of laughter grew louder.

"Oh, shut up," I barked, my face crimson. I crossed my arms and sulked in the back seat.

"You made his day, Kimmer," Garner teased, patting my knee. "Now that's international relations!"

CHAPTER 17

Death Threats

Death threats were common in postwar Iraq. Intelligence sources infiltrated the cells of the remaining Saddam death squads and intercepted their transmissions. When we first entered Iraq, the daily intelligence briefings and the number of threats were overwhelming. If I thought about them, I would never have ventured out of the Green Zone or into the countryside. But you can't rebuild a nation by staying behind concrete walls, and Garner knew it.

I told the C-2 (intelligence officer) that he should brief our protection team on the local threats from now on. Like others in the intelligence community, he refused to share intelligence briefs with the South Africans because they didn't have the appropriate security clearance. *You've just got to love the Army.*

"Okay, but John, the South Africans are hired to protect us. If they don't have the correct information, how can they protect us?" I reasoned. Still, the C-2 was reluctant to share any information with the team. It took a couple of days, but I finally convinced him to give them the daily threat assessments. I had enough to worry about and I didn't need death threats added to the list.

It was the professionals' job to keep us alive, and it was my job to support Garner and our mission.

In early May, the J-2 pulled me off into a hallway. "Look, this is serious," he whispered. He explained that coalition forces had just arrested a cell member from one of Saddam's death squads. During the interrogation, he confessed they were targeting General Garner's convoy within the week. I swallowed hard, knowing we were on the road every day this week.

The informant outlined the planned ambush. When the SUV convoy traversed a roundabout or intersection, a car would crash into the first SUV, trapping the remaining vehicles. A small truck was then supposed to pull in front. A man armed with a RPG launcher in the bed of the truck would fire the RPGs into the center SUV's windshield, while a passenger inside the cab unloaded a machine gun into the first SUV. The probability of killing everyone in the center SUV was 100 percent.

I sighed. "What do you suggest?"

"Don't go out for a while," he advised.

I shook my head. "We can't do that—then the enemy wins. Besides, General Garner will never agree. Especially now that some idiot reporter wrote that he was holing up in the palace. What a bunch of crap."

The C-2 shrugged. "Maybe we can get some military backup." We had been traveling with only three SUVs and no military support for the last few weeks. It was what Garner wanted.

John made a couple of calls, and for the next week we traveled with two gun-mounted Humvees as bookends for the convoy. Garner asked about the added protection and I explained that the Army troops needed to gain familiarity with the Baghdad streets. I didn't exactly lie. Besides, the general had enough to worry about without these death threats to keep him awake.

After three days of traveling around Baghdad and no evidence of an impending attack, I began to relax. I had grown accustomed to and comfortable in these SUVs.

My comfort was short-lived.

On day four, we rounded a corner when a small, rusty, dark blue car slammed into the side of the lead Humvee and bounced off. It happened so fast. Instead of stopping, the blue car hit the Humvee again. This time, it caught its left front fender. The Humvee driver gunned the engine, dragging the car. The entire convoy lunged forward as each driver stomped on the gas pedal. When the car's fender ripped off, we swerved left to miss colliding with it. As we passed the blue car, I could see two men in the front seat and a wide-eyed woman cradling three small children in the back seat.

Oh no!

Garner saw her, too, and yelled, "Hey, we need to stop!" Hector ignored him. I tore my eyes away and swept the trailing traffic. There, fours cars back, was a white pick-up truck closing in on us.

Oh shit, here we go.

Derick rolled down his window, extended the AK-47, and released the safety. I could see Neil and Cecil, the bodyguards in the rear car, doing the same.

"Don't shoot the family," I ordered, as I crawled over the back seat to reach for the flak vest.

"Hold this," I said, shoving it at Garner. I groped for the medical kit, but fell over when the SUV veered to the right. I clawed back over the seat to shield Garner.

He was yelling, and tapping on Hector's shoulder. "God damn it, we need to help those people. I said 'Stop!'" His neck and cheeks were getting red. We were almost through the intersection. The white truck had advanced and was two cars back. I held my breath.

"Who the hell is in charge here? Stop this damn car!" the general bellowed, spit flying from his mouth. I patted his arm in an attempt to calm him. He jerked away.

Derick was trying to get a shot off, but the third SUV maneuvered to block the white truck. The last Humvee got caught in traffic. We were swerving so much that no one had a clean shot at the truck. Besides, the streets were too crowded.

Cars honked at us and Hector jumped the vehicle onto the sidewalk to get around traffic. He was on the bumper of the lead SUV, which was glued to the Humvee. I saw the last SUV and Humvee closing the distance between us, jockeying with the white truck.

"Hurry," I whispered.

We made the intersection and had open highway in front of us. Our speed was nearly fifty miles an hour. The white truck slammed into a parked car and disappeared behind a traffic jam.

"KIMMER!" Garner bellowed because he'd been ignored. I was still looking out the rear window as the scene faded from my view. I rested my forehead on the car seat.

Derick spoke up from the front. "Sir, it is Army policy. When their vehicles get in wreck, they report back to an officer and the officer settles the accident." This answer seemed to appease the general and he sulked in his seat.

My eyes met Derick's. I found my voice. "Derick, tell the general about capturing rhinos in Africa." We needed a distraction.

"Ah, yes. In order to capture a rhino, sir, you must sedate the animal. Now this is dangerous for both the rhino and me," he began, as he rolled up the window.

He voice blended with the hum of the tires. I saw the terrified face of the woman in the blue car. *And the children die.* The drumbeat of words echoed in my head.

When we returned to the palace, I sought out Derick. "Was that true about the Army policy?"

"No, I made it up. The general is having a tough time and he needed to save face," he answered.

I stared at the leader of our protection team for a long time. I did not see the paid mercenary, the ruthless warrior who had taken on "special jobs" and led troops for hire against rebel forces in unstable, violent, and poverty-stricken countries—places the UN and the rest of the world had given up on. I focused on the scar across Derick's lip, a small sign of those past battles. He interrupted my thoughts.

"I have much respect for your general."

"I can see that."

I walked away, knowing we had escaped death again. *How much longer would our luck hold out?*

Rumors of the traffic incident spread throughout the ORHA staff and people refused to ride with Garner. I didn't blame them, but I had no choice. I was his exec, and this was my job.

CHAPTER 18

Commander, Pilot, Wife, Mother

B
ut we all have choices I entered in my log as I concluded the story about our convoy's brush with death.

I chewed on the pen tip, gazed out of the dirty window, and thought of my best friend, Nancy. She had been there throughout my military career. Tonight, I needed her reassuring and comforting words. A tracer cut through the night sky as I wondered how she was doing in her command tour in England. I envied her situation—the cool English temperatures, a support staff, an entirely different daily routine, and concerns so different from mine in Baghdad. I thought of sending her an e-mail, but I was too tired. Instead, I lay down on the metal cot and thought back to our discussion two years back, when she was weighing whether or not to take on that command tour.

It was a heated conversation on the deck of my suburban home on a warm summer day in Virginia. Kent had made us frozen margaritas, but he excused himself the minute we began our debate—one of many, when it came to the Air Force. I sipped the cold drink and played with the salty rim, flicking the grains onto the table. I stared hard at this woman I had known for almost twenty years. We had been stationed together only twice and now she was finishing her assignment in northern Virginia. As she contemplated her next career move, the adrenaline coursed through me. I felt very strongly about the path she should take and I cut her off in mid-sentence.

"The Air Force does not promote you to lieutenant colonel to sit in a stupid staff position. They promote you to command." Nancy reeled back as I pressed on. "Damn it, Nancy, the Air Force needs women like us out there doing the tough jobs. You have to show not only your bosses but also those who work for you that a woman can lead. And lead in the tough operational jobs. And if you don't do it, who will?" Mentoring was something that came naturally to me, but it had been my experience that most women didn't mentor other women well. I knew I was being unsympathetic.

"It's easy for you. You've already done your command tour and it was a huge success," she protested. "You know, sometimes it's hard to be your friend," said the woman who had stuck with me all these years.

Nancy had started her career as an enlisted crew chief on the flight line and later earned an officer's commission. She, too, had come a long way in the Air Force. Although we were the same age, Nancy's crystal blue eyes and soft, fair skin made her look ten years younger than me. I never took the time to cultivate friendships with women. In my younger days, I didn't think I needed them. Now that I was in my forties, I was much wiser and knew the value of a best friend. Little did I know how much I would truly need her support.

I softened my approach. "You'll be successful, too. It is the greatest job, and trust me on this, you will truly regret it if you never command. Come on, girl, you can do this. I am here for you, and once you are in it, the Air Force backs you all the way." Nancy nodded, and I knew her well enough to see the determination bubble in those blue eyes. I smiled as I sipped my drink. "Besides, I'll live vicariously through you." She laughed.

That July, Nancy took command of one of the toughest and most demanding logistics squadrons in the Air Force. She rose to the challenge, supporting one of the busiest operational fighter bases in the world. Under her leadership her squadron won numerous awards, including Best in Air Force for logistics plans and Best in Command for fuels and transportation. She commanded men and women, not for ego, but to inspire them to build a better Air Force for our nation.

In the Air Force, most pilots begin command when they make lieutenant colonel, some fifteen years into their career. During my tour as a squadron commander, I had outlined my philosophy of leadership right from the start: I'll take care of you and help with your family, and you'll take care of the mission, your family, and your community. I believe strongly that military members should balance all three.

It sounds simple enough, but the military is not organized to care for service members' families, especially when the members deploy. My staff and I worked hard to support the families. In my first year of command, our squadron made a major deployment to Saudi Arabia to support Operation Southern Watch, which protected the Shiites in southern Iraq. In preparation for the deployment, which would occur over Thanksgiving, Christmas, and New Year's, we worked to bring the families together in various social functions and gatherings. The idea was to encourage them to become a team ahead of time, so they could support each other when we were gone. As a military spouse himself, Kent helped both the squadron wives and me. He made me proud.

My staff and I generated support from all the agencies on the base to help the families when the member was deployed. All of my troops' spouses came to the pre-deployment parties, and they were most appreciative of our efforts.

The biggest challenge for an Air Force flying command at that time was the retention of pilots. Military pilots can leave after about eight to ten years of service, and many were exiting the Air Force, leaving us critically short of experienced aviators. Kent and I discovered through discussions with the pilots' spouses that it was the wives who had the greatest influence on whether male pilots stayed in the military or separated. I focused my energy on keeping those wives happy and cared for, especially when we deployed.

I thought I had disguised the caring commander well, but my troops were not fooled. During a pre-deployment Christmas party skit, a young female copilot playing my role had a sign hung around her neck. On one side, it read Jetmom (the license plate of my convertible); on the other side, it read Jetjox (the license plate of our station wagon).

When the Jetmom sign was displayed, she said, "Now, if you have any problems, feel free to come talk to me, and we will work it out. I am here to help."

When she flipped the sign, displaying Jetjox, the dialogue was, "If you step out of line, I will kick your butt into next Tuesday."

Jetmom: "I have an open door policy; you just come in any time."

Jetjox: "Are you in here whining? Get the hell out of my office!"

The crowd at the party roared, and I sat stunned. Kent whispered, "Boy, they got your number."

A senior officer once told me that your ability to be happy in this business is directly proportional to your involvement in it. I pulled in the spouses and they got involved. My efforts did not go unnoticed by the senior leadership at the base.

A new wing commander replaced General Lichte, and that replacement quickly recognized my passion for my troops and my commitment to defend them to the end. One day, I was summoned to his office to convince him that we needed our existing space in the building. I sat across the table from him and outlined the logical points for the space allocation, concluded my argument, and sat back with confidence. But the wing commander appeared unconvinced and asked question after question.

As he challenged me on whether my squadron deserved the office space, I leaned forward in my chair to reemphasize my points. I continued pressing forward until I was on my feet, leaning over the table, and almost in the commander's face. My boss, who was sitting behind me, kept pulling on the Velcro tab of my flight suit, trying to get me to sit down. Frustrated, I finally plopped back, thinking I'd lost the argument.

The next night, the wing commander was on the flight line ramp and I was on duty as the supervisor of flying. He called me over and asked me to sit in his car. I crawled in, flipped the air-conditioning vent back and forth, and waited, certain he was going to yell at me for yesterday's show. I had never gotten a warm feeling from that general. It wasn't that he would do anything to hurt someone's career, but he just wouldn't do anything to help them. But tonight, he smiled over at me and said, "I really had you going."

I looked at him as the amber glow from the dashboard reflected off his face.

"You did that on purpose?" I asked.

"I just wanted to see how far you'd go to defend your troops," he smirked.

"You're lucky I didn't come over the table."

"No kidding! We all laughed after you left." He was a tall, regal man, not known for his sense of humor, so his comment surprised me.

"Glad I could entertain you, sir," I replied.

"You know, Kim, what makes an exceptional leader is knowing when to come over the table and when to just sit down," he advised.

"Yes, sir." He started the car. It was my cue to leave. As I stood on the cold, wind-swept concrete and watched his taillights disappear behind the hangars, I reflected on his comment. I had spent most of my career coming over the table. Maybe it was time to sit down. Although I had made it, sitting down was easier said than done.

I demanded a lot from my troops, but I gave everything. One of the things I did early in my command tour was to write a note to the parents of every one of my troops. The card made three points. First, it boasted about what a great job that person was doing. Second, it explained how proud I was to be his or her commander. Third, it thanked the parents for raising a son or a daughter who served our country in an Air Force uniform. The notes were a big hit. My troops would wander into my office, telling me it was the first time their parents had heard from someone in the Air Force. One of my flight commanders told me his father was going in for heart surgery and had gotten the card the day before the operation. Tears welled in his eyes as he thanked me.

The cards had another consequence. It put the troops on notice that I would write or call their parent without hesitation, and I used this a couple of times to keep them in line. One incident reminded me how powerful parents truly are.

When we deployed to Saudi Arabia, the leadership staff briefed the troops repeatedly about the written and video material allowed in this Muslim country. Saudi customs were very strict: no porn, no R-rated movies, and no provocative magazines. Even the *Sports Illustrated* swimsuit edition was forbidden.

Sure enough, when we arrived in Saudi, my senior enlisted advisor, known as the First Shirt, brought one of the young troops into the office. He had tried to smuggle in a *Playboy* video of swimsuit-clad women, the Saudi customs officers had found it, and now they had our entire cargo pallet quarantined. My luggage happened to be on that pallet. I was not a happy commander. The young airman stood in a brace before my desk and I read him the riot act.

"Tell me what you think our mission is here in Saudi Arabia," I asked the frightened airman.

"To support the Air Force," he answered tentatively.

"And what is the Air Force's mission?" I shot back.

"To support the no-fly zone." He grew confident.

"And what is the no-fly zone?" I pressed.

"Ummm, keep airplanes from flying?" he guessed.

"Why?"

"To protect the people on the ground," he said.

"That's right, airman, we are here to protect those Iraqis who live in Southern Iraq. Why? Because the leaders of the United States of America gave their word, and the Air Force is here to honor that promise. Our squadron is here to support those aircraft that enforce the no-fly zone and keep the word of our country." I paused. "You with me, airman?"

"Yes, ma'am." He bobbed his head.

"Tell me what you see out there," I said, pointing out the small window to the long row of KC-135 refueling aircraft.

"Our jets, ma'am."

"That's right, airman, and what is your mission here?"

"To fix those jets."

"Why aren't you fixing those jets right now?"

He looked confused. "Because I'm in here talking to you."

I cocked my head and stared at him.

"Because I screwed up, ma'am."

"So, your actions reflect not only on this squadron and our wing, but our Air Force and the United States of America. *And* the worst part is, it keeps you from fixing our jets!" I barked. "You have shamed us all, and I have a good mind to call your mother."

His knees buckled. "Oh, ma'am, please, no, she thinks the world of you. Please, she'll kill me," he pleaded.

I glanced over at the First Shirt. He raised one eyebrow and a corner of his mouth.

"Please, ma'am, I am so sorry. I'll do any detail, just don't call my mom!" he bargained, looking over at the Shirt.

"You just better keep our jets flying. Dismissed." I returned his crisp salute and he ran out the door.

The Shirt put his feet up on the opposite chair. "You're good, colonel. I think you're on to something."

"I doubt you'll have any more trouble from that kid," I answered.

Following this and my subsequent deployment to Italy to lead refueling efforts for the Bosnia campaign, in the blink of an eye my two-year command tour was almost over. Nancy decided it was time to brag about my accomplishments. In 1999, she nominated me for the Exceptional Leadership Award, sponsored by the nonprofit Federally Employed Women (FEW) organization.

"I don't want to do this," I complained.

"This is not about you, Kim. It is about what you represent. You are the vanguard for women leaders. You have to get out there on a national level, so others can see that women are indeed doing well in military command position. It is part of being a trail blazer," she urged.

A month later, I received notification that I had won the award and was expected to accept it at FEW's annual convention in Washington, D.C. Kent, my mother, and Nancy all joined me at the banquet in the ballroom of the Hilton Hotel. Up on the dais were the award recipients, including the commandant of the Marine Corps. So there we sat, an old male four-star general being recognized for his support of women in the Marines and a young female lieutenant colonel being recognized for her leadership accomplishments. We were both caught off guard when we were asked to give brief acceptance speeches. When the general received his award, his words were short and to the point. "I am really, really honored to get this award. Thanks." Polite applause answered his comments.

After the presenter read my citation and announced my name, I approached the microphone and placed the engraved glass plaque on the lectern. I waited for about ten seconds until the audience of several thousand, seated around hundreds of tables, quieted.

My voice, loud and clear, filled the large ballroom. "This morning I walked the halls of the Women's Memorial. As my footsteps echoed around that beautiful structure, I could almost hear the whispers and stories of all those women who made it possible for me to serve my nation." I paused and leaned over the lectern. "But as I look out at this audience tonight, I am once again reminded that it is because of women like you that I get to fly jets, I get to command troops, and I get to wear this military uniform and defend my country. So tonight, it is I who thank you." I was nearly shouting over the applause when I finished.

The crowd exploded, jumping to their feet with thunderous clapping. I drew back from the mike and squinted past the bright stage lights. Nancy, who was sitting up front, gave me an "I told you so" look. The applause lasted for about three minutes. When I finally sat down next to the Marine general, he reached over to shake my hand, but his eyes gave me a "go to hell" look for upstaging him. I smiled in response.

As I ended my command tour, I was ranked first out of twenty-one commanders at my base. The Air Mobility Command nominated me for the coveted Lance P. Sijan Award, given to the most exceptional leader in the entire Air Force. I was selected to attend the prestigious National War College (NWC) in Washington, D.C., the Ivy League of military senior service schools. In addition, the Air Force promoted me to the rank of colonel "below the zone"—in other words, I was promoted to this rank a year before my contemporaries, placing me in the top 5 percent of those eligible. The Air Force as an institution had acknowledged my accomplishments and my potential for higher command with this type of promotion.

I finally felt accepted. My success validated the belief that women could not only command and lead successfully but also could be role models for others in balancing work, family, and community. It also showed that a nurturing style of leadership worked, even in the hardened branch of military aviation.

The NWC was a great break from the demands of command, and the time in Washington allowed me to concentrate on my own family. While I was there, Nancy pressed me again to accept recognition, this time from an even more prominent organization. "I don't know."

"Trust me," she said. As usual, she was right.

The Ford Foundation, the Center for American Women and Politics, and the Partnership for Trust in Government co-sponsored the Good Housekeeping Award for Women in Government. It was intended to honor ten women in government whose outstanding contributions improved people's lives, displayed innovative approaches to today's leadership challenges, and served as positive role models for all.

Nancy's nomination described my recent command tour and my leadership style (including those letters to the troops' parents). She mentioned some of my appearances in the media, including an interview I had given on the NBC Nightly News with Jim Miklaszewski advocating equal treatment and career opportunities for women in government. She also described a seminar I had led for sixth- through twelfth-grade girls to encourage them to develop science, math, and technical skills. When I was a twenty-one-year-old fretting over the choice between flying and classroom teaching, I didn't realize I might be able to have it both ways. Two thousand girls had taken my seminar so far.

I was the first woman in uniform to receive this award. My picture appeared in the May 2000 issue of *Good Housekeeping*. The award came with a cash prize of $2,500. I used it to establish a scholarship fund at my alma mater, Ohio State, for minorities pursuing aviation careers.

The summer before I attended NWC, Kent and I had gone to a party where the tables were decorated with small silver stars. Kent picked up two stars from our table and laid one on each shoulder. "They look good on you."

I smiled and placed them in my wallet. If I got promoted to general, I would make them into cuff links for him. It could happen. After all, I had an exceptional command tour behind me, the right school ahead of me, and the talent to make it. I knew I could handle the next round of challenges in the Air Force.

After I graduated from NWC, I was assigned to the Pentagon. This eagerly anticipated move should have propelled my career, instead, it ground it to a halt.

CHAPTER 19

And Still It Burns

There were no breathtaking sunsets in Iraq to inspire great paintings or poetic works, no brilliant blue skies with fat white clouds. Instead, on most days the horizon was filled with black smoke ascending diagonally across the sky. There was always something burning in Baghdad—garbage dumps, abandoned cars, grassy fields, or ammunition stores. The pungent, acidic smell left a metallic taste in my mouth and unsettled me the first day I caught a whiff. Rarely did I allow the memory to surface that the smell always triggered. The bitter taste awoke the recollection of a crystal-clear day in September a year and a half before.

The sky was a sparkling blue, but like most Americans that morning, I was glued to the TV. I watched in disbelief as two commercial airliners slammed into New York's twin towers. Little did any of us in the Pentagon know that American Airlines Flight 77 was skimming the earth's surface at 685 feet per second on a collision course with the west side of our own building. Leaning against a window frame in the inner ring of the Pentagon, my chest ached as I witnessed the destruction reported on the news channels. The time was 0938.

Suddenly, a shudder rocked the building, followed instantly by a muffled explosion. The floor shook under my feet and the walls rippled and expanded. Ceiling tiles peppered the room. At that moment, the impact of a fully fueled Boeing 757 ended the lives of 189 people, 64 on board and 125 in the building.

The plane imploded as it entered the E-ring, the outermost portion of the Pentagon, and continued slicing through the structure, settling just short of the B-ring. My office was located in the A-ring. Glancing out of the window where I had been leaning, I could see thick black smoke crawling skyward above the roofline, marring the clear blue sky. I turned to my stunned colleagues. "We have to leave, *now!*"

Tearing through the hallways, we were stopped by a heat blast like an oven set on broil. My clothes, legs, and face were scorching. The flight-or-fight instinct had kicked in—every cell in my body screamed, *Run, run for your life!* All my military training as a pilot had not prepared me to meet death in a Pentagon hallway. My heart hammered, my fingers tingled, and I coughed from the intense smoke. I summoned all my control, drew a ragged breath, and steeled myself. Retracing my steps, I found a stairwell and escaped. Before realizing it, I was outside. Looking back, I saw an enormous cloud of black smoke billowing from the opposite side of the building.

Thousands of people in uniform or civilian clothes tumbled out of the exits as screaming police cars, ambulances, and fire trucks raced to the scene. No longer was I an individual, but part of a mass of humanity, moving now in shocked disbelief toward the river's edge. Someone said, "Here's America's wake-up call." Eventually, we stopped within the confines of a grassy strip bordered by Boundary Channel Drive and a watery finger of the Potomac River. Sirens wailed from every direction, people mumbled prayers, and an eerie calm came over the crowd. Just then, the air cracked with announcements of a second plane inbound for the Pentagon.

"Get down! Get down!" the urgent voice from the loudspeaker shrieked across the lawn. The crowd moved closer to the river and bent down on their knees.

Incensed, I refused to cower. I reached for the hand of my NWC classmate Charlie, a veteran Air Force fighter pilot who had flown missions in the Gulf and Bosnia.

"I am *not* dying on my knees," I vowed. He nodded in agreement. We remained erect as if to defy this unknown enemy and his weapon of choice. No sooner had the murmuring mass taken cover, than a U.S. Air Force F-16 fighter jet roared overhead and pulled a tight spiraling circle around the blazing building. White contrails poured off the aircraft's wings as he wrapped around the ascending column of smoke. *My God, it's like he's escorting the souls to heaven.* Tears sprang from my eyes as I witnessed thousands of people rise to their feet and cheer. I swelled with pride at being an American, an officer, and an Air Force pilot. That moment is seared in my memory for all time.

"We're gonna be okay," I whispered, my eyes still glued on the rising fighter.

"We're gonna be okay," Charlie echoed.

We were not the only ones in the crowd to respond that way. The next day, more than fifteen thousand people returned to the Pentagon. Their nation needed them back at work in a building that was still burning from the September 11, 2001, terrorist attack.

Now Baghdad burned with the same acidic odor that lingered in the Pentagon for months. How could I have known then that less than two years later I would help rebuild one of the countries where we went to war after this heinous attack?

CHAPTER 20

Mother's Day

I t is 0100. I am panting and gritting my teeth like a snarling dog. Bearing down, I give one final push and a blue creature emerges from my body. My eyes fly open and the delivery nurse reassures me that the creature will change color. Sure enough, as the infant draws in her first breath to cry, her skin transforms into a soft pink and her gray face lightens up. She has no hair, wrinkled hands, and a slimy body. Kent wipes the sweat from my brow as I lie back, exhausted from ten hours of labor. *I've got a boy and now a girl. No more,* I think, as I reach over to hold Kent's hand.

Anxious grandparents wait out in the hallway for their first granddaughter. Papa is handed the girl and cradles her as he carries the six-pound, screeching newborn down to the nursery. Our doctor chats in his French accent. I look to Kent to see if he understands him. He doesn't. We nod obediently and laugh when he grins at us. Finally, he pats my thighs and wishes us luck. With that, our family is complete with a baby girl and a two-and-a-half-year-old boy. It is May 10, 1991.

It was May 10, 2003. Instead of watching my daughter blow out twelve candles on her birthday cake, I was a passenger in a C-130 cargo plane flying from Iraq to Kuwait. Lifting off the Baghdad runway, I closed my eyes to catch a quick nap. As I heard the familiar grind of the landing gear retracting into the belly of the aircraft, a sudden shudder, followed by two quick explosions, rocked the airframe.

NO! my internal voice screamed, *not on her birthday!* My eyes popped open and I grimaced at the intense white flashes pulsating through a small window in the aircraft escape hatch. The two enlisted loadmasters positioned at the hatches jumped back. I dug my fingers into the metal rail of my troop seat and waited. Several of the passengers, unsure, glanced at me for clues. They knew I was the only pilot among them.

If the aircraft defensive systems had just pumped out flares to confuse or draw away a shoulder-launched missile, I figured we had about five seconds to live. The aircraft was too low to the ground and its airspeed too slow to take any evasive maneuvers to ward off the missile. A C-130 pilot had tried that during Desert Storm. He stalled the aircraft and killed everyone on board. The senior pilot flying this aircraft held the climb angle, but I heard the engine power increase.

"Please, God," I whispered, keeping my face devoid of emotion.

Seven, eight, nine. . . .

Ten seconds passed and the aircraft continued its turbulent climb. I closed my eyes as if nothing had happened. My heart had stopped pounding by about the time we leveled off at fifteen thousand feet. The C-130 had ejected its defensive flares because an enemy tracking radar was targeting our aircraft. Either the missile had missed, or it was a false alarm. We never knew.

Earlier in the week I had promised myself and Katie that I would at least send her an e-mail message. She would hear from me on her birthday, no matter what it took. Now I could keep that promise.

Garner had been instructed to meet in Kuwait with Ambassador L. Paul Bremer, whom President Bush had appointed as the civilian authority for Iraq. The general had been relieved early from his mission. The ORHA staff and military commanders did not take it well; Garner was a much respected and admired leader. President Bush had announced the change in leadership in the postwar rebuilding of Iraq without warning. When the president spoke, we had been in Baghdad for exactly fourteen days. I shook my head at the game of politics.

My admiration for the general soared as he took this public dismissal with such dignity. Those in power in Washington had no clue about what it took to make things happen in Baghdad. Looters crippled the city; the basic infrastructure of electricity, water, and fuel did not exist; our military forces were shoring up crumbling defensive positions; and there was literally no communication or public radio system. A relatively short-lived power failure later in 2003 would bring the East Coast of the United States to a standstill for days. Iraq had been without electricity for months. Not to mention, some of Saddam's military forces were still shooting at us. Oh yes, the new guy was in for some surprises.

As we landed in Kuwait City, I knew my job was not to judge the actions of those in power. My job was to take care of the man who looked all of his sixty-five years today. Garner would soon have no mission, but he had done so much to make another's achievable.

In his short time in-country he had made it possible for a nation to keep going. He had built trust and loyalty through the power of one-on-one relationships. Secretary Rumsfeld's staff had tasked me with writing the narrative and citation for the medal they would be awarding him. It was the Distinguished Civilian Public Service medal, the highest honor a civilian in DoD could receive.

What should I say about a man who tried to put an entire nation back on its feet? How could I explain the way he took a team of a thousand strangers, motivated them, and steered them in the right direction? Were there words to describe how General Garner's leadership made us want to follow him anywhere? And we did—along the ruined streets of Baghdad, through the dangerous alleys of Sadr City, into the houses of Sunni leaders, over the golden hills of Erbil in Kurdish country, and across the empty ruins of Ur.

Since I was so close to Garner, I could see how it pained him to lose power and be marginalized when there was so much more he could accomplish. News articles about his impending departure were inaccurate, brutal, and written by reporters sitting on their butts in the United States. They said he was failing, but the southern gentleman ignored the criticism, put on a professional face, and forged ahead. After working with him for months, I recognized the frustration and heard the anger.

It was difficult to watch as he struggled through his emotional ride. I wanted to call the reporters and shout, "Do you know how hard this is, given the dangerous obstacles, the inflexible interagency process, the inept policy makers, the lack of military personnel, the lack of resources?" But I didn't make that call. Instead, I settled into the hotel and began planning a tour through Iraq, stopping in all the respective regions to give the general a proper send-off. I would do everything but order the tea sandwiches. *You'll go out in style, sir*, I promised.

That afternoon I knocked on the general's hotel door and entered. He was sitting on the floral couch gripping a small glass half-filled with amber liquid—scotch. His face red and bloated, he slurred, "Kimmer, get me on the first plane back to the States. I've been on the phone all day. I'm being set up to be the fall guy for DoD."

I sat down in the chair opposite him, laced my fingers, and leaned forward on my elbows. It was the second time we were completely alone.

"Sir, listen to me," I coaxed, in my nurturing tone. "No one will remember those damn newspaper articles, but history will sure remember if you run. You are better than that. Stay. Stay and at least give the new guy a chance—Iraq needs both of you."

He grunted.

"Besides, there are hundreds of people who are working their butts off in Baghdad right now. They deserve a chance to tell you good-bye and we owe them thanks for following you into that war-torn country."

"You tell 'em. They respect you." His breath was sour.

"*No!*" I snapped. I stood up and poured scotch into a wine glass. "They need to hear it from *you.*" Garner's eyes followed my hand as I threw back the shot and promptly coughed as it burned the entire way down. *How do you drink this stuff?* He grunted and smirked. I chased the scotch with a glass of water.

Silence set in until I asked, "Sir, why do you think President Hussein refused to leave Iraq?" After that drink, my voice was raspy and low.

Garner looked at me for a long time. "Because he surrounded himself with people who only told him what he wanted to hear."

In that moment, I wasn't sure which president he was talking about, ours or Iraq's. Was there an ironic parallel between the two leaders?

I nodded. "You're right, sir."

"Call me . . . Jay." He leaned back on the couch and drifted off to sleep. I placed a cover over him and closed his door.

Down in the hotel business center, I found an empty computer and typed my promised note to my daughter.

Happy birthday Katie,
I am sorry I can't be there with you. I miss you terribly and wish I could snuggle with you. Right now, my sweet girl, someone needs me. Someday you might understand.
Love, Mom.

I pressed the Send button and the message disappeared from my screen. I rubbed my temples as a message from the minister of our church at home popped into view. He was re-sending an e-mail I had never seen. It couldn't have come at a better time.

Dear Kim,

    Kent gave me a new address for you. Said the Pentagon one was not the best one for us to use at this time. I sent you an email about a very wonderful service we had the Sunday after we entered Iraq. Katie was an important part of the service. I decided to have a special Scripture and Prayer service with candle lights. Besides the altar candles, we lit seven candles after seven specially focused prayers. Katie was front and center throughout the entire service lighting those candles. I love to watch her because she really has a spiritual hunger at this time in her life. I truly sense that church has a special meaning for her. I can relate to that because when I was her age I felt the same and maintained that feeling through those early adolescent and teen years. I was still a rebellious kid but my faith was still important to me. Well, the end of the service was a real "tear jerker." You know how people go to the altar during that closing hymn. Katie went to the altar and knelt and prayed. It really gets to me when I see a young kid go to the altar. I had to look over at Kent who was sitting in the choir loft to see what he was up to. He looked at her as she knelt and then looked away quickly. I'm probably reading into it but my guess is, with you in Kuwait, the war started, he probably would have lost it if he had kept looking at her praying. Well, bottom line is, I knew you would be safe that day with Katie's prayer going up to God because you know it was for you and the other soldiers. . . .

    Pastor Dave

This time I rubbed my eyes. A big tear plopped on the keyboard. *Oh God, please keep my children safe while I serve my country.*

A second message appeared in the inbox. *You are being considered for a position in Korea. It is a remote 12-month tour. You are eligible to move in two months. Signed—AF personnel assignments*

Oh, that is just f—ing perfect. I slammed the laptop closed and stomped off to rest before dinner.

I curled up in bed and clung to Woffins and Penny, trying to quiet the ghosts in my head. My marriage would never survive a yearlong separation. Deployments take such a toll on marriages. I remembered the early days.

Our wedding day had everyone crying with joy, as Kent's small home-town of Mineral Wells, Texas, came to watch us marry. His parents and brothers were such gracious folks and loved me dearly. We made a hand-some and powerful couple. I still laugh at our honeymoon night, when Kent left the hotel key in the outside lock of the door—lucky for us that his mis-chievous brothers did not know where we were.

When we were stationed apart in our second year of marriage, with Keegan on the way, Kent decided he had had enough of the Air Force. He got hired by a major airline and this allowed him to follow me to seven bases, enduring ten moves, and stay employed. Military spouses have a difficult time maintaining professional careers. Kent stood by me through all the ups and downs of military life. He remained my biggest fan and supported me during the roller-coaster ride of a female aviator's career. We had finally made it in the Air Force, but the last two years had strained our family.

I realized that it was not only my daughter's birthday, but tomorrow was Mother's Day.

"Happy Mother's Day, Kim," I whispered to my reflection in the mirror as I brushed my thin hair and dressed for a dinner party given in the gen-eral's honor. Tomorrow, he would relinquish his authority to Bremer. That night, after dinner, the guests gathered around the table and began to sing.

"Happy Birthday to you. Happy Birthday to you. Happy Birthday, dear Katie. Happy Birthday to you."

The host of the dinner party brought out a chocolate cake in honor of my daughter. It was all I could do to hold back the wall of tears that threat-ened to cascade down my face. I looked over at Garner. He winked.

CHAPTER 21

Test of Wills

"What an arrogant j—," I whispered, as we rushed to make the aircraft before it left us in Kuwait.

"No, Kim, give the guy a chance," urged our historian, Dr. Gordon Rudd.

I knew I was being unfair. Ambassador Paul Bremer had answered the call of the president just as General Garner had. Who the hell was I to judge this man? It didn't matter who replaced Garner, however; I wasn't going to like him.

After we flew out of Kuwait and landed in Basra, Iraq, we took a windshield tour of the town. Then we continued on to Baghdad in our Special Ops C-130 aircraft with its blackened windows and sophisticated defensive systems. Both Ambassador Bremer and General Richard B. Myers, the chairman of the Joint Chiefs of Staff, were on board. I ended up sitting across from my Pentagon flight surgeon, who was traveling with the chairman. It was the first time I had seen him since I had deployed more than three months earlier. The doctor grilled me about my excessive weight loss and pale skin tone and eyed my trembling hands. I teased him that Iraq had a great weight-loss program and pretended not to hear his warnings over the loud engine noise. Wanting to escape his assessing medical eyes, I walked toward the front of the bird.

There in the galley stood an old classmate of mine from Naval Command and Staff College days, when we were both majors. Randy was now a colonel, the commander of the Special Ops group out of Hurlburt Field, Florida, and the command pilot of this flight. "Small world," he said loudly as he came over and hugged me.

"Randy, come meet General Garner!" I yelled. We walked back to where Garner was sitting.

"Sir, I've heard a lot about you. It is an honor to finally meet you," Randy said. The general just smiled at the Air Force colonel.

I told Randy I was avoiding the flight doc. He nodded knowingly. "Come up front." I climbed into the cockpit and visited with him for the remainder of the flight across Iraq.

When we landed at Baghdad International Airport, it was midafternoon. The ambassador smoothed his dark black hair and straightened his tie. He wore desert combat boots with his suit and a flak vest under his starched white shirt. Surrounded by his black-vested protection team, he sauntered off the ramp of the C-130 toward a sparse press corps. He stopped briefly for a photo op and said a few words before moving on. Garner walked on Ambassador Bremer's left side, giving him the position of authority on the right. The general had relinquished his power during the twenty yards we walked to the cars.

Garner and I moved to our waiting SUV, but the ambassador insisted that the general ride with him in a large, special-order, armor-plated, goldcolored SUV. It was the same one that Garner had refused to get near when the offensive vehicle arrived earlier in the month.

"Save it for someone who thinks he needs this protection," Garner had commented.

Now, he was forced to ride in it.

"How's it going?" Hector asked, as I climbed into our SUV.

"It's tough," I answered.

That evening we held a staff meeting at 2000 hours to brief the new boss on the status of the rebuilding efforts in Baghdad. Bremer made bold statements about shooting looters on sight and the staff shifted in their seats. I watched Garner and the military commander clench their jaws. *Yeah, right. Sounds aggressive in the confines of the Green Zone. But can you imagine a young Army soldier shooting an unarmed man in front of his young son because they were stealing a chair?*

Coalition forces had lost control of the looting immediately after the war and now we were into damage control. Every time we would get some critical infrastructure components fixed or a building repaired, looters or saboteurs would disable or destroy it. The number of military personnel was simply inadequate for the rebuilding effort.

Instead, large defense contractors brought in a tidal wave of foreign security workers to protect their employees and guard their sites. The rapid influx of private security firms introduced a span of control issues for the new staff. Without protection, though, civilians could not go out of the Green Zone and construction projects would sit dormant.

Security remained the number one problem for all the leaders, but without more manpower, every decision had to be weighed as a risk-benefit choice. The next morning, Garner held a meeting with the senior military and ORHA leaders. There, he reemphasized the eleven issues that were now most important to address. In addition, Garner publicly praised Ambassador Bremer. He assured his fellow generals and the ORHA staff that he'd support the transition and would work here as long as the ambassador needed him. The staff seemed to relax at his words. I knew better.

Every day that week, I received several positive press articles, including an excerpt from *Congressional Quarterly.* The pieces praised Garner's efforts in Iraq, but the damage was done. He was looking for a way to leave with grace and self-respect, but while he remained in-country, there was no slowing down. Every morning at 0730 Bremer held a staff meeting. By 1000 hours, Garner was out of the palace and didn't return until later that night.

One evening I sat in Gordon Rudd's room. Garner wasn't feeling well, and Gordon and I had promised him we would patrol Baghdad later that night and report back. I took a swig of warm beer and gulped the bitter liquid. I could almost feel the alcohol enter my brain cells. Gordon sipped his scotch and declared, "Baghdad is not big enough for the two of them." I nodded. He smiled. "But Iraq is."

I respected Gordon. He lived in the room next to me and traveled a lot with us. As I mentioned earlier, it was Gordon who suggested that I keep my own personal notes during our mission—the notes that later made it possible to write this book. Now retired, Gordon W. Rudd, a former Special Forces officer, was a professor at the Marine Corps' Command and Staff College and had also been Garner's historian during Desert Storm. This time, he had left his teaching position in Quantico, Virginia, to follow the general back to Iraq. A dignified man, Gordon looked like a college professor, with gray hair, sympathetic eyes, and a gentle nature. He was always scribbling in his composition book, interviewing people, and studying events with a curious expression. I had sought his counsel on a few occasions; he was smart and kind and he knew Garner well. Tonight, as I sat on the dusty floor, I wanted his booze and advice.

"What more can we do for him?" I drained the beer and threw the empty can across the room. It rattled in the trash bucket.

"Let's get him out of Baghdad for a while. It helps Bremer establish his authority and we get General Garner out of the city. He can be Bremer's man on the street, winning the hearts and minds, taking the message to the people."

"Hmmm, what message would that be? Bremer will just step on Jay's toes. I don't know, Gordon. That doesn't work in the Air Force. The much-loved military commander always leaves the scene when the new boss comes in."

"Yeah." He glanced at his watch. "Come on, it's time to go."

It was 2300 and the curfew was being enforced. Gordon and I drove around visiting the MP checkpoints. Sometime around midnight, we heard gunshots a block away and rushed to investigate. As we rounded the corner, two dead bodies lay sprawled on the pavement. Under the bright lights of the checkpoint, I could see a third body slumped out of a car, red blood seeping into a tan shirt.

"What happened?" asked Gordon, the historian.

"Sir!" yelled the tense MP. "Yes, sir, we were attempting to disarm these civilians and they failed to respond to our signal." The young soldier was shaking as the adrenaline pumped through his veins. "We gave them several warnings, but they refused to comply with our orders." His baby face was flushed and covered with sweat.

"So, you had to defend yourselves," Gordon, the officer, interjected. I couldn't tell if it was a question or a statement.

"Yes, sir!" barked the nineteen-year-old American boy, dressed in fifty pounds of battle rattle and gripping an M-16. For a moment, he looked like my son.

We stared in silence at the dead bodies still oozing blood. It pooled on the concrete road and mixed with the dripping oil from the car. The night air smelled of smoke, dust, and sewage. The other MP held up an AK-47 he had pulled from the trunk of the car. I felt no emotion at this gruesome sight. *Have I become so jaded and numb that a five-minute-old death scene does not faze me?* I glanced at Gordon, who patted the young man on the back. He said, "Good work, soldier. You probably saved lives here tonight." The MP flinched.

"Thanks, sir." His youthful face grew solemn as he looked at the dead bodies and slung his gun over his shoulder.

When we got of earshot, I challenged our historian. "How can you say he saved lives, Gordon? You don't know if that's true."

"You're right, Kim, but that young soldier needs to believe it's true."

I had much respect for Dr. Gordon Rudd.

Was he right? Did the U.S. troops save lives tonight? Was there a deeper meaning in the fact that these Iraqis would risk death instead of surrendering their weapons? What were we risking? Gordon and I climbed back into the SUV and drove on through Baghdad, a quiet, dark, and deadly city.

CHAPTER 22

Testimony and Last Letter Home

The morning of May 13 was a disaster. Garner held a meeting with the senior generals and members of the CPA staff. (With Bremer's arrival, ORHA had been renamed the Coalition Provisional Authority, or CPA.) Fifteen minutes into the discussion, Bremer's deputy interrupted the meeting and said the ambassador would like to visit with one of the Army generals. Shortly after that general had excused himself, the deputy returned to request that another general leave. This continued until all the generals and most of the senior civilian leaders were gone. The only people who remained were Garner, a couple of mid-level staff members, and me. Garner rose from his chair, dismissed us, and marched straight to Bremer's office. I heard the large wooden door slam and Garner's loud voice echoing in the very room that used to be his office.

Ten minutes later he reappeared and spit, "They can live without air-conditioning. What they can't live without is security." I was not sure what Garner meant, but I assumed this new leader was predominantly concerned about his personal comfort. The next day a small construction team sealed off Bremer's office and a few surrounding offices. They ran ten-inch ducting from small air-conditioning units outside for Bremer and his staff. Next, they installed a metal detector and posted guards outside the office doors. The military Joint Task Force staff constructed their offices on the other side of the palace and required a special badge to gain entry. So began the transition to the CPA, with Bremer and his staff sealed up on one end of the palace and the military support structure sealed up on the other. The rest of us continued working in the heat and the dust.

Late that afternoon, I escorted the general into a room set up for a video telephone conference (VTC). He would be addressing the House Committee on Government Reform's Subcommittee on National Security and answering a list of questions they had sent.

I leaned against the wall out of camera range and chewed on a fingernail. We had worked on the testimony all night long. I suppressed a yawn.

The communication technicians sat against the window. Perspiration stains spread on their brown T-shirts as they watched the signal strength. I had bitten their heads off for losing the satellite signal during Garner's speech to President Bush and his cabinet earlier in the week. The highlight of that VTC was when Ambassador Margaret Tutwiler popped her head in front of the camera and announced to the president of the United States, "Look what a month in Iraq does to your hair." I nearly fell over laughing. I liked Margaret. Today, there was no comic relief.

The Military Radio Satellite (MRSAT) system picked up signals from communications satellites orbiting the earth. When one moved out of range, another was supposed to appear. But when the signal jumped to the new satellite, our reception would often drop off, requiring several minutes to reacquire the new satellite. I had told the technicians I would have their asses on a plate if they didn't fix this problem. The general was not a patient man these days, and he did not care about the limitations of the communications equipment. They had devised a plan to have two signals running off the MRSAT, hopscotching the reception. That way we wouldn't lose the signal as this testimony was being taped back at the Pentagon.

The atmosphere in the room was tense. It was also brutally hot.

"Let's get this over with," Garner demanded. I laid his testimony on the table, signaled to the technicians, and pointed at the camera. I knew Garner was suffering from blinding headaches. I begged him to take the IV solutions to rehydrate; it was the quickest way to rebalance the electrolytes in the body. With temperatures at 120 degrees, you simply could not drink enough water to recover once you got dehydrated. It would take two more days and my threat of calling his wife before Garner let the medic give him three bags of fluid.

"Sir, just read the words," I instructed.

"I know what to do, damn it," he grumbled under his breath.

"Yes, sir." I pulled away, my face growing hot with embarrassment.

As the general began to talk, I could see his shoulders were tight and his cheeks ruddy. He had a death grip on the paper and his glasses slipped down on his nose.

> *Mr. Chairman, I want to thank you for arranging this session today. I regret that I am unable to testify in person to you and your committee, and I would say that were I able to be in Washington I'd do so. But to be honest with you, there's no place I'd rather be right now than in Baghdad. . . .*

> *I'd like you to take two points with you. One is there is no humanitarian crisis. Now, there are humanitarian issues, and there are some serious humanitarian issues. This organization we have over here will work through all of those. But the crisis that was predicted . . . never materialized. We are very fortunate there.*

> *Second, we arrived in Baghdad three weeks ago today with ten people. In those three weeks we have gone up to over eleven hundred people. Since that time, a lot of things have been accomplished.*

I gazed out the window to the dust-filled sky. I thought about the previous morning's staff meeting, during which Ambassador Bodine had gone on a ten-minute tirade. Her other outbursts and public berating of several colonels had the military leaders tight jawed. Garner had even spoken with her about her leadership style. "You have made it, now be the queen," he advised, but her behavior remained the same.

In her tirade Barb predicted an uprising from the Iraqis if we could not accelerate the rebuilding and economic development; she accused the Army of not supporting the rebuilding efforts; and she cursed the ORHA military staff for their ineffective and inefficient management (she, of course, was part of the civilian contingent). She expressed frustration with just about everyone in the room. The fact was, we were all frustrated at trying to accomplish a peacetime mission in an environment plagued with conflict. Her blue eyes burned at the end of her speech. You could have heard a pin drop. *That is one way to get your point across,* I thought. I liked Barb and wanted her to succeed, but my efforts to help her had failed, and after we arrived in Baghdad, she grew distant. When we adjourned the meeting, Garner called me over and gripped my arm.

"Get Powell's office on the line," he ordered.

"Sir, you don't . . ." I closed my mouth when I saw his cold, decisive look. A voice echoed in my head, *You have to know when to sit down.*

"Yes, sir."

I dialed the secretary of state's office, handed the satellite phone to Garner, and walked away.

Today, Barb was packing. The ambassador was being recalled to the State Department for a special assignment.

I brought my focus back to the general as he continued his testimony. "In both the north and the south today, many of the Iraqi people have more electric service than they've had in the last twelve years. In fact, in the town of Basra they have electricity twenty-four hours a day for the first time ever. Only in Baghdad are we really suffering from electrical shortages which are below pre-conflict levels."

The heat in the room was unbearable. I think I dozed off. Garner expounded on Iraq's hospitals—now functional, but in need of reliable electricity—the distribution system, the cell phone service, and the security environment. The general took a drink of water and I suppressed another yawn. He shifted in his seat, wincing in pain, but forged on. I wrote in my notebook, *Call Connie.* "The Iraqi people are highly educated and their technocrats are extremely skillful. Their doctors are very good, their engineers are very good, their law people are very good, their administrators are very good."

A helicopter flew low over head and rattled the windows, and the technicians looked at me. "It's okay," I mouthed. *Let them hear that we are in a war zone.* Garner described our plan to refurbish the city's convention center as the Iraq Forum, a center where international organizations and non-profits could work and coordinate their efforts with the Iraqis and the coalition. Then he returned to the issue of security. "As you'd expect, we're encountering some barriers in getting assistance to the Iraqi people. The primary barrier is security. It's still not a permissive environment. Every day it gets better, but right now, in order to move people to the ministries, I have to have two MP vehicles move with them. They have to wear body armor. They have to wear Kevlar helmets because it's not safe out there."

That was putting it mildly, I thought. It was important to get the real story out and not rely on media reports.

Garner pressed again to lift the UN sanctions on the sale of Iraqi oil. Without oil sales, the pipelines and storage tanks would stay full, preventing further oil refining and its vital by-products of fuel oil, LPG for cooking, and gasoline. "If the situation does not change quickly," he said, "one of the most oil-rich countries on earth will find itself in a fuel crisis."

The general concluded, "This will be a democratic society. And what we're doing here, the success we have here, will—I predict to you—change the whole Middle East. If we fail, it will change the whole Middle East in a way we don't want to see happen. So with the people we have here, with your help, we'll get this job done. God bless you. Thank you very much."

The testimony was over. He paused and looked up. The technician shut off the camera.

"We're done, sir." I patted his shoulder.

"I feel like I need to take a shower," he responded, shrugging off my hand. "Let's go out tonight," he ordered and rubbed the bridge of his nose.

"Yes, sir," I answered, in an exhausted tone.

I found the boys at dinner in the crowded chow hall. As I approached the noisy table, the men stopped eating. Derick was not there, so I addressed Johan. "The boss wants to go out again tonight."

They looked around at each other. "What?" I heaved a sigh.

Johan cleared his throat. "Ma'am, not to be disrespectful, but is there a purpose to these nightly drives around Baghdad?" I could feel the anger rise in my throat, but I inhaled deeply.

The table grew quiet. "All right, what's on your mind?" I demanded, pulling out a chair and straddling it.

"Colonel, we have much admiration for the general and you. . . ."

"Yeah, yeah, what's your point?" I interrupted.

Johan glanced at Hector. "But we believe. . . ." He looked to the group for agreement; they nodded. "We believe the general is trolling for a fight. He goes to the most dangerous parts of the city with no military escorts. It is like he wants to draw fire. We have seen it before. When a great man falls from grace, he invites injury or death."

I sat, stunned, my mouth dry. "This is what you think, that General Garner wants to die? Have you lost your fucking minds?" I spat through gritted teeth. The men froze and stared down at their plates.

Johan flinched, but he pressed on. "Please, ma'am, why patrol Baghdad? It is craziness. We don't visit any U.S. troops. There's nothing to see after midnight. Besides, these Iraqis know our Suburbans, and it's not worth the risk." He drew a long breath. "We have families, too. Why do you think no one else but you rides with the general anymore?" he finished in a whisper.

I jerked back the chair and leapt to my feet. "You listen up. We pay you to protect us and if this mission is too tough for you *boys,* then I suggest you quit. I'll find someone else who's not afraid." I stomped off, my face hot and tight. They had struck a nerve.

Trying to calm down, I marched about the compound. Garner's anger with life, my inability to make it better for him, a discontented ORHA/CPA staff, and now an open rebellion from the bodyguards was more than I could take. I found a vacant wall and sat on it. The concrete was so hot it burned through my pants and stung my legs. I jumped off and kicked the wall several times. *Shit, shit, shit.*

It was less than five minutes before he found me. Even in the shadows, I knew his walk.

"Listen, colonel, we have a problem," Derick started.

"I'll say," I said, my voice thick with sarcasm. "My job is to support this general and his staff and if he wants to patrol the streets of Baghdad, then we'll patrol the streets of Baghdad. The last thing I need right now is a psychological evaluation of my boss from a bunch of South African mercenaries."

I could see Derick's jaw clench as I let loose on him. "You better get your men in line. I do not appreciate having to convince people to do their jobs around here. And another thing, the vehicles are trashed out. Your guys look like hell—half the time you all don't bother to shave. I saw Louis and David shoving each other outside the bank yesterday. How the hell do you think that looks to the Iraqis? And you'd better get Cecil to drown his sorrows in something else besides rum. I can smell him a mile away."

My face burned and perspired, but it felt good to unload. "We work our asses off eighteen hours a day, trying to keep everyone focused on the mission, and now some snot-nosed political hacks think they can do better. Well, they can knock their socks off. General Garner is working miracles, given the odds against him and the lack of support from the very people who sent him here. *That's* craziness!" I yelled, my voice quivering. I turned away.

In the thirty seconds of silence that followed, a machine gun echoed in the distance. "I understand," he whispered. I spun around to see a face void of emotion.

"How the hell can someone like you understand?" I glared at him.

His look grew dark and he leaned into me. "Ma'am, we are afraid of nothing and we will take you and the general to hell and back." He exhaled and chose his words carefully. "But this is about *our* families."

I gritted my teeth and broke eye contact.

His voice was flat. "We've been working for two weeks with no contract. The men don't worry about money; they worry about life insurance. Right now, we have none."

I threw up my arms, "Jeez, this is just what we need. We can't even keep our security team paid long enough. This is so screwed up. Have you talked to the contracting guy?" I knew the answer before he spoke.

Derick grimaced. "I tried. He says it is not his problem."

Of course it's not his problem; his fat ass never leaves the Green Zone.

"Remember, we're subcontractors. This is between us and the prime. We have seen no renewal contract or a company representative. This is about protecting our families."

Self-conscious, I looked at the ground, my anger completely spent. "Two weeks. Why didn't you say something?"

"You have much on your plate." Derick's voice softened. "Our team voted to continue to work for the general even if we don't get paid."

I leaned against the hot wall. *So much for worrying about loyalty.* "Your guys must think I am such a witch."

For the first time he smiled. "No, we think you are a great person. Like General Garner says, 'an angel.'"

"Well, an angel shouldn't lose her temper. I'm sorry; it's so unprofessional." I pulled my fingers through my dirty, sweat-drenched hair.

"It's okay. We've seen you pee in a field," he teased.

"Shut up!" I gave him a friendly shove. "Okay, Derick, let me see what I can do." I walked back to the palace feeling the weight of the day on my shoulders. Time for some help.

"Is that what the South Africans said?" asked Garner's chief of staff. A fellow lieutenant general and his friend for thirty years, he had been coordinating with the coalition military force on behalf of the ORHA organization. He was the only general I felt safe confiding this information to.

"Yes, sir," I answered, rubbing my palms together and tapping my foot.

"I'll talk to him," promised the tall, well-built general with gray-streaked hair.

I sat there and blinked several times.

"Don't worry, I won't tell Jay you said anything." He had read my thoughts.

"Sir, we just don't want to send him home in a body bag."

"Or you," he replied.

We did not leave the palace that night. Instead, I finished my third and final letter home.

13 May 03

Hello from Baghdad,

        We have been in Baghdad three weeks. Our first
impressions remain our lasting impressions—Iraq is
a country of contrast and complications. As hard as
we try, this is a most difficult process. I would
offer that the military action tends to be easier
when compared to the challenges of rebuilding a

nation. So, what makes this so difficult in Iraq you ask? Well, several assumptions we relied upon in our prewar planning proved untrue in postwar realities.

The number one issue for Baghdad and greater Iraq is and continues to be security. Now, if you talk to a military type, security is okay. There is no Iraqi army to speak of, few people are taking on the coalition forces, and we can move freely within the city. As a military commander, you'd be satisfied with the security situation. Now, talk to an Iraqi in the city and security is out of control, because to them security is about law and order. Looters still threaten neighborhoods and office building. It seems every time we get something up and running, looters, or better yet, saboteurs, destroy or steal items. Carjacking is an everyday occurrence and people are fearful of the gangs that are forming. Who is responsible for law and order? Well, the police are, but most of them ran away. We have hired new policemen, but there are training requirements, we must develop an officer corps and teach these people about civil liberties, humane treatment, and basic human rights. The police are very afraid of the Iraqi population and will only do mounted patrol and only with US forces. Instead of spreading out our forces we consolidate them and in a city of 5 million, it is not very effective.

One might ask, so why not give the law and order to the US forces? The 3rd ID fought up and into Baghdad and to be honest they are tired. They do not want to do foot patrol. They probably believe it is not worth the risk and are in a defensive posture. Besides, they are a heavy division and tanks are not appropriate for patrolling cities. We went out the other night for 2 hours and did not see one policeman and only 4 soldiers. The second problem is that even if we catch looters there are no jails or court systems to send criminals through. So you see our problem: no security, no safety for

workers; no workers, no rebuilding or establishing
the structure; no rebuilding, no economy; no economy, extremists emerge. What is the answer?

The DoD leadership is sending 4,000 light in-
fantry soldiers to help with patrols. We are planning on swapping some of the 3rd ID forces. We need
to begin a disarming program and become very aggressive about the looters and saboteurs. A curfew
is in order, but there is no one to enforce it. We
try neighborhood watches and grassroots programs,
but they do not take hold because of the central-
ized, top-down mentality this country was subjected
to by its recent leadership.

There is some good news in all this. We have
electricity and water to places in Iraq that never
had it. We have more oil than we can store (gasoline and LPG is a by-product of oil production,
because we have no oil production we have gasoline
shortage). Pictures of long gas lines in the rich-
est oil country should shame the UN into relieving
sanctions so they can sell off the excess oil. We
are paying the $20 emergency payments and standing
up the Ministries to run the country. We held elections for the university presidents and the students are going back to school next week to
complete their exams. The city of Baghdad is beginning to provide services such as garbage removal,
emergency services (911), and traffic cops. . . .

Tonight we are having the third meeting with the
leadership with Iraq. These groups represent Kurds,
Shia, Sunni, clerics, tribal leaders, and Christians. They are beginning the governance process to
establish an interim Iraq authority. An explanation
of how that is going is a whole other letter.

I so enjoy hearing from you all. We should be
out of here by 1 July and I am looking for a job. My
dream would be to guest lecture at the war colleges
in the military and other colleges that would be
interested.

By the way I ran into Col Jeff Smith in a
bunker in Tallil AP during a sandstorm. His unit was
grounded for weather. The NWC grads are everywhere.
     Kim Olson
     Col, USAF

A couple of days later, I received an excerpt of a question-and-answer session with Secretary Rumsfeld and handed it to Garner. He handed it back. "Read it," he ordered and coughed several times. His mood had not improved.

"FYI, thought this might be helpful. Please share as appropriate," I began. The transcript continued with some comments about the microphones. Then came the first question.

Q Good afternoon. I'm Menno Kampoese. I have a question for the Secretary of Defense. Can you elaborate, because there's some confusion, about the return of General Garner to Washington and arrival of Ambassador Bremer to Baghdad?

A I'm trying to think when it was, think it was late last year, the President, the Vice-President, Secretary Powell, and I talked and we asked General Garner to undertake a task of beginning to prepare the ground for a post–Saddam Hussein Iraq and the kinds of reconstruction and humanitarian activities that might be necessary in the event that there had to be a conflict, which we hoped would not be the case.

Jay Garner, God bless him, agreed to do that and left his business responsibilities, came into the Pentagon, began that work, did a superb job. And at the time he did it, we talked and agreed that he would not be able to stay at it for an extended period, and that he recognized that it made sense to have a senior civilian serve as the presidential envoy in that post at some point in the future.

"July," Garner interrupted. "They were supposed to give me until July, bastards." I waited. The general waved his hand for me to continue.

He then, when the conflict ended, went to Kuwait, in fact, I think before it was even over and began the process of getting ready to move into Iraq when the environment was sufficiently permissive. He has done a superb job; there is just no question about it. And this nonsense in the newspaper is unfortunate. It's unfair to him.

I paused. The general rolled his eyes.

It's unfair to the process. It is terribly confusing for the people of Iraq. This is an outstanding American who is doing a spectacular job for this country.

And I know that Ambassador Bremer, who the President selected for that civilian post, is a first-rate individual. I've known him. The Vice-President's known him. I know he used to work with Henry Kissinger years ago. And he will do a terrific job.

Jay Garner has agreed to stay on during the transition period and assist in that process. And for that, we are deeply grateful.

So, they're both first-rate individuals. The articles suggesting that Jay is being replaced by somebody for some reason [are] just plain not true.

"HA!" Garner laughed, rubbing the bridge of his nose. I cleared my throat and continued reading.

This was part of the concept when we first began this process, and I'm personally deeply grateful to Jay and Jerry Bremer for undertaking this service to the country.

"It has a quote at the end of the signature, want to hear it?" Without waiting for Garner's response, I continued. "It says, 'For none but the shades of Cavalrymen dismount at Fiddler's Green.'"

"Do you know what Fiddler's Green is?" Garner asked.

"Yes, it's heaven," I answered.

The general looked at his drink. "Yeah, the ballad of the U.S. Cavalry begins

Halfway down the road to hell,
In a shady meadow green,
Are the souls of all dead troopers camped
Near a good old-time canteen.
And this eternal resting place
Is known as Fiddler's Green."

"The secretary said some nice words here," I said, upbeat. "I think Margaret and Larry were working the phones late last night."

"It's too late." He shuffled to his room to get his bag.

I followed him. "You know, some famous king once said it is just as important how you fall from power as it is how you rose to power."

"Kimmer, that was Louis the Sixteenth, and he got his head chopped off." I wanted to tell Jay I knew how he felt.

CHAPTER 23

Why Iraq?

"I am so dead." Static filled the void on the phone line. For the first time in our nearly twenty years of friendship, my best friend had no plan or words of encouragement for the face-shot I had taken from the chief of staff of the United States Air Force.

That was two years earlier—my second year at the Pentagon. I stood right at the threshold of the next level of command for an Air Force officer and pilot. I was ready, I had earned it, and it was time to take group command. It had been just within my grasp.

I hung up the phone with Nancy and let the reality of the previous afternoon replay in my head.

My foot began its nervous tap as I remembered how, not quite twenty-four hours earlier, I had cradled this same phone to my ear. It was late afternoon, 1600 hours. Two rings. "Colonel Olson, OSD legislative office; may I help you?"

A woman's brisk voice replied, "Colonel, please hold for General John Jumper."

"Sure," I responded in a confident tone. Like the chief of staff of the Air Force, one of the most powerful four-star generals on earth, charged with leading an organization of half a million people and equipping them with the world's most expensive, sophisticated, and lethal weapons, usually called me on a Thursday afternoon.

It could happen.

I had been working some tough Air Force budget issues on the Hill with the defense appropriation committee members. I'd been successful in keeping money for some of the Air Force's critical programs. For a brief moment, I thought General Jumper might be calling to give me a small pat on the back. The thought was fleeting.

"Colonel Olson?" His low voice boomed through the receiver. I leaned away from the earpiece.

I answered with a cheery "Hello, sir," still hoping for an accolade.

"I got a call from your boss," he barked. *All right, here it comes.*

My smile froze and the blood drained from my face at his next words.

"I don't need your boss calling to tell me you're unhappy with your assignment."

"What?" I grunted, as if punched in the stomach.

"You'll go where the hell the Air Force sends you. You got that, Colonel!"

"Of course, sir. I. . . ."

"You need to keep your mouth shut, get off the net, and let the system work. We'll decide to take care of you. Don't make me question your loyalty."

My stomach twisted in a knot and my throat constricted.

"Jeez, sir, I bleed blue. I am honored to be on the commander list. I'll go wherever. . . ."

He cut me off in mid-sentence.

It was clear this was a one-way conversation—a monologue, not a dialogue. I listened in stunned silence for the remaining sixty agonizing seconds.

He continued his harsh lecture. The shock of it all rendered my brain useless. It was all I could do to get in a "Yes, sir" when he stopped to take a breath a couple of times.

I wanted to fight back, to scream, "NO, YOU'VE GOT IT ALL WRONG!" But the voice in my head cautioned. *Don't make it worse. Just take it, Kim. He's not interested in any explanations.*

I squeezed my eyes shut and drew in a deep breath.

"Do I make myself clear?" Without waiting for a response, a sharp click ended the call and my career.

I sat there with the dial tone humming in my ear, then let the phone slide from my sweating hand. I felt light-headed. Bile rose in my throat. I coughed several times in an attempt to keep it down. That lasted about five seconds.

I sprinted out of the office, barged into the rest room, and slammed open the stall door. I dropped to my knees just before vomiting my entire lunch and small remains of breakfast into the toilet. Tears streamed down my face and I gagged again, but nothing came out. Gripping the toilet seat, I closed my eyes and willed my heart to stop its rapid pounding. A searing pain cut through my chest and throat. The overpowering smell of vomit mixed with urine and disinfectant made me gag a third time. I spit out sour saliva. Reaching out, my fingers wrapped around the cool metal handle, with a shaking hand I flushed the toilet. A swoosh of water drowned out the groan that came from deep within me. Through watering eyes, I watched the swirling brown-yellow mess disappear and be replaced with clean water.

It's gone! Twenty-two years, gone.

Large tears dropped into the bowl and rippled the still water.

Oh my God. All the sacrifice. All the work. All who believed in me.

I spat out bitter saliva.

Everything—gone. Please God, this can't be happening. It just can't end like this.

But it had. *The most sickening part is—have I done it to myself?*

My legs protested, cramped against the hard tile floor. I sank back against the stall wall. A chill washed through my body. I drew up my knees and leaned my damp forehead against them. Then I banged the back of my head against the wall in three rapid hits.

Stupid! Stupid! Stupid! What had I been thinking?

My civilian boss had asked me what I really wanted for an assignment, and I had told him. How could I have misread his interest and let down my guard?

Three months earlier I had made the group command list. This was the big time. I was one of only six women aviators and among the top 1 percent of the colonel force who made the command list. Now the placement to command jobs was in full swing.

The grapevine had it I was matched with a command assignment to a base in Hawaii. Hawaii! Who wouldn't love an assignment to Hawaii? Sun, surf, sand—the kids were excited. My sister and her family were stationed there and they were thrilled we might join them. My husband and brother-in-law even talked about buying a boat together.

Everyone was happy—everyone but me.

The command assignment to Hickam was away from the primary airlift mission—away from the core mission of the Air Force, flying aircraft. In my mind, Hickam was a sleepy base that only served as a replenishment point to the Far East. I wanted to command an operational aircraft group. I wanted a tough, no-shit flying mission. Without command of an operational flying group, I believed I could not compete against my peers; my career goals would grind to a halt.

Historically, women had only commanded in the training or nonoperational jobs. The last thing I wanted was a typical "girl's job." Besides, commanders out of Hickam, Hawaii, did not get promoted to general or continue to influence the future of the Air Force. I wanted to lead troops. I wanted the power to shape policy and effect change. I wanted to make a difference for both men and women. I wanted to make a lasting impact. *Well, I'd made an impact, all right.*

When my boss, a powerful political appointee, had asked me what I really wanted to do, I told him in my cocky tone, "To command the biggest and most demanding flying group in the Air Force!" I knew full well that only colonels promoted to rank six years ahead of their peers and sponsored by the most powerful Air Force generals got those plum command jobs. I had neither. However, I did have a boss who was the number four man in DoD, charged with responsibility for the entire military budget of $480 billion. He could make or break a service's programs with the sweep of a pen. The services and his office had a love-hate relationship, each needing the other to make DoD's gigantic budget palatable to the authorizers and appropriators on Capitol Hill. Military generals treated him with caution and disdain, as they did most political appointees in OSD.

I knew this next command assignment was pivotal for me in achieving bigger things in the Air Force. I was ready. When given the chance, I had proven I could play with the big boys. I could stand toe to toe with them and excel in everything—flying jets, commanding troops, and even working in the complicated world of the Pentagon. My passion to make a difference, to influence the Air Force and to lead its people, burned in me.

Did my desire to succeed drive me too far? What had worked so well throughout my career and in the operational world had just failed miserably in the building. My boss, thinking he was helping, had blown through the delicate maneuvering required to secure military command jobs and had gone right to the head guy. He had seen nothing wrong with telling General Jumper exactly what he thought.

Instead of helping, those efforts had landed me on a bathroom floor, with the ghosts of my past popping up before me like a cheap carnival shooting gallery. All those who had made my Air Force life difficult came to visit me.

The cigar-chomping commander: "I told you women had no place in the Air Force."

Male pilots with accusing fingers in my face: "Told you women couldn't handle combat."

Senior officers: "Women can never lead men."

The faces of my children appeared, asking that haunting question: "Mom, do you have to leave *again?*"

Anguish, pain, and disbelief suffocated me. My head ached.

I had come over the table and fallen flat on my face. And now it was five minutes before the weekly staff meeting, a meeting I dared not miss. I combed through my tangled hair with shaking fingers and pressed my damp palms against my cheeks. I didn't look in the mirror as I washed and rinsed my mouth. Then I shuffled on trembling legs into the briefing room.

Dazed, I sat through the crowded staff meeting. I watched the mouths moving, but I couldn't hear a word. It was like being under water. All noise was muted.

The only voice was in my head. *This can't be happening. This can't be happening.*

I fixated on a ragged fingernail and tapped my foot. Someone from far away was calling my name. I looked up, trying to mentally surface and find the speaker.

"Kim!"

"Yes, sir." My eyes focused on my boss's proud, grinning face.

"I called Jumper for you." His chest puffed out.

I nodded. "So I heard." I wanted to slap him, but he really thought he had helped.

"What's the matter?" His frown cut a deep furrow across his brow.

"He called me." I shifted in my seat, aware that twenty pairs of curious eyes stared at me.

"Well, what did he say?" His smile widened.

Clearing my throat, I leaned forward and whispered, "Can we talk about this after the meeting?" The twenty pairs of eyes glanced away.

"Sure," he said, grin all but gone.

In the culture of the Air Force, it was an unforgivable sin. It is one thing to battle the military system by breaking into the all-male world of flying. It is another for a political appointee to try to influence your command assignment, whether you asked for it or not. It simply was not done.

The best operational command assignments were made by generals— not just any generals, but three- and four-star generals. It was one of the few functions generals had total control over without meddling from civilians, congresspeople, or the public. They guarded their right to choose who would lead the Air Force in the present and the future. Anyone who interfered with their game plan would get cut off at the knees.

As my boss described it to me later, the call probably would have been okay had he just told General Jumper I was doing a great job and left it at that. But, thinking he was doing the right thing, he didn't stop there. No, he had told the general that I had better get a good assignment, and the Air Force had better send a good replacement for me, because these jobs in OSD were really important—a sentiment General Jumper probably did not share.

The truth really didn't matter now. General Jumper obviously thought I had put my boss up to it. I had crossed the line. No matter how good my record, no matter how much I wanted to serve, no matter how much I was willing to give—I had suffered the same fate as any officer who appeared self-serving and tried to game the system.

To complicate the matter, the timing of my boss's call could not have been worse. The Air Force had just lost the lawsuit brought by Lieutenant Colonel Martha McSally challenging the requirement for military women to wear abayas when they went outside a U.S. base in Saudi Arabia. The issue pointed to the double standards the military forced on its female members. After much debate and embarrassment to the Air Force, the leadership had reluctantly changed the policy. General Jumper must have perceived me as another female challenging the system and moved to crush any dissension in the ranks. One day after my boss tried to help, I received the career-ending phone call. From hero to zero in less than twenty-four hours.

I was never awarded a group command, nor would my name appear on a command list again. I had been blackballed by the Air Force leadership.

My boss might have felt guilty that his call destroyed a career. If so, it didn't show. But I was a professional, and I continued to work hard for the office. I may have fallen on my face, but I wasn't giving up, and my boss knew it. It was in my third year at the Pentagon that the deputy asked me to work with General Garner and the emerging ORHA staff.

Here was a chance to do something on a big scale—Iraq. If I deployed on this dangerous, important mission and did a great job, then the Air Force would have to let me back into the fold.

But the Air Force leadership was not impressed with our efforts to rebuild Iraq. It seemed no one was. The message about the remote assignment to Korea proved it. I wanted to tell General Garner I knew the heartache of failing to achieve your goal.

CHAPTER 24

Safe

Although he had asked, I never told Garner the story of why my career came to an abrupt halt. It didn't matter. The transition with Ambassador Bremer was not going well. He was dismissive of the progress the ORHA team had made. "He doesn't listen," came the comments.

Bremer did not listen to Garner, and why should he? The president had picked him and he had his marching orders. Within a week, against the advice of both Garner and the CIA station chief, Bremer dismantled the Iraqi Army. Garner and others had been working to reorganize it into a defensive force and use some of the professional troops as police officers. Bremer then fired the very civil-service workers whom Garner had coaxed back to work to help run the Iraqi ministries. Bremer also implemented a blanket de-Baathification policy that insulted a majority of the senior leaders in Iraq. The final blow came when he dismissed the Council of Seven with a wave of his hand, basically telling them, "I'm the government of Iraq."

The speculation in newspaper and online news articles was that the Pentagon's favored expatriate did not want to share his power base; when Garner established the Council of Seven, he complained to the Pentagon leadership.

The leadership then accelerated Garner's removal and announced Bremer as his replacement, effectively making Garner a lame duck leader.

Within five days of his arrival, Bremer had fragmented the ORHA (now CPA) staff, pissed off the U.S. generals, and angered a large number of Iraqis. These actions gave credibility to those who opposed the coalition occupation, and the insurgency gained momentum. Garner took it personally.

I was trying to get Garner out of Baghdad and away from Bremer. So we took another trip to Al Hillah, about sixty miles south of Baghdad. I planned a visit to the ancient city of Babylon just to give Garner a break. The entrance was a blue painted archway into another time. Bab-il, meaning "Gate of God," was etched on a bronze plaque. The crumbling ruins still held their majestic beauty and impressive architectural forms. This city was at its greatest in the year 580 BC Under the rule of Nebuchadnezzar, the magnificent complex was said to be seventeen miles long and the center of culture and civilization. Our tour guide explained that "Iraq was rich in historical significance."

Pointing south, he continued, "Mesopotamia was the suspected spot known as the Garden of Eden. Ur is the birthplace of Abraham. Predating the Babylonian era by about two thousand years was Noah, who lived in Fara, a hundred miles southeast of here. In northern Iraq was the vast Assyrian empire. They were known to be warriors, so the first wars were fought there, and the land has been full of hostility ever since." The elderly man ended his narrative on a note of sadness.

We had seen the ancient city of Ur on our journey to the Tallil AP. The building traditionally identified as the birthplace of Abraham consisted of a brick house with an archway, said to be one of the oldest arches in the world. It is truly amazing that the architects of early biblical times could construct such a structure.

Equally amazing was what we saw now within the Babylon gates. The Baathist regime had built directly over the ancient ruins and flooded the rectangular moat to replicate the original city. Although that accelerated the deterioration of the outer walls, many of the interior buildings remained intact.

The walls were constructed of mud, straw, and a tarry substance to hold the mud bricks in place. They had stood for thousands of years. Bulls and antelopes decorated the walls, standing fifteen feet high. It took four bricks to form each animal and they were thought to represent fertility and strength. I ran my hands over the rough surfaces that had been constructed before Christianity or Islam. The stories these chambers could tell.

By the end of our three-hour guided tour through the ruins of Babylon, the harsh heat had sucked the strength from everyone. Garner's face was sunburned and he nursed yet another throbbing headache. He finally accepted the medic's advice to take the IV solution we had been pestering him about, but not before he barked out instructions for me to explore the local market square. I was to assess the security situation and judge whether the economy was recovering.

"Start with the shopkeepers," he ordered as the IV dripped into the long tube. I had to wait for the evening because the Middle Eastern sun drove Iraqis into their homes all afternoon. Their towns lived at night; most stores opened around six and closed after midnight. Later, when the sun went down, I ventured into town with two translators and four bodyguards in two SUVs.

As I wandered through the township, I encountered sidewalks lined with wrinkled men sitting in dingy plastic chairs. Smoke from unfiltered cigarettes swirled above their heads as they sipped warm, sweet tea from thin glasses. The sleeves of their white robes flapped as they argued and laughed. In the street, teenage boys wearing tattered brown sandals played tag or kicked a weathered soccer ball.

I approached both groups and made friends with the help of my digital camera. I coaxed individuals into posing for me while I snapped their pictures and revealed their faces a second later in the tiny window display. Some children and adults gathered around me, pointing in amusement at their frozen expressions in the photos. It was fun to entertain the group with a simple camera and modern technology.

I strolled down a crumbling walkway with a small crowd in tow. An American woman shopping in their stores was probably a first for this town. The news of my presence spread quickly, and the bodyguards grumbled about the number of men gathering across the street. I ignored their concerns and was drawn into a store by the lingering aroma of warm bread.

It was a closet-size shop with a small window through which customers ordered their bread. In the corner, fifty-pound bags were stacked to the ceiling, and flour as fine as talc drifted in the air. A blazing brick oven dominated the back wall. Young Iraqi boys with sweat-stained shirts kneaded the dough into pita-sized forms. Puffed bread came out on a large wooden paddle and steamed as it tumbled into plastic bags.

I inhaled the rich smell of baking bread and let its aroma take me back to my grandmother's kitchen. For a moment, I was there in her red farmhouse in northern Iowa. The delicious Iraqi bread melted in my mouth, and before I knew it, I had eaten several pieces, savoring both the bread and the memory. The young bakers grinned playfully as I snapped their pictures. I smiled back, content with the simple scene before me—a baker and his family providing food for the local town. Iraq was going to be okay.

With my stomach full, I pulled myself from the bakery and strolled down the narrow sidewalks. By now, half the town was trailing behind me. I peered in several storefront windows and settled on a drapery stop. As I peeked in, an array of colors exploded before my eyes. Burnt red, chocolate brown, sunflower yellow, and navy blue bolts of fabric decorated the walls. I recognized the hum of a sewing machine as a young man fed the material under the pulsating needle.

I relaxed again to the familiar sound of the machine's hum. It pulled me back to my grandmother's small sewing room, just big enough for the Singer machine and my bed. A basket of colored threads and a box with paper patterns sat stacked on the floor. I stood in the doorway and watched my grandmother's wrinkled fingers push the fabric and her foot create the rhythmic motion of the treadle. She smiled at me and held out the dress she was making. It was yellow with small white flowers.

It should have been a pleasant memory, yet a sense of foreboding overwhelmed me. I steadied myself against the shop's center pillar as a sudden wave of dread passed through my chest. Shaking my head, I concentrated on the stocky Iraqi man who boasted of the numerous drapery orders he must fill. He had inherited this store from his father and business was good because after the war, looters had stolen everyone's curtains. I listened to him elaborate on the different fabrics and styles.

As he pointed out his wares, my eyes moved toward a green drapery that dominated the corner. It hung from ceiling to floor like a waterfall of stagnant pond scum. The shopkeeper followed my gaze. Trying to impress me with his client list, he bragged that this drapery was a special order for one of Saddam's palaces before the war. I nodded my head. I was not surprised. It represented all that was vulgar and ugly about Saddam's regime. Like all of Saddam's palaces and furnishings, it was purchased at the expense of the Iraqi people.

The fabric reminded me of the bottom of the water trough when I would forget to fill it for the farm horses. I tried to think back to the farm, where I was free to ride and explore life in the cornfields. I labored to recapture that memory, but whatever pleasant feelings had lingered were now gone. I forced a smile at the shopkeeper.

In an instant, my world shattered.

The store's front glass window exploded in an onslaught of gunfire. Bullets slammed into the concrete walls, sending biting particles around the shop. I tucked behind the concrete pillar and plastered my back against it. The roar was deafening, and time distortion took effect, making everything appear to move in slow motion. I had heard stories of pilots in emergency situations experiencing this sensation, giving them the illusion that they had all the time in the world. I watched the back door open and shut in what seemed like ten minutes as the employees made their escape. I thought of following them, but I didn't know what might await me beyond the door. Bits of white plaster from the walls erupted as bullets grazed them, falling like snow to the floor.

Hector's six-foot-four frame burst through the front doorway as he returned fire with his AK-47. "Stay behind the pillar," he yelled over his shoulder between the bursts, then disappeared. His voice snapped me back to real time.

No shit! I squeezed my eyes shut. Screams echoed outside and I dug my fingernails into my palms. *What had happened to my safe world?* I blinked to see the shop deserted, except for the green drapery, which swayed as bullets brushed it. Taking on a life of its own, it leered and slithered toward my feet. I kicked at it. *Get away! If I get killed, they damn well better not put you over my body.*

Tires screeched at the store entrance and Hector came back through the door. His dark, intense eyes burned into mine. I gulped. *My daughter! Oh God, she's only twelve—I was twelve when my dad died. I wore that yellow dress with the white flowers to his funeral. I can't leave Katie without a mother.*

"It's okay," Hector mouthed. His bearlike hand grabbed the back of my neck and buried my head in his chest. Using his body as a shield, he enveloped me. With my feet barely skimming the floor, he dragged me across the room like a rag doll. Bullets continued to whistle above our heads and ricochet all around. I could feel the concussion pinch my skin as the bullets slammed into the walls. I went rigid, expecting a barrage of hot piercing metal to rip me open.

Engulfed in darkness, I felt the night air change as we exited the store. Hector and I plunged into the back seat of the Suburban, just as the driver gunned the engine. My back slammed into the seat belts as Hector's body fused into mine. I bit my lip to keep from crying out. Arms wrapped around waists, legs intertwined, and my face buried in the center of his chest. I was pinned in the back seat, completely covered by this man. Breathing hard, I could smell the sweet tea, the bread, and, somehow, our family farm on him. As we raced down the highway, the shooting faded and stillness set in.

Wrapped under this 220-pound body, I was content. Amid the danger and the dance with death, there was something very calming in being rescued and protected. The fact that this brave young man was willing to die to save me aroused a deep longing. As his solid body covered mine, love radiated from him—or was it my imagination? I clung to him, pulling his shoulders close. His hipbone pressed into my belly. I gasped for air, then shuddered against his chest. Was it terror, relief at being alive, or grief from long ago that washed over me? I didn't know, but a deep, animal groan escaped my throat.

Appalled as these feelings bubbled to the surface of my consciousness, I released my grip on Hector's shoulders in an instant. Seconds passed. Still pinned under this rescuer, I felt the blood pound in my ears and my left foot begin its nervous tap against the floorboard.

"Hec?" I questioned in a hoarse voice.

"Kim," his warm breath stroked my temple. His body lightened, shifting ever so slightly from protector to admirer. He had misread the cue. *Oh no! No, don't do this.* His fingers widened against my waist and squeezed my flesh. My face grew hot and I struggled. I struggled to suppress the vulnerability. I struggled to regain control. I struggled against the helplessness. *Get up,* my mind screamed to him, *get up!*

Helpless, vulnerable, and out of control—it was too much.

"GET UP, GODDAMN IT!" I screamed. My fingers clawed at Hector's biceps, shoving him away. He lunged back as if he'd been electrocuted, and retreated to the far car door. He had just saved my life and I had hurt him with my reaction. Gathering myself, I slid to the opposite side and pressed my cheek against the cool glass. I inhaled and bore down, forcing my hammering heart to slow, and those painful memories back into the sealed compartment where they belonged. *Breathe, just breathe,* I told myself.

I cast a sideways glance at Hector, his face twisted and contorted as though I had slapped him.

"Sorry, ma'am, I . . . " he stuttered.

"No, no, it's my fault. I . . . I panicked; it was hard to breathe." I wanted to lean across the darkness that separated us, to pat his forearm and say, "Hector, you saved my life—thanks for keeping me safe." But the words caught in my throat. His troubled face searched mine. I looked past him as we sped down the highway. My father's death had shattered my world, just like the bullets shattered the shop window. Some memories don't fade away.

Home. . . . I wanted to go home to the warm smells, the comforting sounds, and the place I belonged. But that world of my childhood was gone forever.

I stared straight ahead, numb and unaware of anything around me. Then Hector's rough thumb reached out to catch the single tear that slid off my jaw. He cupped it in his hands, as if to hold it like a captured butterfly. We huddled in silence, each in our respective corners, holding onto a memory.

CHAPTER 25

Men

I caught up to Hector at dinner the next night. His face flushed, and he was clearly uncomfortable in my presence. The previous night's encounter had changed our relationship.

"About the other night," I began in my take-charge voice.

"We must not speak of it." He looked down and kicked the ground with his foot.

Men!

"Look, Hec, I didn't imagine that." His silence answered my suspicions. "Hec, look, I've got a younger brother and I miss him terribly. You are so much like him. You can treat me like your older sister and I'll think of you as my younger brother. That way, we can express affection and concern without . . . you know."

He looked at me like I was speaking Chinese. "Say again?"

"Hector, we can't deny there is an attraction, but we both have a mission here. We both work for General Garner and you keep us alive. It is the best way to frame this friendship. Brother." I pointed toward him. "Sister." I pointed to my chest. *Besides, I am old enough to be your mother.*

He certainly wasn't the first man to think he had fallen for me. After two decades of flying and deploying with men, I knew the signs. Some are subtle, others blatant. When I was a T-38 instructor pilot, a young student named Bob had a crush on me. I had been tough on him from the beginning. He was the kind of student pilot that the harder you pushed, the harder he tried. We formed a unique bond. The night he received his assignment to the C 130—a prop-driven cargo plane—he got toasted, really staggering drunk. He stumbled up to me at the officers club and flopped an arm over my shoulder. He smelled of beer, cigarettes, and overused Brut deodorant.

"You," he pointed his bottle of beer at me, "are the s-s-sexiest wo-man I ever met."

I wiped his spit from my cheek. "Yeah, right, Bob, now let's go find your buds."

"No, really. . . ." Pulling me to his tall lean frame, he leaned in to plant a kiss on my lips. I turned my head. His mouth rested on my ear. "I would kill for you, ma'am."

"That won't be necessary." I patted his back, looked over his shoulder, and searched the crowd for his classmates. They materialized at his side.

"We'll take him, ma'am," they said, pulling Bob's arm from around my neck. Pilots take care of one another when they get too drunk. They cover each other's six.

"Nooooo. I love this woman," he slurred as they dragged him away, arms outstretched to me. I shook my head and laughed at the silliness of the exchange.

I had heard of students becoming infatuated with their instructors, but I was so strict with my students. Maybe for that very reason, I liked the reputation of being a "Hammer." How could a guy fall for a woman who had yelled at him, scolded him, grilled him, and demanded 100 percent every day? I was not a nurturing instructor, but I did care for my students and wanted them to succeed. I decided I would pay more attention to the impact I had on men.

Get them in a box, was the solution. If I was to survive the advances of men in the military, I needed a way to stroke their egos and protect myself. I had heard the stories of senior male officers preying on junior female officers. Military pilots drank a lot in the early days of my career. Many women found themselves in strange beds with flyboys after a night at the officers club. I was determined not to fall victim to decisions I would regret later.

Within the Air Force world of flying, certain officers club bars had reputations for being wild. On the weekends, pilots would take cross-country flights to those bases so they could pick up women in the bars. That was the game pilots played—hence the term "players." Joc night at a base near Sacramento, California, was notorious for wild women and wild drinking. The Auger Inn in San Antonio, Texas, boasted of dancing bears (strippers). The Nellis bar in Las Vegas, Nevada, the site for advanced combat fighter training, was the most dangerous from a female aviator's perspective. Throughout the 1980s, it was the last bastion of male dominance in the flying world. There were no female fighter pilots and most military men wanted to keep it that way. When a female flyer walked into the Nellis bar, she took her life and her physical safety in her hands. I always went to Nellis with very large men in tow. Fights broke out in my wake on several occasions. The arguments centered on whether women should fly in combat. I rarely backed down, but when beer bottles came slinging across the room, I made a hasty retreat. "Live to fight another day" was the classic pilot motto.

When some notorious male pilots went on temporary duty (TDY) to other bases for flying or training exercises, they transformed into different men. A devoted husband and father of three became an alley cat on the prowl. Inhibitions, judgment, and accountability went right out the window. Picking up women and drinking to excess dominated their nights and bragging about their escapades was a ritual.

The rule was, "Whatever goes TDY, stays TDY." Translated, that meant that whatever happened during a TDY tour was never discussed or revealed at the home station. I found it difficult to watch my fellow pilots hustle women in a bar one weekend, then go to one of their houses for dinner with the wife and kids the next. I didn't buy into those traditions.

Women did more than break the barrier surrounding the previously all-male world of flying; we changed it. In the early 1990s, alcohol lost its glamour. Barhopping slowed and the aviators' behavior improved over time. When women rose to leadership positions, they refused to tolerate promiscuous and irresponsible conduct from their troops. As a squadron commander, I, too, held mine to high standards.

At one point, one of my young copilots informed me that a married pilot was visiting local prostitutes. This presented a real problem. Not only was it against military regulations for an officer to hire a prostitute and commit adultery but his behavior could also prove deadly; 75 percent of these women were HIV positive. This called for some shock treatment. Instead of holding a commander's call and lecturing my 125 military personnel on morals and proper conduct, or threatening punishment, I called in the doc. Our squadron's flight surgeon, Captain Blane Tuft, was a quiet, gentle man with a calm demeanor whom my aviators respected.

"Today, we are going to talk about sex," the doc announced as he approached the lectern. Nervous giggles danced around the room. The troops were slumped in their seats and looked ready to fall asleep.

"This is the penis of a man with STDs, if left untreated." A large, purple organ with nearly black testicles flooded the screen. The troops' heads snapped up as if they had been stung, and low groans replaced the laughter. *Now we've got your attention.* The doc continued on for an hour, each slide worse than the previous one. From my vantage point in the back of room, I could see that the men were getting the message. They squirmed in their seats and looked at each other in disbelief as the pictures unfolded before their eyes. Some even covered their faces at the final picture of skin sloughing off the back of an AIDS victim.

"Questions?" Dr. Tuft looked around the room. You could have heard a pin drop.

The slide show had quite an impact. The troops talked about it for months, and it appeared that the trips to the local call girls stopped.

Moving Hector into a "brother" role was a piece of cake. However, true families are never created, they are born. By its very nature, our pretend family would not last long.

CHAPTER 26

The Bags

Men are pigs. It was the only thing I could think of as I surveyed the grisly scene. The area was filled with scattered garbage bags. From a distance, it looked like a typical dump, but barbed wire and Army soldiers surrounded this one. It turned out to be not a dump, but a graveyard.

Each bag contained the skeletal remains of someone's brother, father, son, or uncle, buried for more than ten years. Their relatives had begun digging them up with their bare hands soon after the war ended. Now the U.S. Army was determined to rebury the unearthed bodies. Off to my right, a bulldozer idled and coughed gray smoke. The bags made a soft clapping sound as the hot wind blew across this field. Women clad in black abayas cradled clear plastic garbage bags and rocked as they wailed. Iraqi men in white clothes wandered aimlessly. The men from the ORHA leadership team and the bodyguards remained beside the cars.

"You guys coming?" I asked. They shook their heads no. The scene was too much, even for these combat-hardened Army veterans and the guards. Stepping across the wire fence, I waded in among the graveyard of bags. On closer examination, the skeletal remains were curled in the fetal position.

A typical body had a blindfold around its eye sockets, hands wired behind its back, and a bullet hole in the skull.

As I drew near to one of the Iraqi women, she raised her tear-stained face and cried out. I hesitated, then met her sorrowful eyes. She reached for me and I squatted down, pulled out a tissue, and offered it to her. She grabbed my hand and kissed it. I leaned over the bag she cradled, wrapped my arms around her, and whispered, "I'm so sorry." I glanced down and saw that the bag contained the small bones of a child. She sobbed out words I couldn't understand, but there was no need. Grief is a universal language. We rocked together for only a moment, and then I untangled myself and stood up. I blinked away hot tears. I'd seen enough. Rage seared every cell in my body.

With clenched teeth and narrowed eyes, I stomped toward the vehicles. The men parted to let me pass, exchanging worried looks at my silence.

No words could convey the seething anger that boiled within me. A million people were killed after the failed uprising against the Baathist regime in the early 1990s. America had just walked away from the Shiites in the south and left them to die horrific deaths. (The no-fly zone that my squadron had supported did protect the south, but it was imposed years later.) They were shot or buried alive in ditches they themselves were forced to dig. Others were bound, gagged, and executed in front of their families. Some were burned to death in cramped buses. The butchery at the hands of men went on and on. I wanted to scream at someone, "How could we have let this happen?"

No one spoke as we returned to the hotel. When we arrived, Johan moved to help me out of the car. "Don't touch me," I hissed. He flinched and blushed.

I stomped over to the Euphrates River and paced along the bank like a caged animal. Incensed, I screamed across the flowing river, "What do you want from us?" But I knew it was the wrong question. Garner would be gone in two weeks and there was nothing I could do. The strong current of ancient water offered no answers. I started heaving stones toward the other bank, and each splash was swept away in the swift undertow. I threw rocks until the tears blinded me and streamed down my checks.

I was physically and emotionally exhausted. My skin had blistered in the heat, my curly hair fell out, and my hands were always trembling. I was tired. Tired of traveling, tired of sweating, tired of this wretched place. Mostly, I was tired of men. In hindsight, I recognize the killing field wasn't really about gender; human nature itself was to blame. But that's not how I was thinking that day. *It was always about men. What they wanted, what they needed, and what they would do to get it. They used force, laws, religion, money, power, and repression to control. Men were cruel, ruthless sons of bitches.* It seemed as though I had battled the darker side of men my entire career, and now I knew why. I had witnessed what happened when men were left to hunt and kill at will.

Were we having no impact here in Iraq? I spread my arms out. *What do you want me to do?* I sighed and waited for the answers that did not come. A bird cried out in the distance and water trickled at the bank. A warm breeze tickled my skin.

Give me peace. But Iraq was no place to find peace.

I plopped down on the grass at the water's edge and buried my face in my hands. My shoulders wracked from the sobs. It was the first time I had cried in more than a year. My anger had turned to tears and I grieved for the loss of American soldiers, the loss of all those buried in the fields, the loss Garner was suffering, the loss of faith in a system, and the loss of myself.

I heard someone approach from behind. Without turning, I held up the palm to warn the intruder. His footsteps stopped. He cleared his throat and said, "Ma'am, I was sent to see if you're all right."

"I'm fine," I lied. "I am just fine. Now leave me alone." His mission was completed; his footsteps hurried away.

Great, now they will think I'm a wimp. Women cry when they're angry. It is something you men never understand. Pulling my knees into my chest, I continued to stare at the flowing river until the sky turned blue-gray. I could feel the sight of the river draining the anger and frustration from me. I began to hum an old hymn. Where it had come from, I didn't know. *When peace, like a river, attendeth my way,/When sorrows like sea billows roll;/Whatever my lot, Thou hast taught me to say,/It is well, it is well, with my soul.* My soul—it felt dead and scattered like those bags in the field.

Much later, a dark figure emerged from the shadows. I could hear him clear his throat. "Colonel, please come inside. They have a serious sniper threat here at night," came Johan's concerned voice.

I reached out my shaking hand and he pulled me up. A worried crease wrinkled his brow and he chewed on his lower lip. I brushed the grass off my pants, shoved my hands in my pockets, and glanced back at the dark, flowing river. "If anyone ever doubts why we're in Iraq, they should wade among the bags just once."

"Yes, ma'am. Wade among the bags," he murmured, and handed me a tissue.

CHAPTER 27

Ode to Jay

In the last week of May, we arranged a farewell party for Garner and the CPA staff. Most of Garner's senior staff had already left Iraq. As he drafted his letter to President Bush, I worked with some local Iraqi restaurant owners, a beer distributor, and a DJ to plan quite a party. It would be the first social event for the staff since we had arrived in Iraq six weeks earlier, and they deserved a break. It was supposed to be a surprise party for Garner, but he got wind of the festivities.

"I don't know what you're planning, but I'm not going." He sulked as he jammed clothes into his suitcase. His departure was scheduled for June 2, 2003.

"Sir, these folks left their families to follow you into this harsh place. One, you asked them to, and two, they believed in you. The least you can do is come down, say your good-byes, and thank them for their service." I pressed on. "The party starts at 1830 and I am coming up here at 1815 to get you. I'll be bringing the boys. You've got two choices. You can walk down, or they will carry you down, but, sir, you are going to that party." I softened my voice. "Sir, the transition is hard on the team, too. They need you to tell them it's okay."

"Call me Jay, and I'll think about it," he answered in a gruff voice.

I stomped out of his room. "I'll be back."

"I could just hide, you know!" he called out after me.

I spun around and motioned to the Gurkhas guarding the halls. "Do you really think you can hide from *me?*" I shouted back, and continued walking down the hall.

Men.

At 1815, I tapped on Garner's door and pushed it open.

"Well?" I asked with a slight smile.

"I'll walk, damn it," he said mockingly, and patted my back.

That evening, the staff, U.S. troops, the Gurkhas, local Iraqis, and even Ambassador Bremer paid their respects to Garner. The general's own words were elegant and to the point. He thanked the staff and asked them to support the new leadership team in its mission. We feasted on shwarmas, watermelon, flat breads, and sweets, washing down our meal with Heineken beer, scotch, and Jack Daniel's whiskey. We ended the evening by dancing and singing into the late hours. After four Heinekens, I staggered off to my room sometime after midnight. Johan emerged from nowhere.

"That was a good party," I slurred, as he led me up the two flights of stairs.

"Good party," he repeated.

I stopped and swayed. "Now what am I going to do?"

"Come on." He pulled me into my room and I sank to the bed.

As he bent down to slip my shoes off, he answered, "You'll be okay. God will take care of you."

"What do you ask God for, Johan?" I swayed to the side.

"A child," he responded in a soft voice, "and a chance to show you my country." (Within a year after leaving Iraq, Johan would get both his wishes.)

He pulled the sheet back, swung my legs around, and gently patted my damp forehead. I gripped his hand and held on for a moment. "Thanks for being there."

"You did a good thing tonight. Sleep well, colonel." Johan shut the door behind him.

I wasn't too sure about God taking care of individual people. I believed you took care of yourself; God just provided you with the gifts and the free will to use them. And where had my gifts gotten me—a has-been colonel who was losing her boss to the political whims of the administration? I sat up, reached for the bottled water, and washed down the self-pity that stuck in my throat.

The next morning, with a throbbing head, I finished Garner's civilian medal nomination package for DoD.

Lieutenant General (retired) Jay M. Garner is nominated for the Department of Defense Medal for Distinguished Civilian Public Service for exceptionally meritorious service and supporting the Department of Defense while serving as the Director, Office of Reconstruction and Humanitarian Assistance, Baghdad, Iraq, from 15 January 2003 to 5 June 2003. During this period, General Garner's leadership, dedication, and selfless service were the driving force behind the postwar efforts in Iraq . . .

General Garner accepted a mission that the United States had not attempted in 60 years—bringing democracy to people who haven't had it in over 600 years. To begin this daunting operation, he prioritized the key tasks needed to stabilize and rebuild Iraq. He immediately tackled improving security, restoring public services, and building confidence in a transitional administration.

Within three weeks, the Baghdad team grew from 10 to 1100 people. In a country the size of California with a population of over 23 million people, General Garner faced a nation that had endured three wars in the last decade and shameful neglect of basic human needs.

The story of his accomplishments took three pages. I concluded the citation:

General Garner has left Iraq a better place for him having been there. In the words of Secretary of Defense Donald Rumsfeld, Jay Garner is an outstanding American who did a spectacular job for this country. The distinctive accomplishments of General Jay M. Garner reflect great credit upon himself and the United States Department of Defense.

I forwarded it to the Pentagon staff. The president would award him this medal later.

Garner spent the last five days of his time in Iraq traveling back and forth from the northern border to Baghdad, with a final stop in Al Hillah. Following a dinner with the local Iraqis, a white-robed, dark-skinned cleric stood up and read a poem, first in the original language, then in English. This English translation was distributed to us so we could follow along as the older man read it.

A great man from a simple heritage grew.

As a young man, no one knew

That one day he would give breath to freedom,

That a people, long repressed, would look to him

And see themselves blessed.

This man sits among us tonight,

Representing not the might

But the compassion

Of a caring nation.

What currents of divine wind carried him

To this distant place?

Did he stand as one with Abraham at Ur?

And Nebuchadnezzar and Hammurabi at Babylon?

It matters only that he was here now,

When the need was greatest.

When our future was in doubt,

We looked beyond the carnage

And saw his light of hope.

We honor this man tonight.

We pray that God keeps him safe

As he wings his way home,

And we pray that he will sleep the gentle sleep

Of the blessed few who have

Touched the present and given life to the future.

The next day, Garner and a few officers from the former ORHA team made the final four-hour drive to Kuwait City. Riding down the dirt road, blinded by dust and sand, we wove our way through a fifty-truck convoy. We passed young boys selling AK-47 bayonets and small kids in torn, dirty clothes begging for water and food. As miles and miles of dead desert rushed by, I couldn't help but wonder, after six weeks in-country, *What had we accomplished?* I fingered the gold cross around my neck.

On June 2, 2003, at 1900, I stood at Kuwait International Airport and watched him walk away.

Before he turned to go, Garner hugged me tight and whispered, "Love ya, darling." It was the first time we had hugged. Sadness washed over me. But so did relief; I was sending him home alive. "It's been a privilege, sir," I said to one of the finest men I had ever known.

As I left the airport, a sudden calm swept through me. Later that night I wrote in my log: *It has been an experience to say the least. It is amazing to have worked with someone 18 hours a day for nearly three months. You learn all their ways and bend to them. Jay was always kind, yet demanding. He had been a general a long time, and this gave him the view that things just happened. We were an interesting team. I hope he remembers me with a smile. I know he will be in my thoughts.*

Maybe one person can make a difference. You just don't see it at the time.

I clicked the pen and closed the chapter on my military life. I knew then that it was done. I just couldn't say it out loud.

CHAPTER 28

Just a Routine Mission

The large chow hall clattered and clanked with the crowd of soldiers and contractors eating lunch. I hunched over my bowl, slurping the cold, bland broth. Colonel James S. Steele, U.S. Army (Retired), leaned over the table and stared down at me. "You ready to go on a mission with us?"

I nodded, spoon poised at my mouth.

"Be ready at 2330, sharp," he commanded. I watched him disappear into the crowd. Steele was an appropriate name for this tall, slender Texan with thick gray hair, a taut face, and piercing blue eyes. His hard expression spoke of the lessons learned fighting the drug war with U.S. Special Forces in the jungles of Colombia. Steele was a political casualty of Iran-Contra, which had cost him a general's star. Now, in retirement, he was fighting another war. Steele had shouldered the responsibility of training the new Iraqi police SWAT teams. Rumor had it the mission wasn't going well. From his strained demeanor, I guessed the rumors were true.

After Garner left, I worked for the Iraqi Ministry of Interior (MOI) as it tried to rebuild the police departments. The CPA was now completely in charge of rebuilding efforts in Iraq. For the past week, I had asked Steele to

let me accompany him on a SWAT training mission. I missed the excitement
of working on the streets of Baghdad. Steele's answer was always the same:
"This is no place for a woman." I would roll my eyes and explain all the reasons why a woman was an excellent addition to any team.

"No, no, no, the culture is not right for a woman. You'll get hurt, or you
might panic," were his other excuses. I was actually shocked at finally being
asked to join this elite, all-male team that included Emad, a heavy-set Arabic
translator who was the complete opposite of Steele. Emad was a bald, round
fireplug of a man with an outgoing personality and the gift of gab. Two
weapons specialists from South Africa were also on the team. Marc and
Jacque were tough men cut from the same mold. Marc, nicknamed "the Tas-
manian devil," had wavy black hair and wild brown eyes. He was all brawn.
His hands flew at a hundred miles an hour and he rushed everywhere.
Jacque, another short, stocky man, was quiet and an internationally
acclaimed expert sniper. Several young Iraqi police officers rounded out
the team.

I learned from Emad that tonight's operational mission might have a
special need for a woman. Earlier in the day, a distraught Iraqi father had
come in, begging the Americans to save his daughters. It was commonplace
in the days just after the war for Iraqis to settle old scores with their neighbors. Commanders were cautious about getting involved in private matters,
but the sixty-year-old man with a weathered face and a quiet demeanor
unfolded a sad story. Tears streaked down his cheeks as he told of his daughters' disappearance sometime after the war ended. Three months prior, the
family had sent his children to Amman, Jordan, for safekeeping. They never
returned. Convinced that Republican Guard thugs had kidnapped his young
daughters to force them into marriage, the father had scraped together just
enough money to hire a private investigator.

Soon, he discovered the location of his beloved girls. They were being
held in an apartment building in a poor suburb of Baghdad. At the end of
the story, the father held out a trembling hand. In it was a tattered piece of
paper with a scribbled address. Emad translated the father's final plea. "If
only the Americans would rescue my children, my prayers to God would be
answered." With that, the father clung to Steele's hand and began to sob.

Emad said Steele never flinched, but sat stone-faced during the father's
discourse. However, we both knew Steele would help this man, for he had
daughters of his own. So, at 2300 hours the SWAT team planned and briefed
this straightforward, routine mission. Yep, it seemed straightforward enough
at the time—save two Iraqi girls and return them safely to their father. From
my own military experience, I knew few missions go as planned.

At 2330 on the dot we drove into Baghdad's abandoned streets, still dark from the lack of electricity and still dangerous from the infiltration of armed gangs. The moonless night added to the gloominess that penetrated a city already thick with dust and smoke. Killing the headlights of the three Suburbans, we coasted into a cluttered back alley wedged between old apartment buildings. Gravel crunched under the tires. As soon as the vehicles stopped, the SWAT team piled out with the father in tow and sprinted toward a narrow stairway, guns raised and flashlights burning. They vanished into obscurity, leaving the car door wide open and the dome light shining on me like a spotlight. *What the h—! I can't believe we don't disengage those dome lights.*

I blinked. As my pupils constricted in the brightness, I caught the movement of several tall silhouettes materializing from hidden corners. Slamming the doors shut and pressing my body flat on the seat, I buried my face in the rough fabric. The smell of dirt puffed from the cushion. An eternity passed before the timer on the dome light switched off. My foot tapped nervously on the floorboard and sweat beaded on my forehead. I peeked out of the car window and held my breath. *This is not good!* The menacing silhouettes continued their advance toward the cars until sharp voices echoed in the darkness. Then they halted and faded back into the shadows. I exhaled, blowing fog on the window.

Alone and anxious, I slid on my flak vest and questioned my judgment in volunteering for this mission. *Why hadn't I brought a weapon? Didn't think I needed one with those specialists and Iraqi police around. I hadn't planned on being deserted.* My hands groped around the vehicle for anything to protect me. Bottled water—*nope, can't drown them.* Sticky candy wrap—*gross.* My fingers felt something cool and metal—*these men, they just leave weapons everywhere.*

Lucky for me, a lightweight MP-5 lay under a seat. This sleek black submachine gun could fire thirty 9-mm bullets in five seconds—it was absolutely lethal at close range. I stroked the barrel and could feel the safety aligned with the arrow. *Good, the safety was off . . . no, was it on? Crap! Sure wish I'd paid more attention at the firing range.* Who was I kidding? If I wasn't careful, I would shoot my foot off. I sighed and resigned myself to the fact that if I were attacked, I would have to swing the MP-5 like a madwoman, because I had no clue how to chamber a round. Sitting erect, I held the weapon against the window for any lurking Iraqi to see, and then cradled it in my lap. My fingernail tapped the cool steel barrel, making a sharp clicking sound. It broke the dead silence that enveloped me. I sat trapped, annoyed, and sweltering in the back seat of this vehicle.

Five. Ten. Fifteen minutes dragged by and still no SWAT team. *Damn, I can't believe I got left in the car. So much for needing a woman.* I craned my neck to scan the apartment complex, hoping for a sign. The gray, six-story structure looked abandoned. Many of the windows were broken, sheets of metal swung from the roof, and crumbling balconies protruded from the outer walls. The absence of electricity rendered the building lifeless, almost creepy. Although I could see small candles flicker inside the windows, it was the red glow of cigarette butts in the darkened doorways that concerned me most. They represented men watching and waiting.

Gray smoke from a smoldering trash fire just down the alley spread out like fog. I could smell the acidic odor as it seeped into the vehicle. Beyond the haze, silhouettes of children playing soccer darted across the street. I looked at my watch—half past midnight. *Those kids should be in bed.* I rubbed my itching eyes. The silence nearly suffocated me. *Come on, come on. How long does it take to rescue two women?*

Finally, I heard shouts. The SWAT team burst from the darkness. The car door tore open and I squinted against the momentary blindness caused by the dome light. Two dazed young women were pushed into the seat next to me. The irate father was close behind, scolding them in Arabic. Ignoring him, I patted the girls' arms and cheered, "We saved you! We saved you!"

My enthusiasm deflated the instant they sobbed, "But we love them." I widened my eyes at Steele, who crawled into the front seat.

"Seems we have a domestic situation," he growled through clenched teeth.

I glanced at the weeping girls. "You home wrecker, you," I whispered under my breath.

"Let's just get everyone down to the police station and straighten this out," he ordered. I suppressed a smile. *Just a straightforward, routine mission indeed.*

As we raced through town at 0100, my mind was miles ahead. They'll need a woman to straighten this out, all right. This mission was getting more interesting by the minute. As we bounced through the streets of Baghdad, the frightened women huddled together. "We are married," they repeated in broken English. "We love them." The father started yelling again and the girls clung to each other, whimpering at the harsh words he spat out. I had no idea what he was saying, but anger and disgust have a familiar ring. The woman closest to me whispered that her father was threatening to kill them. I spun around to our translator. "For crying out loud, Emad, tell that old man to *shut up!*"

In the silence that followed, I noticed the girls were wearing tattered house slippers and mismatched sweatpants and shirts. "It will be okay." I patted their arms, turned my eyes to the irate father, and stared at the back of Steele's stiff head.

"It will be okay," I said louder. No one spoke.

Fifteen minutes later, we arrived at the stucco police station with its four-foot-high cinder block wall that extended only across two sides. In Iraq, public buildings were rarely completed. Empty window frames lined the front of the station and a single lightbulb dangled in the doorway. Like most structures in Baghdad, it looked deserted, until two policemen wandered outside to greet Steele. The two alleged kidnappers were dragged into the building. The girls hurried out of the car and began to wail.

"Nooooo, we love them," they cried. They had good reason to panic. In Saddam's Iraq, if the police took you into custody, you were rarely seen alive again, unless you paid a steep bribe or turned in a neighbor for a minor offense. Even if you survived, the brutal torture you had endured would scar you for life. One of the girls started to faint, her eyes rolling back in her head. I caught her on the way down.

"Help me with her!" I yelled to Marc, before she hit the ground. He slung her over his shoulder and laid her in the back seat. Her sister crawled into the car and cradled her head.

"Shhh." I stroked her hand as she whimpered. "It will be okay." My heart ached for these young women, hauled out of their beds in the middle of the night by men with guns. First their angry father threatened them and then they had seen their mates get hauled off in handcuffs. I might have fainted, too.

"Please," the elder sister pleaded. "Our father has hunted us for weeks. Save us from him."

I was torn between protecting these women and respecting Steele's leadership decision. When Steele shuffled out of the police station, I could tell it hadn't gone well. It was a case of he said, she said. The men claimed they were married and had certificates to prove it. The father contended that the girls were lying to protect the family, because their "husbands" were Republican Guards whose friends would kill them all. Steele's dilemma was deciding which party to believe.

He called me over and leveled his cold, blue eyes at me. "Olson, I need you to talk to the girls."

"No kidding. It's not right," I replied, looking back over my shoulder at them.

"I know, I know. Let's just validate the girls' story. Talk to them. You're a woman, you're good at that," he declared, kicking an imaginary rock.

I wanted to challenge him. *Good at that? What's THAT supposed to mean?* But I held my tongue. "Roger that," I snapped, annoyed at the stereotyping, but glad to finally be of use. So, at 0130 in a rundown suburb of Iraq, I crawled into our Suburban, slammed the door, and switched on the dome light. I blinked and stared at the two nervous Iraqi sisters, knowing I held their fate in my hands. The artificial light bathed their smooth, pale faces and reflected fear in their liquid brown eyes, which were on the verge of tears. They smelled of sweet tea, sweat, and smoke. Both sisters recoiled from me and sucked in sharp breaths. I studied them for a full minute, and then asked my first probing question.

"So, how did you all meet?"

They exhaled audible sighs. "College," they answered in unison, their lips curled in slight smiles at the memory.

After thirty minutes of "girl talk," the intimate details these women shared convinced me they were not hostages, but indeed newlyweds. I learned that one of the sisters was a doctor of internal medicine and the other a geologist. They were in their early thirties and had met their husbands in school. It was an Iraqi *Romeo and Juliet,* a made-for-TV saga. The older sister explained that they had been dating in secret for more than nine years.

"Nine years in secret! Why?" I asked.

"Because under the Saddam regime, Christian girls didn't date Muslim boys," the older sister explained. "Iraqi laws forbid such relationships and our father was afraid of what would happen to the family if we were caught. He said no when we asked to marry, even after the Americans arrived."

"So, let me guess, you guys did what lovers have done all over the world?" I shook my head.

"Yes, we eloped. Iraq is free now and we have waited long enough," she whispered forcefully. Even in a closed vehicle, she appeared afraid to verbalize her thoughts.

Unfortunately, their marital bliss was temporary. When they called from Jordan to tell the family, the father demanded they return home immediately. After much arguing, they refused, and that is when their father threatened to disown or kill them. Honor killings are a harsh reality in the Middle East, so the husbands hid their brides in a cramped one-bedroom apartment in Baghdad. Both couples were trying to save enough money to move away and, eventually, buy houses. They had been living safely until tonight.

On the night of their three-month anniversary, the SWAT team kicked in their door, shoved guns in their faces, and unleashed their cursing father. After they had been jerked from their beds, thrown into cars, and whisked away to this police station, I wanted to ask, "So, how do you like Americans so far?" Instead, I stated, "I believe you."

"Thank you. I told you a woman would understand," the younger one said to her sister.

I understood, all right. There was no doubt in my mind they were married. Now all I had to do was convince Steele.

I left the women sitting in the car and strolled back to where Steele was leaning his head on the wall, staring at the sky. "Well?"

I followed his gaze skyward. "They're married."

"Are you sure?" he challenged.

I tilted my head, set my jaw, and jammed both fists into my hips. "They met in college, dated in secret, and eloped to Jordan. This is their three-month anniversary party. They're married, Jim."

He raised a palm. "Okay, okay, I figured as much. Sometimes you try to do the right thing and. . . ." His voice trailed off. I almost felt sorry for him—almost.

I patted his arm. "Yeah, we got sucked into this family saga. Well, look at it this way; you probably saved these girls' lives. At least you got to them before their old man. Now, someone's got to convince him that Iraq has changed and he needs to accept the marriages or leave the girls alone."

Steele nodded. "I can't get the husbands out of jail before morning."

"Morning? You should throw that father in jail—" I stopped.

We glared over at the father, cowering next to the car.

"Just give me a minute to impress upon him that hurting these girls is not in his best interest." With that, Steele marched away and whispered instructions to Marc. I watched Marc drag the father behind the vehicles. I later learned he had brandished his knife and thrust it against the man's throat, threatening to slit it if anything happened to the girls. It appeared this was a language the Iraqi father understood.

When Steele returned, I suggested we get the girls to a local Iraqi who had a safe house. He nodded in agreement. "We'll get everyone back home tomorrow. It's been a long night." Steele ran his long fingers through his short gray hair. Now I did feel sorry for him.

After dropping off the sisters, we drove back through the gloomy, vacant city. The car was quiet. I leaned forward to settle a score and slugged Marc in the arm. "You idiot! What the hell were you thinking, leaving me in the car all alone and unprotected!" He flinched at my assault and stammered in his thick Afrikaans accent. "Y-y-you was protected," he answered, keeping his eyes on the road.

"Really, how's that?" I demanded, leaning over the seat.

"Ma'am, I stationed Jacque on the balcony overlooking the vehicles. You was in no danger. Was the colonel in any danger, Jacque?"

"No danger," echoed Jacque.

Squinting my eyes and furrowing my brow, I conceded the point. "Oh. Good planning." Steele cupped his mouth with his hand, suppressing a smile. It was the first time I had seen him smile all night.

"What are you laughing at?" I pushed on his shoulder. "Leaving me like that. You guys were just lucky I was here tonight. Routine mission. *Ha.*" I sat back to gloat as the streetlights and guardrails flew past outside our speeding vehicle.

After a minute, I opened my mouth to thank Steele for including me. Before I could speak, his callused hand reached back and gripped my arm. "Seriously, Kim, I'm sure glad you were here tonight."

I smiled and squeezed his hand. "See, Steele, there's always a place for a woman." We both chuckled.

CHAPTER 29

Time to Go Home

Everyone has his or her limits. I had reached mine. After Garner left, I worked to integrate the former ORHA staff with the newly arrived CPA staff; to reduce and reorganize the Iraqi MOI; and to help the Ministry of Finance with building a program review process. I wrote award justifications and performance reports until my wrists ached. At one point, I worked for three different bosses, all demanding and impatient. It was too much. Exhausted, discouraged, and drained, I called Nancy, who was finishing her successful command tour in England.

"Something is terribly wrong with me," I whimpered to my best friend. I could get reception only on the satellite phone outside, so I hid behind a tree to make the call, ashamed of my tears.

It had happened over time. My hands trembled and wouldn't stop. The excessive weight loss, the acid in my throat, the sleepless nights, and the suffocating dread that gripped my chest—what was wrong with me? The adrenaline ride was exacting its price and that price was my health. It seems that not all casualties of war come home dead or physically injured; some return with other wounds. I had suffered mine. Maybe they came from witnessing traumatic events or coming close to death too many times, maybe it came from the unrelenting stress and the extreme physical environment. It didn't matter; the damage was severe.

"Get out of there," Nancy urged. "You have done your part. No one will question your leaving or your loyalty." I flinched at her words. "Your whole life you've taken care of everyone else. It is time to take care of yourself." I heard the logic, but I did not want to listen.

Later that night I curled up in a chair, drained and emotionally spent. A gentle knock rocked the door open. The electricity was out again and the room was lit with a dull flashlight reflecting in the mirror.

The protection team had been transferred to the MOI to train the Iraqi police force and to provide protection for the senior advisor to that ministry. I did not travel with them any more.

"Are you all right?" Derick's words were laced with worry. I rolled into a fetal position, trying to pull a blanket of darkness around me.

"Listen." He sat beside me, his face gaunt and anxious. "Go home. You don't belong here any more. You're like an exotic animal caged up. You'll die if you're not freed."

"You and your animals." I brushed away the tears. "Derick, I don't know where I belong."

"I know the feeling." He folded his hands as if to pray.

I sighed and studied the leader of the team who had kept Garner and me alive for a hundred days. In the colorless light of the room, his black eyes looked soft and sympathetic.

"Tell me again about the rhino," I whispered, wanting to change the subject.

He leaned forward as if he were addressing an eager student.

"First, I must dart the rhino with a powerful air rifle using a drug called atropine sulfate." He sighted an imaginary rifle across the room.

"It takes about six minutes to affect the animal. Then the rhino falls to its knees and over to one side. So, you sneak up on it and throw a towel over its eyes, but you must be careful, because you don't want a fifty-five hundred-pound animal to start chasing you." My eyes grew wide and he gave a half smile.

"Ah, but once the blindfold is in place, you attach a braking rope to one hind leg and a steering line to the head with a slipknot. Now we must move the rhino."

"But he is on his side," I declared.

"Yes, so I carefully inject a stimulant into a vein on his leathery ear. The rhino wakes back up and is helped to his feet, but he's still sleepy. The two ropes steer him to the open wooden crate. Once in the crate, we use a crane to lift him onto a truck." The shadow against the wall looked like a giant claw as he demonstrated lifting the crate with his hand.

"Before the truck drives off, I climb into the crate with the rhino and give him more drugs to lift him out of his daze. I also take off the ropes and the blindfold. Then he gets even more drugs to calm him down for the trip."

"You get in the crate with a rhino?" I asked, shaking my head. "Jeez."

He grunted and continued. "When we arrive at the other side, I wake him up with an antidote. Now he is totally alert and we open the crate so he runs free once again. All creatures should be free," he concluded, looking back at me.

"Why do you move them?" I asked.

"To save them from poachers," he spat, his face hard and distant. I flinched. "We also move them to a new game preserve when there is over-crowding," he offered.

"Wow, what an interesting line of work. You must like animals." I stud-ied the outline of his face and for a brief moment his compassion returned. Then it was gone.

Derick stared at the floor for a long time before he answered. "Better than people. I know what it is like to be trapped, Kim." He patted my hand. "But sometimes you must free yourself from the demons that haunt you; conquer them."

"Have you conquered your demons, Derick?" I asked, thinking back on the nightmares he had told me about.

"No, they come in the night and wait. This is why I do not sleep. Being a warrior has its own sentence." He paused. "I just don't know how to stop running. It cost me my family." He looked pained. "Kim, being here and see-ing what you tried to do makes me want to do something besides carry a gun. Can you help me?"

I studied his battle-scarred face and I appreciated his confession. These men whom I had developed a great affection for wanted a shot at a better life. I thought I could help them with that dream, but I was mistaken.

"Oh, thanks for saying that." I reached up to pat his shoulder and he gave me a hug. A sob caught in my throat. I swallowed it down.

So there we sat again, an Air Force colonel and a mercenary from South Africa, more alike than different.

It was time to go home.

Colonel Glenn Collins approached me a couple of days before my July 2, 2003, departure date. "We want to give you a party," he said.

"I'm really not up for it, Glenn." I sighed, my hands tucked deep in my pockets.

"Hey, Kim, you've done so much for everyone. You deserve a royal send-off. Come on, it'll be fun," he smiled.

"Where on earth would we have it? We're restricted to the al-Rasheed Hotel." Most of the staff now lived in a fifteen-story hotel on the edge of the Green Zone.

"Uday's disco," he joked.

"You're kidding!"

He wasn't. The night of the party, I walked into a room on the second floor of the hotel that took me back to the late 1970s. Scarlet crushed-velvet walls in quilted patterns surrounded the room. Hazy mirrors with thick gold frames hung on the walls. Cherry-red vinyl booths and black tables encircled the parquet dance floor. A large silver mirrored ball hung in the center of the room. The DJ's booth blared music through speakers that crackled. I could feel the bass in my chest. Multicolored lights bounced off the rotating ball, and smoke swirled among the soldiers crowded at the tables.

Iraqi waiters hustled around the room, carrying trays of canned beer and shots of liquor. I worked the room, thanking people for coming and toasting them with a swig of beer.

Glenn came up and hugged me tight. "Glad you came," he whispered. "You look nice."

I had put on makeup and it had stayed on for the first time in a hundred days. My skinny legs protruded from under a tan skirt Nancy had sent me; I had dropped three clothes sizes. My brown hair was soft with curls. "Who'd want to miss discoing at Uday's?" I chuckled. "Why, it's the hottest club in Baghdad!"

Had I come full circle from the officers club bars of my early days of flying jets? I surveyed the room. Tonight, I doubted any woman was worried about someone biting her on the butt. Most of the female soldiers had side arms. Now their concerns were the same as the men's—accomplishing the mission and staying alive. *Yep, things sure have changed,* I thought.

The dance floor was packed with soldiers in their tan DCUs and civilians dressed in khaki pants and T-shirts. They were drinking, laughing, and dancing to the rhythm pulsing through the room. It could have a bar in any U.S. city, but here we were in the middle of Baghdad, Iraq.

"Put your hands in the air, like you just don't care," the lyrics blared. Faces glistened in the bouncing lights and for a while they looked like they didn't care. Tonight, the young soldiers, old civilians, and tired officers moved and rocked to the disco beat. They didn't care about the frustration of the rebuilding efforts, the dirty guard posts, the long separations from their families, or the heat and dust awaiting them beyond this room. Gone were the disappointment, loneliness, exhaustion, and boredom. Tonight, they were just people having a party.

Right before midnight, Glenn grabbed the DJ's microphone and quieted the rowdy crowd. He called me up to the cleared dance floor as a hot bright light shone on my face. I squinted at the brilliant light and put my hands on my hips.

"We are here tonight to say good-bye to a great American, Colonel Kimmer Olson." He winked, and the crowd responded with the classic Army HOOAH! and loud applause. Fists pounded the tables and grunts rose from the crowd. "Hoo! Hoo! Hoo!"

Glenn continued, "For over four months, Colonel Olson has done a hell of a job and made our lives easier. You are truly awesome. Thanks for taking care of us." He lifted his beer over his head as the cheers continued. I raised my warm beer and toasted the crowd. *You all have done well,* I thought, but it felt good to be recognized.

Glenn bowed low and invited me to dance to the next song. I did not leave the floor for the rest of the evening. Some time after 0200, the DJ announced last call, shut down the rotating mirrored ball, and brought up the overhead lights. The drunken, loud crowd was in no hurry to leave. By the end of the night, my fingers ached from shaking hands.

When I collapsed in bed, the amber clock light blinked 0257. For the first time in three months, I slept through the night.

CHAPTER 30

Home

I stepped off the airplane at Dulles Airport. I had come home—home to my family, who met me with flowers and balloons. Kent's shocked face betrayed how bad I really looked. I was a walking skeleton with yellow skin and hollow eyes. My hands shook so badly that I couldn't grip the flowers. When my children hugged my skinny body, I winced.

Nancy had just returned from her command tour in England and was staying at our house until hers was ready. When she saw me, tears sprang to her eyes. "Oh, Kim, what have they done to you?" It was not the homecoming I had fantasized about some five months earlier. She took my hand and squeezed it. "I know the way out." I didn't understand at the time what she meant.

My first month at home was difficult. Adjusting to a normal family life, the time zone difference, and the change from everything I had left behind hit me with full force. At work, I was back at the Pentagon, assigned to an office overseeing Iraq policy in OSD. I was so sick that I was not very effective.

I was also trying to clear up some tasks I had been given by the leaders in Iraq: find soccer balls for the Ministry of Education, finish the award packages for the military staff, and help Garner with his after-action report.

I accomplished the first mission through the efforts of my neighbors. We gathered more than 150 donated soccer balls from our local youth league. Each team wrote messages on the balls with Magic Markers. These words from American kids to the kids in Iraq were heart-warming. I later found a company that would pay for the shipping expenses to Baghdad, and the balls arrived a month later.

Next, I worked on several Bronze Star and other award packages. Some of the enlisted soldiers' medals would take more than two years and several resubmissions to get approved, but I was determined to recognize those who had served our country during this difficult mission.

Garner's after-action report was still in draft form. Within a week of my return, the general and I met for lunch. He looked rested and relaxed; I was pale and emaciated. His concern was written on his face when I told him that Bernard Kerik, advisor to the MOI, had called and asked me to return to Iraq to help him with the police budget. Kerik, a self-made man, had started his career as a New York street cop and later became the New York City police commissioner. He, too, had endured the September 11 attacks and we shared a unique bond.

When we first met in Iraq, he had originally wanted me to be his executive officer. Garner discouraged the idea, mentioning that Kerik had stated he had come to Iraq partly to get more speaking material. I could not be sure of his intentions, so I resisted his request, but I offered to help organize the MOI as they hired people for that Iraqi ministry. Kerik worked hard at the MOI, but quickly got frustrated with CPA and left within three months.

"What did you tell him?" Garner asked.

"I told him I had female issues. That'll make him back off," I answered.

Garner laughed. It wasn't female issues, though; it was the overwhelming sense of dismay that gripped me for days. But I wasn't about to admit that to anyone, not even myself.

Garner asked if I would come down to Florida. "I want you to meet my family, and more importantly, I want them to meet you."

"Sure," I said noncommittally. By that point, I didn't have the energy to do much of anything.

I finally took leave for two weeks, but I spent most of my time in bed. One night, my daughter leaned in the doorway of the bedroom. "Mommy, I wrote you a poem." Twelve years old and on the edge of adolescence, she still looked angelic.

"Read it to me, sweetie," I coaxed.

She shuffled to the end of the bed and unfolded the wrinkled paper in both hands. "'Tears of a Lily,' by Katie Olson." She cleared her throat.

In the beauty of the meadow, so lovely and green,

Not a harmful word is spoken, nor a violent thing is seen,

Yet deep in the center, one sight is new;

Water falls from her petals, but it's not the morning dew.

Her little soul has been hurt, in this poor little flower;

She cries away her life and only gets sadder by the hour.

Her heart weighs sadder every day, till her voice no longer sings.

Her love and her kindness had left on a pair of wings.

The misery and the loneliness made her heart black with hate.

She no longer worries about her future or worries about her fate.

No flowers will be her companions, nor will the trees or the birds.

No creature will hear her lovely songs or listen to her wonderful words.

Soon the loneliness and the hate drives right through the heart,

And just like the cruel spear, it slowly tears it apart.

She wanders the forest sorrowfully, while all the other flowers stare.

The birds and the trees watch in horror as she runs into a wild mare.

All the animals hold their breath, thinking she'll soon be dead,

But the mare just smiles a loving smile, and pats her on the head.

The water that runs off her petals is now the morning dew,

And so there is a happy ending. You should make your ending happy, too.

Katie lowered the paper and her gray-green eyes looked straight into my soul.

Speechless, I pulled back the covers and patted the bed beside me. She crawled in next to me and snuggled against my body. I kissed her shoulders, inhaled her scent, and absorbed the sensation of her skin under my fingertips as I stroked her back. Her blonde hair fell around her shoulders and I kissed her flawless ivory skin. "Thank you, my daughter."

It was time to get help. I turned to the Air Force flight surgeon who had eyed my trembling hands three months earlier during that C-130 flight over Iraq. As I sat in his office, explaining my symptoms, he smiled with compassion.

"I can't seem to get over this," I admitted, struggling not to cry.

"No, you can't. You've hit the wall," he concluded. I rubbed the palms of my hands together and tapped my foot. His voice grew soft. "War takes its toll, Colonel. You'll get through this, I promise. Just let us help you."

I did. And he was right. It would take time, but eventually the nightmares went away, the sense of dread faded, and I would learn to accept what I could not change.

I did return to Iraq for a short time in August, but as soon as I stepped off the plane I felt the return of the weight and pressure crushing my chest. *What is it about this place?* My mission was to execute a $120 million budget by setting up a system to purchase equipment for the thirty thousand plus Iraqi police force. I was back in the grind; there was still no banking system, no distribution system, no storage facilities, no armories, and no transportation for the equipment. I met with Iraqi police chiefs, officers, bankers, and businessmen. I would joke with Kerik that it was a challenge to my womanhood to spend all the money. Well, I got close. We obligated close to $100 million in much-needed equipment and supplies for the Iraqi police force.

When I returned home, I was assigned to the Secretary of the Air Force Inspector General (IG) office in the Pentagon. The Air Force Academy sexual assault scandal was all over the news, and the IG needed female representation on the team. It was ironic that I would end up working there as a final career assignment. I wondered what Colonel Rush would have thought these two decades after he had got me into pilot training.

The mission of this IG section was to investigate complaints against Air Force general officers and senior civilians. But our team of ten colonels was focused on the sexual assault scandal. The Air Force was under tremendous pressure to release a report on sexual assaults and misconduct at the academy. It was so disheartening for me to learn that after twenty-five years of admitting females to the academy, the system still discriminated. The most disturbing thing was that it had been going on for ten years and the Air Force did little to help the women or punish the men.

I suddenly felt my entire career in the Air Force had had little influence in changing the minds or attitudes of its leaders. I knew I was bitter, but of all the jobs I held in the Pentagon, I disliked the IG job the most. It was like working with toxins every day. I believed they needed a female to show the public that the Air Force team had a cross section of minorities. History will judge whether the Air Force leadership just paid lip service to fixing the problems at the academy. That would have to be someone else's battle. I was done.

On top of that, our team was the graveyard of colonels. Our careers had come to an end, and we were just waiting for our time commitments to the Air Force to expire, so that we, too, could retire and then expire. It was a pathetic attitude, and even at the time, I knew I was wrong. So many things had changed in the Air Force for women. Nearly all career fields were open to women. Females were flying fighters in a war zone and no one even blinked an eye. Women were commanding troops at all levels and held positions within the leadership structure never before achieved. We even had our first female three-star general and our first female pilot to achieve the rank of general. Many things had changed for both men and women in the Air Force. I had done my part, but it was time to move on.

I had known for a while that it was time to retire, but it hadn't been easy to say. I knew it the day Garner left Iraq. Then, in the early fall of 2003, I wasn't selected for promotion to brigadier general. I wasn't surprised, in light of my phone call from General Jumper two years before, my lack of group command, and the struggle in Iraq, but it hurt nonetheless. Once again, I sought safe harbor with my mom at "our" beach. It was late in the evening, but the sand was still warm and the beach deserted. We walked in silence. "How's it going?" she finally asked.

I sighed at her question, shook my head, and waded out knee-deep into the surf. The warm water swirled around my legs and seashells poked my toes. My mom watched from a distance.

I turned to her. "I should have done this two years ago."

I pulled out the star-shaped party decorations Kent had placed on my shoulders four summers before. The two silver stars glistened in the sun. Closing my fist, I extended my arm, opened my fist, and dropped them. They floated on the water's surface until a small wave curled and pulled them under. I stared at the white foam of the churning sea and caught a glimpse of the silver reflecting in the sunlight. I blinked, and they were gone. Turning, I walked back to my mother, who observed me in silence. She hugged my bony shoulders.

"I need to retire. It's time." There—I had said it out loud. "It's been a good run, but I'm done. I don't need to be a general or even be in the Air Force to make a difference. There is something else I am supposed to do in life."

She patted my back. "You fought the good fight. You have so much to be proud of, sis."

I looked back at the sea. Why didn't I feel proud? Was it because I had failed to achieve my personal goals even though I had accomplished so much?

Little did I know, walking on the beach that day, how bad it was about to get.

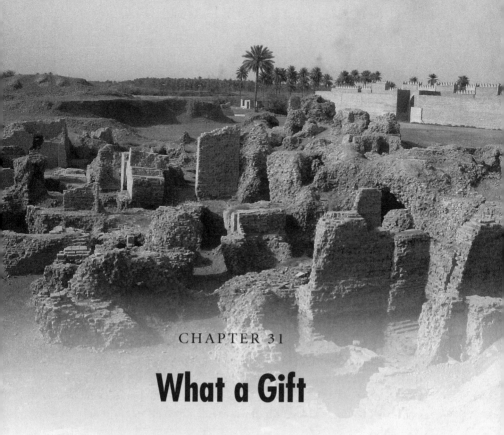

CHAPTER 31

What a Gift

More than a year after I walked on the beach and made the decision to retire, the results of an investigation into my actions in Iraq were released. The outcome was devastating.

The report was dated August 31, 2004, but I didn't see it until late October. From it, I learned that I could face the prospect of a military court-martial. The report alleged a violation of Title 18 U.S. Code, section 208, "Acts affecting a personal financial interest." Numb is the only way to describe my state of being. I walked around in a fog, wanting to escape, but knowing I was trapped in this situation, a captive of a military judicial system.

How do you battle the might of an institution with unlimited resources and people ready to believe the worst of you? These investigations began and ended with the theory that you were guilty until you prove yourself innocent. It was true for everyone.

Over the previous year, I had watched an exceptional colonel in the IG office, an officer I admired, get raked over the coals by criminal investigators. They had arrested him, failed to present a search warrant, and stripped his house of all his Air Force professional gear and documents. His wife, who was recovering from life-threatening cancer, whispered to him as the agents ransacked their home, "This is worse than the cancer."

The colonel, a seasoned combat pilot and a gifted staff officer, was under suspicion of a breach of security. He was appalled that someone would question his integrity and loyalty to the country he had served for more than twenty-nine years. I knew exactly how he felt.

Only after the report was released, and he was threatened with a court-martial, was he allowed to tell his side of the story. Every single alleged violation was dropped. But the damage was done, and he never recovered from the betrayal he felt at the hands of the institution he had served so honorably. I would not even get that outcome.

In the military, there is no investigative system available to prove your innocence. That is up to you. I needed an expert lawyer specializing in ethics law. By the end of this twenty-month ordeal, I would spend $70,000 in legal fees to defend against the allegations in the Defense Criminal Investigation Services (DCIS) report. (The Air Force could not provide the type of counsel I needed to defend me in this situation.) We sold our house to fund my defense and moved the family to Texas, telling my children they needed to start school before my scheduled fall retirement, which was now delayed for six months.

Although the DCIS report alleged serious misconduct, it was packed with errors, misstatements, and unsupported conclusions. My position at that time as an investigator for the Air Force who reviewed allegations against generals and senior civilians gave me insight into the investigative process. In our particular IG branch, we worked endless hours to provide a balanced report for commanders so they could make informed decisions. We prided ourselves on an unbiased approach to investigating. However, after reading the DCIS report, it was clear that they did not have the same approach.

Violating section 208 carried a maximum penalty of five years in jail. If this DCIS report was believed, I could end up in prison. But the report was built on a house of cards that quickly came apart when my legal counsel uncovered the facts. It had been a long, painful, and expensive process—but still I kept clinging to the idea that the truth would prevail.

Jim Cole, my defense attorney, is a trim, fit, handsome man with a thick mustache and dark hair. His calm approach was exactly what I needed. But his greatest professional asset was that he had worked for the Justice Department, where he had prosecuted a federal judge and an assistant U.S. district attorney. He had even been special counsel to the House Ethics Committee investigating Speaker Newt Gingrich. He knew section 208 and was now a defense attorney specializing in ethics cases.

What had I done wrong? After Jim interviewed witnesses and exposed the errors and serious omissions in the DCIS report, he discovered many of the report's conclusions were not supported by the facts. His legal opinion was that I had committed no ethics violations. When he was able to present his findings to the prosecutor, the most egregious charges were immediately dropped. However, even in the absence of criminal violations, the Air Force was compelled to take some action.

What remained were administrative errors stemming from decisions made in postwar Iraq. It was well within the Air Force's power under the Uniform Code of Military Justice to punish me—despite a lack of any violation of Title 18 U.S. Code. I was prevented from presenting evidence to the convening authority unless I pled guilty, because, in the words of the prosecutor, he wanted to avoid a mini-trial. This was in sharp contrast to the normal process in the military. Usually an individual does not have to plead guilty and wait until the punishment phase to present his or her side of the story. The bottom line was this: Unless I pled guilty to some kind of charges and accepted nonjudicial punishment, I was going to face a court-martial.

The DCIS report had already been leaked to the press and reporters had begun trying to question me. It scared the hell out of me. My lawyer informed me it was a classic technique used by institutions to pressure the accused. I could see the headlines, "Female Air Force Colonel Charged with Ethics Violation." This was not the legacy I wanted to leave.

So, what happened?

I thought back on those chaotic times in Iraq. Just before Garner left, he had discovered that the bodyguards were not being paid and he took my head off. "Why didn't you tell me?" he bellowed. It was the only the time he yelled at me, believing there was a very real possibility they would walk. Without the guards' protection, he would be unable to accomplish anything in his waning days in Iraq.

Since my discovery that the guards had been working without pay (and, more important to them, without life insurance), I had been trying to work the problem at an informal level. So far, I had not had any luck. When I questioned the contracting officer on how to get them paid, he told me it wasn't his problem; it was a problem between the prime contractor and the subcontractor. Since he couldn't help, I let it go, thinking we could work it out later. But the team complained to Garner one night when he asked if there was anything they needed. "Get us paid," was their answer.

Garner began calling around the Pentagon and eventually sent me to see one of the attorneys in the contracting department. I explained the situation in Iraq, and he said he would look into it. That was the last I heard of it until allegations about the contract surfaced in the DCIS report.

If those who were protecting our lives had remained under contract, if the system had ensured that the bodyguards received their promised salaries on time, if the rebuilding efforts hadn't been controlled from half a world away, maybe none of this would have happened. Who knows? Instead, my efforts to get these guys paid generated an anonymous complaint and a subsequent investigation. DoD did eventually compensate the bodyguards for their work.

At the time, Garner was also working to ensure a smooth transition with the Bremer team and to uphold his promises to the Iraqi people. One of those promises was safer streets, and that meant trained police officers on patrol and in the public eye. The Iraqi police were in desperate need of training. Every day that the police training plan (CIVPOL) remained tied up in the Washington bureaucracy, violence escalated on the streets of Baghdad. The few Iraqi police who were working would patrol, but only with U.S. soldiers. It was an ineffective use of manpower in a city desperate for law and order.

The general now suggested using the South Africans as one stopgap measure to aid in police training, an idea enthusiastically supported by the leadership in the Iraqi MOI. The MOI deputy was elated, since his repeated requests for military trainers had been denied. The senior staff accepted the fact that men like the South Africans had been hired from the private sector because the powers that be had decided this was going to be a war with a minimum of boots on the ground. Perhaps with the right type of U.S. soldiers in-country, they could have trained the Iraqi police and there would have been no need to outsource this requirement. But we'll never know, and that wasn't the situation we were trying to address.

Shortly after his farewell party, Garner approached the South Africans and asked them if they would consider working for Bernard Kerik, the U.S. advisor to the MOI. He wanted to split the team, with half providing personal protection and the remaining guards working as police trainers. It was then that Garner learned that Hector and Derick and a few others already had their own security company and would welcome the opportunity. No more going through a prime contractor—they wanted to bid directly on U.S. government and other contracts. Let's face it, they knew money could be made in the rebuilding of Iraq. If they could do it for less than the competition, because of their lower overhead, they were eager to compete. In

Garner's opinion, the U.S. government could save $2.4 million by hiring the South Africans.

I handed this over to our legal team, which drew up the requirements paperwork. The contracting officer provided the South Africans with a template contract proposal, and the MOI deputy presented it to the CPA program review team to validate and approve the requirement. Garner and I were not involved in that process. After it was completed, the request was sent back to the Pentagon to the OSD comptroller and the Interagency Executive Steering Group, which included members from the OSD policy office, the Office of Management and Budget, and the Treasury Department. The e-mail documentation included all the right parties for the prescribed decision-making process, with all the proper questions asked, answered, and acted upon in the correct manner. We had dotted the i's and crossed the t's.

Everyone involved in the multilayered approval process was working hard to make this happen before Garner left Iraq. If these guys were not on contract, they would leave the country when Garner did. More importantly, there would be no training assistance and no personal protection for Kerik. His initial request for a protection team was tied up somewhere.

When we returned to Baghdad from traveling through northern Iraq in the last week, the CPA comptroller told Garner the contract was approved and had been done by the book. It would take another week for the OSD officials to sign the request and allocate the appropriate funding. In the meantime, the guards began work protecting Kerik, so he could move outside the Green Zone and provide effective leadership. They also started training the Iraqi police force, putting police officers on the streets within the next week.

After Garner left, the South Africans received a signed contract in mid-June, but not before a competing security company complained to Bremer's chief of staff, a retired ambassador. He reviewed the documentation and the process and, finding no improprieties, elected to uphold the contract award. Everyone involved in the process had done their job—saved the taxpayers' money, protected part of the new leadership team with experienced men in Iraq, and jump-started the much-needed training for the Iraqi police force. It was not only unfair to those who ensured the integrity of the contracting system, but completely ludicrous, to think that one person could circumvent this whole process and force the award of a contract. But that was what the DCIS report alleged I had done.

Was trying to do the right thing, and relying on the system to do it correctly, going to result in my being sent to jail? Sometimes systems within our most trusted institutions get out of control.

There were other allegations in the report about my setting up the U.S. company. After Garner left, Hector and Derick asked me if I would consider joining their company. My answer was no. They came back and said they wanted to establish a U.S.-based company, because they felt it would be more credible and thus win them contracts. When they asked if I would consider setting one up for them, I said I would check to see if it was legal.

Their idea was for me to set up the company and then turn it over to them. Hector wanted to contract with private businesses that would work on the economic recovery in Iraq. It would certainly accelerate the rebuilding process to get U.S. businesses investing in Iraq. In addition, he and another guard were romantically involved with U.S. Army women and wanted to come to the States to work; the company could provide the means to make that happen. Hector would eventually marry the young soldier he had met in Iraq. At the time, I just offered them some advice on how proper businesses should run, and said I would think about their request. After so many weeks together in some dangerous situations, I had a lot of respect for the bodyguards. I certainly considered some of them my friends, and I would be happy to help them achieve their dreams, but only if I could do so legitimately.

In the weeks after my return, I tackled a series of leftover tasks from Iraq as well as my new Pentagon assignment. Right before I left for a much-needed vacation, I sought legal counsel from the senior ethics lawyer in the Standards of Conduct Office at OSD about setting up a U.S. company as the bodyguards had requested. During our conversation, I took notes to make sure I got it right. It was my understanding that I could set up a U.S.-based company. I asked him twice to be sure I understood him correctly. I then asked what the restrictions were and he answered, "You have to recuse yourself if the company works with DoD." He added, "Also, if you are compensated, I think you have to get your commander's approval for a second job."

"Oh, I'm not being paid," I replied. "I'm just trying to help these guys out. I don't know anything about the protective services business. Besides, I'm taking some leave and that's when I'll hire them a corporate lawyer to draw up the paperwork. I want this done correctly and legally. I don't do anything without checking with lawyers," I teased.

He smiled and asked if I would help him contact Iraqi lawyers and put them in touch with a professional legal organization he belonged to in the United States.

"You bet," I answered. After my time off, we worked together on his project for a few weeks.

Ignorance of the law is no excuse, as the old saying goes. I should have sought my commander's approval, but I was unaware that this requirement applied whether I received compensation or not. Had I known this, I would have followed the procedure without question. But I had not pursued it further, and so now I was charged with conduct unbecoming an officer. It didn't matter that I made no money and resigned shortly after establishing the company. The appearance it created for an officer in my position was what mattered. That is what had happened.

The month after I read the report, I went to discuss my options with Jim. I rode the elevator up to the seventh floor of the downtown D.C. law offices of Bryan Cave LLP. Jim met me at the glass-and-chrome door and offered me a seat in the tastefully decorated conference room. The large window looked out on the church next door, where a bell chimed the quarter hours in a melodious tone. I studied the man to whom I had entrusted my legal welfare and, in essence, the rest of my life.

"Tell me again." I sat rigidly in the high-backed leather chair at the conference table, as I had done during my many meetings with Jim.

"Look, Kim, I agree with you completely about how one-sided the process is and how it takes enormous resources to point out all the errors. Those errors are allowed to go unnoticed in most cases because most people can't afford the time, money, and aggravation to set things right. It is not enough in that kind of situation to just say the report got it wrong—you have to prove that it was wrong by doing the job they should have done in the first place. I would be happy to talk to anyone and do anything to start making the system right." He paused and opened his notebook.

"Let's go through their allegations. The most important is the awarding of the contract. The evidence that is referenced points to the fact that the contract award was done by the book, and you had little to do with it. How they can conclude you made that happen is beyond me. Next. Did you try and get the guards paid? Yes. Is this illegal? No. Did you let them use your computer and forward their documents? Yes. Is it illegal? No, it was not illegal, especially when their contract authorized them to have government-issued computers." But the Air Force counsel considered it an abuse of government equipment because I had forwarded their private business documents they had left on my computer back to them.

Jim continued, "Did you set up a company? Yes. Did you check with the OSD ethics legal counsel before you took those steps? Yes. Did you profit? No. You were actually out money."

"What about the rest of the conclusions? How can they say I spent all my time with that company or authored all their documents?" I asked.

"Did you?"

I gave him a look that said *You've got to be kidding me. You know how busy I was.* We had been through every day in Iraq. Jim wondered when I had even had time to go the bathroom.

I was accountable for my actions, but I was not going to plead guilty to things I did not do, even if it meant a court-martial.

"I know, I know. The report's evidence is anecdotal in nature. Forensic evidence shows otherwise, and the witness statements are not supported by any testimony, sworn or otherwise. Look, we've been through the computer files, and most of the documents you were alleged to have authored were done when you were out of the country. I have interviewed witness after witness who refutes their characterization in this report. And what is really disturbing is that those who supported you or whose verbal testimony ran counter to the agents' theory were completely left out of the report. They didn't even interview General Garner, for crying out loud. Besides . . ."

He placed his hand on a folder. "I have interviewed numerous people who verified your unwavering integrity, professionalism, and exceptional leadership. They are unimpeachable sources who were there with you every day in Iraq and expound on how hard you worked and how dedicated you were to the mission. The evidence demonstrates you did nothing that would form the basis for any violations. Kim, you did not break the law."

I tapped my leg under the table and squared my body to Jim. "I want a fair hearing. Why do I have to go to a court-martial to get it? It is bad for everyone—me, my family, my friends, and even the Air Force." My hands trembled as I made my point and he glanced at my fingers. I balled them into fists and shoved them into my lap.

"Forget the Air Force, Kim. This is about you. Trust me—the Air Force doesn't want this on the front page of the paper either." Jim paused to take a breath. He was right. Negative publicity about the Air Force consumed the newspapers. The Boeing 767 tanker procurement scandal continued to rock the Pentagon. The Air Force Academy sexual assault scandal was still under investigation. And the Judge Advocate General for the Air Force, a two-star general, was being forced to retire after confirmed sexual harassment allegations. The last thing the Air Force needed was one of their female colonels dragged through a military court system. *He didn't know the half of it,* I thought. Another prominent Air Force general with serious sexual harassment allegations pending against him would also be forced to retire.

"Besides, it is my legal opinion your actions do not constitute a violation of federal ethics law," he repeated. His unspoken concern was that I wouldn't get a fair trial as a senior female officer.

"Forget the Air Force," he had said. I couldn't forget the Air Force! This was my Air Force, too. I didn't want to battle the institution I had worked so hard to improve, and disappoint all those I had led and mentored. I prided myself on still being a role model and leader, even in the twilight of my career.

"Jim, I accept responsibility for my actions. So, what are my options?" I pressed.

"Okay, let's just talk about what you accept responsibility for. You acknowledged that you were negligent when you withdrew funds using the government travel card, before you were reimbursed for your travel expenses got posted; you did forward four e-mails with the company's documents that you found on your laptop; and you did set up this company. Kim, your option is to plead guilty to these lesser charges and present your side to the convening authority because he determines the appropriate punishment. Otherwise, it is war, and we see them in court."

My face blanched. I had seen enough wars. The room began to spin. I may have had the mental resolve to battle this, but my body had not recovered from Iraq. I could feel my heart begin to palpitate. My pulse was racing at 180 beats a minute. I breathed in and tried to relax.

"I need to lie down, Jim," I gasped.

His face went white as he watched me drop to the floor. "You okay?"

"Just give me a minute."

My heart was hammering so hard that my shirt jumped on my chest and I could hear the pounding in my ears. I inhaled, held my breath, and bore down, forcing my heart to slow, a classic L-1 maneuver for the pressure of high Gs. For a moment, it relieved this emotional pressure, too. But when I exhaled, my heart began racing again. I lay on the carpet, staring at the white ceiling and track lighting. The church bells next door chimed. *God, don't let me die in a lawyer's office.*

"You want me to call an ambulance?" He leaned over the table.

"No." I took deep breaths, trying to ride out the explosions in my chest. A few minutes later, my heart slowed back to normal, but the episode left me light-headed, sweating, and sick to my stomach. It was not my first or last physiological reaction to this experience.

He softened his voice. "Kim, we don't want this to kill you. Your best option is to accept the limited charges, present your facts to the convening authority, and there's a chance of having the entire matter thrown out. The worse is a very limited administrative punishment that would allow you to move on with your life."

It didn't happen as I had hoped.

Three months later, I pled guilty and finally had the opportunity to present the facts and the extenuating circumstances. Despite my optimism, however, the convening authority elected to issue a reprimand and impose a monetary fine. The nightmare was over—or so I thought. A year later, the DCIS report was made public to the press. Although Jim had prepared a memo for the convening authority to set the report straight and outline the facts that corrected the DCIS report, this was not made available. Once again I had to defend myself, but this time in the public arena.

During those weeks, as I screened my calls, I reflected on some correspondence with Jim. He wrote that at one time, "the hallmark of a good prosecutor was someone who suspended judgment on what happened until all the facts were in. In particular, they wanted all the facts, good and bad, before making up their minds. Now, people get an idea of what happened and then only look for evidence to support that theory—ignoring contradictory evidence or thinking it is a product of lying. I feel very strongly about this and would be anxious to help the system improve . . . tell them to call me." Jim fielded those press calls and we made the decision to release the memo he had prepared to ensure that the correct information and evidence were available. His continued, steadfast support and his friendship during those difficult days were true gifts.

Those would not be the only gifts I received at about this time. Early in 2004, as I struggled through the impact of the investigation, I began to receive e-mails from a man I had never met. Years earlier, my father had excelled in high school basketball, track and field, and football in the small town of Mineral, Illinois. Dave Egan, an Illinois highway patrolman and father of five, had become interested in his athletic achievements after hearing anecdotes from his relatives who grew up with my dad. Eventually, he researched the sports records and became determined to get my father and his teammates into the Bureau County Sports Hall of Fame. Dave began forwarding me old newspaper clippings, pictures, and stories about my father that he encountered in his research.

I knew my father only as a coach and remembered the intensity with which he motivated his players. He was something to watch from the eyes of a twelve-year-old. I have images of him practicing with his players, but it was his large hands that encompassed over half the basketball that really stuck with me. Sometimes, during the games, he would let me sit on the bench and cheer for the players. I think this is where I got my best lessons on encouraging and inspiring people.

Dave was not even alive when my father played ball. But something about my dad's athletic exploits and citizenship inspired Dave to pursue this quest. He was successful. Late in the summer, I left behind my worries and met my two sisters and my brother in the tiny Midwestern farming community. Kevin Hieronymous, sports editor of the local *Bureau County Republican*, later wrote that we "were given the gift of seeing [our] dad," then added a quote from me, "'through the eyes of his hometown.'"

I had not been to Mineral in forty years. We stopped by the two-story white house my father grew up in. The long line of cottonwood trees and the swing set I remembered playing on as a child were gone. But there in the front yard was a family with young children chasing each other, just as we had done decades before. The smell of fresh-cut grass filled the air and I smiled at the simple pleasure of watching children play.

That evening, the crowded auditorium could have been that of any high school in America. For the four of us, though, it was a window into the past. I glanced around the noisy room, filled with gray-haired men and women and children of all ages. I recognized one familiar face, then another, and another. Childhood friends long forgotten came into focus, cheered as they saw us, and hugged us tight. The last time we had seen each other was at my father's funeral. I fought back the tears. I had worn my uniform to this event and I did not want to cry with it on.

So there my siblings and I sat, surrounded by past friends, as we traveled back decades to discover a man we hardly knew. It was a rare moment for the four of us. The induction ceremony allowed us to celebrate the teenager, the athlete, and the hometown boy they called Billy and we called Dad. As Billy's young face flooded the screen, the announcer read the history of his athletic accomplishments and his contributions to the town of Mineral. We had learned about some of these achievements in the e-mails Dave had been sending. I heard about others for the first time that night.

My normally stoic sister Kris cried and Kellie, her twin and the nurturer of the family, held on to both of us. Kevin, who was five when we lost our dad, stared in wonder at the man he never knew. It was a bittersweet moment. At the age of thirty-eight, Kevin, single with no children, had just been diagnosed with prostate cancer. "Will I live to see forty?" he whispered, knowing his dad never did. I knew he was afraid and I reached over and squeezed his hand. He looked up at the ceiling.

Later that evening, we found ourselves in a small, wood-paneled bar with booths and an old jukebox playing in the corner. I had changed into blue jeans and straddled a stool. Suppressing a smile, I thought, *Yep, all bars smell the same.* One of my dad's teammates came over and slid me a beer across the bar top. "Let me tell you about Billy. . . ." For the next few hours, as I peeled the labels off the beer bottles, I heard story after story about the great athlete, the mischievous teenager, and the big-hearted man that this small town had known.

What a gift, was all I could think, when I saw that Kris, Kellie, and Kevin were also engaged in conversations with friends of Billy. I strolled over to Dave and hugged him until he cleared his throat. How could he have known that his efforts would bring such joy to my siblings and me? When he began this endeavor, he had no idea that his generous heart would not only help me at a very tough time but also, more importantly, strengthen my brother. By the end of the night, Kevin swaggered over, slung an arm over my shoulder, and whispered, "I'm no longer afraid. I come from good stock and I'm gonna be okay." *We do come from good stock,* I thought, looking at Kevin's handsome face that so resembled his dad's.

Kevin Hieronymous later interviewed my mother about my brother's health. "His mother deeply believes there was some divine intervention as to the timing of the Sports Hall of Fame," he wrote, "as the love and genuine caring from those who knew his father made a significant impact on a young man facing an uncertain future."

Four weeks after the induction ceremony, Kevin's surgery was a complete success. He made a full recovery and married his true love two years to the day after the operation.

The newspaper article said it best. "His father is surely smiling from above."

CHAPTER 32

Retirement

I sat on the stage of the building that houses the Women In Military Service For America Memorial at the gateway to Arlington Cemetery. Now my story, too, would become part of military women's history. From a passing stranger's point of view, I was a living portrait of a successful woman and leader. Only a handful of those sitting in the audience knew about the investigation that had occupied so much of the last several months.

It was May 31, 2005, and I was finally retiring from the Air Force after twenty-five years, nine months, and four days. I had made it. The eagles on my shoulders represented a rank worn by merely a couple of dozen women. Both the command pilot wings, earned by a select few, and the command pin signified a coveted leadership position. I touched the numerous medals and awards displayed in row after row of ribbons on my chest. The three shiny Joint Command badges showed the breadth of my experience in the military.

As my role model and friend Major General Marne Peterson, one of the very first women pilots and the first female aviator selected as a general officer, boasted of my achievements, I looked out into the audience and a lump caught in my throat. Most officers do get choked up at their own retirement. Now I knew why. Facing me from the audience sat the true measure of a leader's success.

There were people with me today whom I had befriended, flown with, mentored, taught, led, and served under. Those in the audience spanned my entire career. The first woman I ever flew with, a fellow copilot from the early 1980s; students from my days as a pilot instructor; an author who had written about me as a pioneering military woman; men and women from the Army, Navy, and Marines; military and civilian colleagues from our time in Iraq; and a dozen troops whom I had commanded six years earlier, gathered together in the second row. Would they remember my leadership lessons when they commanded their own troops?

My lawyer, Jim, who sat in the third row, paid me the greatest compliment when he said he wished his daughter could have been there to listen to my speech and meet me. Even my First Shirt, Dan, came halfway across the country just to narrate the ceremony. Several VIPs occupied the front row, including General Jay Garner. Nancy, who had retired a year earlier, was in the audience, too, wiping tears from her eyes. We had certainly seen happy and dark days together. I was a fortunate person to have a friend like her. I can honestly say I would not have made it through the past year without her. But those who really mattered the most sat front and center—my family.

I brushed an imaginary piece of lint from my skirt, crossed my ankles, and thought back to the last time I wore this Air Force Class A uniform.

It had been more than a year prior, one Friday evening in January 2004. My daughter walked in with the phone.

"Mommy, someone from the secretary of something for you."

"What?" I sat up in bed. "Hello?"

"Hi, ma'am, can you please hold for Secretary Wolfowitz?" the voice replied.

"Yeah, right, who is this?" I answered with a chuckle.

The voice pressed, "No, really, ma'am, it's Cables." Cables is the name of the communication center in the Pentagon. I had spoken to them many times when I was in Iraq.

"Of course." My voice turned stern.

A few seconds later, I heard another voice. "Colonel Olson. Hi, Paul Wolfowitz."

"Yes, sir."

"Listen, we have a Kurdish general who was injured in a friendly fire incident during the war." He went on to explain that U.S. forces had attacked a Kurdish convoy by mistake, killing several people and seriously wounding a Kurdish general. This general was the son of a prominent leader in Iraq who had cooperated with the United States during the invasion. The U.S. military had medevaced the injured man to Walter Reed Army Medical Center, where he was receiving care, but the prognosis was grim. The explosion had damaged his brain, leaving him blind and deaf on the left side and unable to walk, talk, or eat. He had seizures and all kinds of infections from the shrapnel wounds. He was lucky to be alive.

Why are you telling me all this? I wondered.

"Anyway, the family could use some help and Jay Garner said. . . ."

So that's it. "Yes, sir, what can I do to help?"

"Well, colonel, I am going over to meet the family at their apartment. The wife is upset with the way we are handling things and I'd like you to come with me. That is, if you're not busy." *Like I am going to say no to the number two guy in DoD.*

"Of course I'll be there, sir. See you then."

So I put on my Class A, drove to the Pentagon early Saturday morning, climbed into the black SUV with Secretary Wolfowitz, and drove into town. It was just the deputy and me. "Jay says you were his exec in Iraq. What do you think?"

I studied the deputy and thought, *Do you really want to know?* For the next thirty minutes of the ride, I told him exactly what I thought. The lack of an integration plan, the lack of support, bringing in Bremer too soon, the wrong kind of troops on the ground, the lack of funds to get things started, and the general lack of appreciation for how hard people worked over there. I pretty much unloaded on him. I spoke respectfully, but there was no doubt as to what I thought. He nodded and studied my face.

We arrived at the apartment and were ushered up to meet the general's wife and his staff. The general sat slumped in a wheelchair, his hands curled. He grunted in response to our hellos. As soon as the deputy and I sat down, the wife started in on him. Her aggressive attitude surprised me, given my previous experience with Iraqi women. She reminded the deputy of the U.S. government's promise to help her husband after the attack. Now the doctors told her that there was nothing else they could do—that he should go into a nursing home. She leaned on the end of her chair and informed the deputy that her husband was not going to a nursing home. He was going to walk and talk and they would be returning to their home within the year.

The deputy got an earful, but he was gracious and thanked the general and his family for their support during the war. He then assured the wife he would do all he could to help her husband. I actually wasn't paying much attention to him until he said, "And Colonel Olson here will help you with anything you need."

My head snapped around. "Yes, ma'am, whatever you need."

As we climbed back into the SUV, he laughed. "Didn't mean to catch you off guard. Jay says you can get things done."

"Guess General Garner still thinks I work for him," I answered.

"Don't we all," he replied, smiling.

It took some research, but I found a group of effective and smart people in the medical community and they worked long hours to help the family. Sure enough, almost as the wife predicted, a little more than a year later I stood in an OSD conference room as Secretary Wolfowitz presented a medal to the general, who got up and walked to the stage, supported by a cane, and thanked the crowd in a slow, measured tone. The wife hugged me tight and told me they were going home at the end of the week.

So here a soldier gets blown apart and, with the love and support of his family, puts himself back together and goes home. Some warriors receive visible wounds and recover, and some endure unseen ones. Maybe unseen injuries could heal, too.

I stared hard at the faces of my family. I knew it would take time, but their love and support would heal my wounds, too. Each was providing medicine in his or her own way. My loyal, quiet husband, Kent. My tall, gracious son, Keegan. My beautiful, soulful daughter, Katie. My proud mother, always there with her wise counsel and unconditional support. My stepfather, who only yesterday, it seemed, was yelling at me for going to the IG. My younger sister, Kellie, who had made the trip from Wisconsin; the one I could call night or day. They loved me as a wife, a mother, a daughter, and a sister. I straightened my shoulders and thought, *Okay. I can still serve my country.*

I rose from my chair to stand next to General Peterson as Dan read the certificate.

"To all who shall see these presents, greetings: This is to certify that Colonel Kimberly D. Olson, having served faithfully and honorably, was retired from the United States Air Force on the First day of June, Two Thousand Five." Ironically enough, it was signed "John Jumper, Chief of Staff."

And it was done. I walked off the stage and closed another chapter in my life. The following day, I flew down to Texas and began the process of rebuilding my family. They, too, had suffered during the last year.

Several months later, I finally made the trip to see General Garner in his home in Orlando, Florida. I had put him off for two years. That was long enough. Although he had stood by my side, and still does today, I had kept my distance because I believed I had let him down. When I met his wife, daughter, granddaughters, and his female dog, I thought, *You certainly are surrounded by women.*

In his study I was surprised to see a note from Secretary Rumsfeld clipped to a copy of the Iraqi Constitution. He had scribbled his thanks to General Garner, adding, "You made this possible." Even after coming home, Garner had continued to work behind the scenes to rebuild Iraq. By the end of the weekend, Connie commented that she would not have worried so much about his safety had she met me before we deployed.

On the last night of my visit, we sat on the deck of their spacious home. Steaks were sizzling on the grill, and a cool evening breeze brushed the cypress trees. This was only the third time I had been alone with Garner. There were no other staff, bodyguards, or fellow generals, just two battle-weary retired warriors enjoying a pleasant evening.

"Sorry." I took a sip of the cold, crisp chardonnay.

He let out an impatient sigh. "Kimmer, you got nothing to be sorry about." He turned to face me. "I know this." He pointed the spatula at me. "If I could live my life over from 2003, there are two things I'd do again."

"What's that?" I asked.

"Go to Iraq . . . " he paused, squinted his pale blue eyes, then continued, "and take you with me."

The weight floated off my chest. I blinked. "Thank you, Jay."

We clinked our wineglasses together and toasted one another with a silent head nod.

The following week, I sat captivated in our church in Texas as Katie, now fourteen, approached the microphone to sing her first solo. *Now there's an angel,* I thought, as her beautiful, sweet voice echoed through the large room, bringing tears to several eyes—mine included. My son nodded knowingly at me. I looked back and forth at my two children, gripped my husband's hand, and whispered a silent prayer of thanks. The war to find my own peace had ended, and I was right where I belonged.

Index

About the Author

Kim Olson travels the country speaking and lecturing on leadership strategy, political-military insights, and educational issues. She also finds time to serve on civic boards, to work to improve a community homeless teen program, and to mentor kids. After twenty-five years in the United States Air Force, she now flies with her son in their Cessna 150, while her husband teaches their daughter to drive a tractor. The family is growing pecan trees on their "4-K River Ranch" next to the Brazos River in Texas.